A Chance for the World Bank

Anthem Studies in Political Economy and Globalization

A Chance for the World Bank

JOZEF RITZEN
with a foreword by
JOSEPH STIGLITZ

Anthem Press
London

Anthem Press
An imprint of Wimbledon Publishing Company
75-76 Blackfriars Road, London SE1 8HA
or
PO Box 9779, London SW19 7QA
www.anthempress.com

This edition first published by Anthem Press 2005

British Library Cataloguing in Publication Data
A catalogue record for this book is available from the British Library.

Library of Congress Cataloging in Publication Data
A catalogue record for this book has been requested.

1 3 5 7 9 10 8 6 4 2

ISBN 1 84331 161 5 (Hbk)
ISBN 1 84331 162 3 (Pbk)

Typeset by Footprint Labs Ltd, London
www.footprintlabs.com

Printed in Great Britain
by Cromwell Press Trowbridge Wiltshire

Dedicated to Hanneke, always supportive

'The job of politicians is never to get depressed', Peter Mandelson, March 16, 2004 (Den Uyl lecture)

CONTENTS

4, 6, 7, 8, 10

LIST OF ILLUSTRATIONS AND MAPS

LIST OF TABLES

ACKNOWLEDGMENTS

This book is a record of my own edification to which many people contributed. In my years at the World Bank Joseph Stiglitz, Nicholas Stern, Paul Collier and David de Ferranti were more tutors than sparring partners. Koen Davidse provided (unwittingly?) the push to write the book and Justus Hartkamp carries the onus of making that push decisive. Danae Bodewes provided excellent research assistance in particular as she felt that the voice of the anti-globalists should be clearly heard. Francois Bourguignon, Louk de la Rive Box and Martin Koppensteiner commented on the manuscript ruthlessly – greatly contributing in the process.

My friends, colleagues and companions at the World Bank – I owe you a lot for your inspiration and commitment. I am sure that I will omit many if I mention: Jim Wolfensohn, Mamphela Ramphele, Jean Louis Sarbib, Ruth Kagia, Robert Holzmann, David Dollar, Shanta Devarajan, Maarten de Jong, Joan Santini, Phil Hay, Robert Hecht, Hans Boehmer, Manny Jimenez, Jamil Salmi, Yael Duthilleul, Linda Likar, Yordi Seium, Zafiris Tzannatos, Benoit Millot, Halsey Rogers, Coralie Gevers, Margaret Miller, Anne Kibutu, Edith Thomas, Zmarak Shalizi, Charles Griffin, Gary Perlin, Egbe Osito, Oey Mesook, Cathy Cardona, Franny Leautier, Anupam Khanna, Elizabeth Lulae, Callisto Modavo, Chris Lovelace, Linda English, Jim Adams, Deepa Narayan, Lianqin Wang and Annette Dixon. A very special person during my time at the World Bank has been Elaine Botwinick. No one can overestimate her contribution to human development through her personal commitment.

I am most grateful to the University of Maastricht, which allowed me to get my thoughts on paper. The students of the economics classes gave me excellent feedback, MUNDO (Han Aarts) supported the student assistance, Ruben Vroegop carefully edited the English and Eefje Kouters completed the typing.

Maastricht
January 2005

FOREWORD BY JOSEPH STIGLITZ

The demise of the Cold War changed the opportunities for development and development assistance. No longer were the developing countries simply pawns in a global political struggle. Development assistance could be directed towards countries that most needed it, or could use it best, not countries which were of the most geo-strategic importance. Regrettably, sometimes, the new opportunities were seized upon, not to advocate a balanced agenda for democratic, equitable, and sustainable development, but to advance particular commercial and financial interests within certain of the advanced industrial countries. The World Bank, the pre-eminent multilateral institution providing assistance to developing countries, has been among those most successful in seizing the new opportunities and transforming itself. The changes have not always been pursued with the vigor and resilience one would have hoped for, but still given the political and bureaucratic barriers to change, the changes have been impressive. This is one of the main themes which Jo Ritzen pursues in his personal, but highly organized and thoughtful account of the way the World Bank, as the major development organization, works, touching on the main themes in development economics and development cooperation.

Jo Ritzen sets the stage for an assessment of development cooperation as a means to create convergence between richer and poorer countries in what he calls the interbellum between the end of the Cold War (1992) and the start of the War on Terror (2001). Wars stand in the way of development. Development cooperation requires the support of donors that is broader than just money; it entails support for better governance and better policies in developing countries, while richer countries at the same time should reduce their restrictions for imports from developing countries. They can help further by actively policing multinationals to ensure that they do not engage in corruption, including bribery. But during wars, countries become divided along the simple line of 'friends' and 'enemies'. The friends will be assisted with aid and trade facilities even if this means the support of a corrupt regime, even if one can predict that this support may delay development. The 'enemies' will be cut off from aid and trade facilities, even when such support would have reduced poverty and helped the country to grow.

The demise of the Cold War has, unfortunately, not brought with it the success to the development process that many hoped for. There have been some successes: marked increases in per capita income in many parts of Eastern Asia, in some countries in Africa, and in parts of South Asia. Latin America realized higher growth rates in the early nineties than before, but saw these gains disappearing rapidly towards the end of the nineties and in the early years of the second millennium. Many parts of Eastern Europe and Central Asia have yet to benefit from the movement from communism to the market.

The successes in East Asia and elsewhere are first and foremost the successes of the countries concerned and their leadership. The dismal performance in so much of the rest of the world is in spite of the increased effectiveness of aid. No longer is aid allocated on the basis of 'friend and foe'. Increasingly, attention is focused on how well the money is being used. Changes in development strategies, well described by Ritzen, have also helped. These gains have been more than offset by the fact that the world has become riskier and more hostile – Africa ravaged with Aids, and much of the rest of the world ravaged by unstable short term capital flows.

The end of the Cold War not only meant that aid could be better allocated, but also facilitated a less ideological approach to development strategies. The change in the development paradigm has, I believe, contributed to the increase in development effectiveness. 'Country ownership' is key, with development partners (donors) as listeners, bringing knowledge of good practice from around the world in support of the government of a developing country, which must ultimately assume responsibility for and take charge of the development strategy.

There remains a problem of donor 'overload' – the difficulties that developing countries often have in dealing with the differing concerns of different aid agencies. While everyone speaks of the need for coordination and harmonization by donors, it has been hard to achieve.

The nineties saw some improvement in donor coordination, but we are still at an early stage, with major potential gains within reach. To realize these, however, political leaders in donor countries have to abandon their 'flag-planting' mentality and rhetoric. The object of aid should be to help the developing countries, not to provide assistance to those in the donor country, whether it be through subsidizing exports or tied aid.

Under President Wolfensohn, the World Bank has opened its windows and let fresh air into the sometimes stale atmosphere of the past – the projects, programs and policies pursued under the doctrines of a narrow 'Washington Consensus', a perspective that was claimed to be technocratic, but was actually highly political, which claimed to be based on economic science, but was actually based on economic ideology. The World Bank helped to shape the new development paradigm and gradually implement it; the new paradigm recognized the importance of local culture, of the role of partners in development and of civil society.

While the Bank made large strides in reforming its development strategy, Ritzen describes how it often remained too focused on its own internal operations, too embroiled in internal debates; this inhibited its ability in moving vigorously to a different 'business model'. According to Ritzen, the governance structure of the Bank is not to blame, however odd and outdated this structure may seem. The overwhelming influence of the US Treasury is a factor. But, unlike the IMF, where the Treasury has an effective veto, other donors could presumably exercise more influence. Other donors, and some of the receivers of aid, have yet to be sufficiently mobilized to put into action the new development paradigm.

Jo Ritzen analyses and writes with the experience and background of a top economist as well as a politician. He was the Netherlands' minister of education, culture and science for almost a decade – one of the longest serving ministers in the European Union. He brought about substantial change in the education and science system in his country. While he brings the hardheadedness of an economist, he also brings the sensitivity of a political leader to the challenges posed by societal transformation. He understands what needs to be done to enhance development, but he also understands the limits in the 'room for maneuver' that the political process sometimes imposes.

Distinctively, he also understands the role of civil society in the development process – how it can sometimes give voice to those whose concerns would otherwise not be heard, but also how it can sometimes pursue an agenda largely of its own making. He believes that, in a democracy, it is the elected officials who must ultimately take responsibility for the *collective* actions of government, which are central to determining the long-run course of their societies.

Globalization has gradually brought on an increasing concern for the plight of those in the developing world. The advanced industrial countries have made a major commitment to help the developing countries. This book, written by an insider who has worked hard to make these efforts pay off, provides key insights into the way development cooperation has been shaped in the past decade, its promises and its limitations. The image which emerges is not entirely positive, but the critical observations are meant as exhortations to shape up, to do better. They are offered in a spirit of constructive criticism. I too saw some of the limitations, but I too saw how sometimes development assistance made an enormous difference in the lives of the people in the Third World. I share Jo Ritzen's commitment – the convergence in development between the rich and the poor is to the benefit of all; I share his aversion to simplifications which see all aid as wasteful, or all problems of waste as attributable to faults of the developing countries; and I share his optimism: if we understand our failings of the past, if we look realistically at where we have succeeded, and where we have failed, we are more likely to do better in the future.

Joseph Stiglitz
December 2004

LIST OF ABBREVIATIONS

ACP	African, Caribbean Pacific Group of States
CAP	Common Agricultural Policy
CAS	Country Assistance Strategy of the World Bank
CD	Country Director (World Bank)
CIDA	Canadian International Development Agency
CSO	Civil Society Organization
CRS	Corporate Social Responsibility
ESW	Economic and Sector Work (World Bank)
FDI	Foreign Direct Investment
GDP	Gross Domestic Product
GNP	Gross National Product
HIV/AIDS	Human Immunodeficiency Virus/ Acquired Immune Deficiency Syndrome
HIPC	Heavily Indebted Poor Countries
IBRD	International Bank for Reconstruction and Development (World Bank)
IDA	International Development Association
ILO	International Labor Organization
IMF	International Monetary Fund
IPR	Intellectual Property Rights
LICUS	Low-Income Countries Under Stress
NGO	Non-Governmental Organization
OECD	Organization for Economic Cooperation and Development
OED	Operations Evaluation Department (World Bank)
PIC	Public Information Center (World Bank)
PRSP	Poverty Reduction Strategy Paper
QAG	Quality Assurance Group (World Bank)
SAP	Structural Adjustment Program
UN	United Nations
UNDP	United Nations Development Program
UNESCO	United Nations Educational, Scientific and Cultural Organization
UNICEF	United Nations Children's Fund
USAID	United States Agency for International Development
WHO	World Health Organization
WTO	World Trade Organization

1

Introduction: Off on the Wrong Foot

This new decade, the first of a new millennium, has started off on the wrong foot where the poorer countries are concerned. This is – as far as I can see – not due to a failure of *commitment* in rich countries (or for that matter within poorer countries) to make widespread and enduring poverty in the world belong to history. On the contrary: this commitment got a fresh boost at the start of the new millennium with the Millennium Declaration. The declaration was widely endorsed: 188 heads of state signed up to it, while in 2002, in Monterrey, many of the rich countries pledged to supply the funds needed to bring poorer countries along in reducing poverty, and in reaching basic literacy and basic conditions of health for their people.

And yet: the tragedy of this first decade of the new millennium is that most of the traffic lights for successful progress in development cooperation remain fixed in orange or red. The goals of the Millennium Declaration were to bring developing countries faster into the camp of the better off. But now we do not seem to be heading in that direction. The painful lessons learned in the past decades are maybe not forgotten, but they are not applied as diligently as one would expect either. Is it because we are so focused on the war against terrorism? Or is it because I (and many others with me) am losing patience? I belong to the generation of the idealistic and revolutionary 1960s, during which development cooperation became a self-evident part of the life of world citizens. I have seen and been part of the ups and downs of working together with poor countries and felt that, with the fall of the Berlin wall and the disappearance of that ideological rift in the world, there were new chances to speed up the convergence of poorer countries with rich countries. And the late 1990s were indeed hopeful when the cooperation between rich and poor countries became unfastened from ideologies and turned pragmatic. But it feels like September 11, 2001 was a turning point.

This book is about the lessons we have learned in the past on effective ways in which rich and poor countries can work together so that poor countries can emerge from dire poverty. The book pleads for an implementation of those lessons. *They would imply a radical reform in the international context of development cooperation* as a first and decisive step. Continuity is always of importance. But in order to save this decade for development cooperation a quantum leap is necessary. This step applies first to the World Bank, the heart of development cooperation worldwide. This explains the title: a (could we say with the critics who have found the 50 or 60 years of the World Bank's existence enough, 'last'?) chance for the World Bank.

The book is not meant to be an academic monograph, although I try to support my statements as much as possible with empirical evidence. It is not an autobiography either, although it is written from the perspective of my recent experience as a Vice President of the World Bank (1998–2002), as you can see from the additions of my personal experience (in boxes). In reading the book, you will notice the personal touch resulting from my long-run association with and involvement in development cooperation and with education: in my studies (up to 1970) I was 'raised' on the teachings of Nobel Prize Winner Jan Tinbergen, one of the most eminent development economists to believe that a world with less inequality would be a more peaceful and more prosperous world. My dissertation (1977, at North Holland Publishing Company) was entitled 'Education, Economic Growth and Income Distribution', and my first professional job (1970–1) was in what was then East Pakistan (now Bangladesh) in development cooperation (through the Ford Foundation). Most of my work as a professor of economics (at Berkeley, CA, Nijmegen, Madison, Wisconsin and Rotterdam) dealt with the economics of education as part of economics of the public sector. As a minister of education, culture and science of the Netherlands (for almost the whole decade of the 1990s) my attachment to education grew even further.

The book is also personal in the sense of the need I felt to complete my work at the World Bank with a reflection, as I did after my period as a minister (*The Minister, a Handbook*, Amsterdam: Bert Bakker, 1998, in Dutch). I started these reflections on the first day I left the Bank using my extensive notes on my period there, and elaborated them later from the busy but comfortable distance of the Netherlands (as President of the University of Maastricht). I have realized that it is my drive to contribute to the debate which has made me complete this book.

I believe that the time is ripe to re-engage worldwide in poverty reduction. The urgent need to reduce abysmal and widespread poverty has become stronger as abject poverty all the time approaches closer to our doorstep. This is the result of what I see as the nucleus of globalization: the decrease in the costs of bridging the distances between the haves and the have-nots, whether it is the costs of having access to information or the costs of travel. Distance is no longer a wall that shields the rich parts of the world or obfuscates and tempers the expectations of the poor. Decreased distances mean mounting tensions, increased pressure on immigration from poor to rich countries and the hardening of the emotions of the losers of today against the winners.

The years ahead may not be the hoped-for era of fast poverty reduction in the world, despite all efforts, despite all development cooperation and all development aid. There are fortunately some exceptions, like the mammoth countries India and China as well as some of the Asian Tigers. But overall we lack the context and commitment to apply the lessons of the past: *we lack a platform of worldwide cooperation* to achieve a better position for developing countries in trade, to reduce corruption effectively, to engage in development cooperation in a coordinated and harmonized way, to rely on the country's ownership if the country has shown a reliance on 'good governance', and to focus with diplomatic and if necessary policing forces on countries which are in civil conflict. More aid might then easily be argued for, even more so if the case for aid were also better argued (through – let us call it – marketing or public relations).

Part of the platform involves improving public relations in rich countries on development cooperation. Protests against the World Trade Organization, the World Bank or the IMF have become muted after September 11, 2001. Yet the reality underlying those protests has not changed: major parts of the population (and among them a substantial part of our youth) simply no longer believe that the official avenues for poverty reduction, through the official agencies of development cooperation, are going to be successful. One need only to witness a discussion on the World Bank in any university around the globe and one is quickly convinced that a major information campaign is long overdue.

Creating such a platform would have a tremendous impact on poverty reduction worldwide. First, such an approach would help poor countries directly. Reducing trade barriers in rich countries for products from poor countries alone would have a benefit to poor countries four times that of the existing flow of development aid. Second, the rise in efficiency of aid which would result from such a platform would in turn help a large number of countries to get much further in poverty reduction than they can at the moment, either directly by growth of income in the poorer part of the population, or through the improvement of the foundation of income growth, namely improved human development. Third, such a platform might stimulate the developing countries, which now lag behind because of poor governance, to faster join the successful ones. Nothing succeeds like success.

The development community might also shift its attention to those countries who are lagging behind because they are at war, involved in civil conflicts, or otherwise in a state of unsatisfactory governance and where, as a result, development aid (other than humanitarian aid) cannot be effective. Diplomatic solutions, peacekeeping or other similar kinds of solution might be the point of concentration for these countries.

The World Bank – as the most important player in development cooperation – would need such a platform. The Bank (as it is commonly called by insiders) is bound to have little chance to be effective in this decade, unless the major changes mentioned above take place in the attitudes and political positions of the countries participating in the World Bank's Board (practically all countries). These changes require worldwide agreements and require clear decisions and choices, in particular in the rich countries. Indeed, I focus on the changes in the rich countries, for while the poor countries still have to do a lot as well, it must also be recognized that these poor countries have already done so much in past decades in struggling to redress corruption, inflation and budget deficits, while the prices of their export products often plummeted.

Is it a kind of whistling in the dark when one asks for a new platform, for what might look like a renewal of the 1944 Bretton Woods agreements that led to the introduction of the notion of development cooperation and the founding of the World Bank? In contrast to the time of the founding of the World Bank, the climate for international agreements that might provide the framework for effective poverty reduction may not seem beneficial or supportive. However, when Keynes launched his ideas for worldwide agreement in the 1930s and early 1940s, there was a von Hayek who fought those ideas tooth and nail. One should not overrate the public and political support for the winds of change at that time. And equally, one should not underrate the public and political support for changes now. For example, youth groups are highly committed. There is also a strong scientific community supportive of change, led by great thinkers like Joe Stiglitz and Amartya Sen. And – maybe for the first time – there is a business community which has increasingly realized that its future is more certain with corporate responsibility on a global scale, that corporate responsibility (as a shared standard) contributes to the profitability of firms.

Not acting now implies not doing what we know that has to be done. The war on terrorism should not be an excuse for not acting, for putting the lessons of effective development cooperation in the fridge and rushing again to buy friendship. On the contrary, let us remember that only 20 years ago the West used the vehicle of development cooperation to buy Iraq's friendship, because the West sought to fight Iran. We are in danger of repeating those mistakes nowadays in our development cooperation with, for example, Uzbekistan or Tajikistan.

We should also realize that the present state of the world is likely to lead to a continuation of imported discontent in the rich world with – as a result – increasing insecurity. Immigration is in a substantial part the result of globalization in the face of great inequalities in the world. The awareness has grown that immigration might be accompanied by a transfer of tensions rather than a reduction. Rap songs of UK born and bred musicians, who are immigrant descendants, preach hatred and violence against the evil forces of Western imperialism. Muslim religion often provides the cloak for hardened opponents of the rich countries, attacking their economic and political dominance and – in the process – sometimes threatening their very accomplishments of enlightenment, of individual freedom and democracy. In the end, the tensions need to be resolved by open dialogue in the face of equal chances for human development.

This book analyses trends of the recent past and present in inequality in the world, with a focus on the cooperation between rich and poor countries in undoing dire poverty and with specific attention to the World Bank and its role in development cooperation. It sketches an outline for a way forward, with the World Bank as the focal point: the World Bank as the 'throbbing heart' of development cooperation, in the sense of the political, intellectual and financial leader among the community of agencies involved in development cooperation.

The way forward is to be brought about by a common concern of the world community for poverty reduction (whether based on true altruism or on long-run self-interest). This is the topic of Chapter 2, which leads to the conclusion that there is nothing wrong with the basic commitment in the world to poverty-reduction worldwide. The generosity of rich countries towards the poorer parts of the world remains sizeable even if it is little compared to their incomes. Also it was a major step forward to adopt worldwide the Millennium Development Goals. The world would be much better off if these were achieved. The world has been less successful in translating that commitment into action. Chapter 3 makes clear that it was hopeless to rely on the forces of globalization as a means to give poor countries a boost in the world economy: the kind of globalization of the past did not automatically lead to poverty-reduction. Agencies of development cooperation – among them the World Bank – have operated (and still operate) in this complex world of globalization where the rules are not yet set in a way that creates a level playing field. Rather, the rules of the jungle, those of power and privilege, prevail by and large. Rich countries impose on poor countries trade rules that allow easy entrance of their products, while they are still not willing to abandon their trade barriers for imports from developing countries. Also, rich countries do not speak with one tongue when they demand good governance, while at the same time not effectively preventing their companies from engaging in the tango of bribery and corruption.

Chapters 2 and 3 are the setting of the stage (Part I) with as main conclusions: first, that there is a tremendous urge for poverty reduction worldwide, but that the type of globalization we have had does not support the realization of this goal; second, that development cooperation has done too little, too late, to tie in with the goal of poverty reduction and needs rapidly to be brought onto the right footing.

Commitment to poverty reduction and the failure of the present type of globalization to fulfill that commitment: these notions set the stage for the second part of the book, which deals with the World Bank (Part II). The Bank could be a leader among the agencies of development cooperation, not just because of its financial strength. It could also lead by being a good learner, sensing quickly why prevailing development paradigms failed or were insufficient (Chapter 3). Perhaps one of the greatest talents of the Bank is its analytical capacity. But where the Bank was a quick learner of the theory, it turned out to be slow in adapting to what it knew it should do. In part this is the result of its governance structure. The Bank is 'owned' by countries, which are heavily involved in the day-to-day decision-making at the Bank. The dominance of the US in the Bank's work is particularly worrisome (Chapter 5). But equally disturbing is the lack of European cohesion in the Board of the Bank: because the EU countries act by themselves in the Bank (and not as one), they allow the US dominance. As a result, the individual European countries condemn themselves to a marginal contribution.

Internally, there have been decisive attempts at the creation of an organizational culture that could be the fertile ground for effective development cooperation. But the change process has been often chaotic, with little attention to good management practices (Chapter 6).

With the appointment of a new President (likely in 2005) it is important to guarantee a mandate which allows a fully effective Bank, both in terms of its governance, in terms of the inside organization, and in terms of the context in which the Bank operates. Bank President Wolfensohn has laid the stepping-stones during his term in office (1996–2005) for such a renovated mandate.

Part III looks into the gradual spinning of a network of organizations that shape the global economy. These are the 'official' partners. Multilateral development banks (like the African Development Bank), but in particular the 'bilaterals' (the development aid organizations of different countries, like USAID for the US, the Japanese JICA or Canadian CIDA, etc.) are part of this network. The IMF – the neighbour and sister of the World Bank – is in the same way part of this arena for the World Bank. It is amusing to see that the office-buildings of the IMF and World Bank in Washington are connected by a tunnel. A tunnel is the epitome and symbol of secrecy. The IMF–World Bank relationship surely requires the maturity of a bridge between the buildings. Their success is entirely dependent on the cooperation with the other.

More generally: whatever the strength of the World Bank in political, intellectual and financial perspectives, the Bank can only be successful in partnership with other organizations, like the United Nations organizations (think of the WHO, UNICEF or UNESCO), and like the bilateral agencies and like-minded organizations (Chapter 7). Likewise, these organizations can only be successful in partnership with others, including the World Bank.

Increasingly, civil society has become a partner of official development agencies (Chapter 8). This is a logical reflection of the recognition of the role of civil society in rich and poor countries alike. Transparency, advocacy and private initiatives are part and parcel of development around the globe. The term 'civil society' opens up a broad spectrum of all kinds of different organizations, all with their own place in development cooperation. Some are very close to the development paradigm of the official organizations. Others have quite different ideological perspectives (this is, for example, the case for a small part of the protest movement, which rejects outright the market mechanism as a means of organizing international economic relations).

Part IV contains a prospect for development cooperation. This part sketches the way forward, by learning the lessons of successful development cooperation (Chapter 9). And even though the task may seem huge, this decade need not represent a lost opportunity (Chapter 10). Applying the lessons from the past requires drastic, one may even say radical changes; yet such changes are needed for the World Bank to stand a chance of realizing its mission. In his comic presentation 'My speech to the Graduates', Woody Allen speaks of mankind facing crossroads: 'One path leads to despair and utter hopelessness. The other, to total extinction.' This is not the scenario I envisage for development cooperation, even though the challenge is huge.

PART I

WHY DEVELOPMENT ASSISTANCE: SETTING THE STAGE

2

Poverty Remains a Universal Concern

I will argue that there is a fundamental willingness among a considerable part of the world's citizenry to improve the fate of the very poor in the world. At the same time, the world has not organized itself well enough to engage effectively in development cooperation in such a way that the goal of poverty reduction is realized.

Poverty in the world is still widespread as we show in Section 2.1. This ought to be sufficient reason to be actively involved in development cooperation, and rich countries should be expected to be generous in alleviating this poverty. Section 2.2 deals with the existing transfers from rich to poor countries. Although the present flow of 'Official Development Assistance' (ODA) may seem large with around US$50–60 billion a year, it is quite small in terms of the incomes of rich countries, namely only two cents out of every *ten dollars* earned. It is also small in terms of the incomes of developing countries, namely in the order of magnitude of about one per cent of the GDPs of poor countries (or one cent for every dollar of income). This is at odds with the professed generosity. The only likely explanations are that, on the one hand, citizens may not be convinced of the effectiveness of development cooperation or, on the other, that the appeal in rich countries to the generosity of its population is insufficient. Or could it be that rich countries are shortsighted and egoistic?

ODA is dwarfed by foreign direct investment (FDI) and by remittances. Those two are also flows from rich to poor countries. Yet ODA remains important, definitely for those countries with little FDI or with few remittances.

To get more support for development cooperation requires (in my view) an increase in the effectiveness of ODA in reducing poverty. It also requires better transparency in how aid is used. It is also a question of communication; there is a dire lack of awareness in the rich countries of development cooperation (Section 2.3). There is a decisive under-spending in the 'marketing' of effective development cooperation.

There was a time when people believed that globalization would do the job of poverty reduction. This was not unreasonable. Globalization, leading to more open markets holds a potential: in principle poorer countries might have better chances to compete internationally, because of lower wage costs. However, we know that it has been the other way around (Section 2.4), namely that certainly in the first decades of fast globalization (1960s, 1970s and 1980s) the developing countries lost out on the global markets.

I define globalization as the reduction of physical and psychological distances in the world. During the period of fast globalization, expectations in poor countries rose. Also the visibility in rich countries of poverty in poor countries increased. One might then have expected convergence between rich and poor countries. And yet the opposite (namely, divergence) took place (for a more elaborated reflection, see Chapter 3).

As a result we conclude that the potential of globalization for poverty reduction has been underutilized. The era of fast globalization (1960–2000 and continuing) is characterized by globalization with – what have become evident as – unsatisfactory rules of the game. The market mechanism became dominant, but its application created major advantages for the haves and major disadvantages for the poor: a less than level playing field.

The debt crisis in developing countries and their failure to make substantial progress in human development are – together with the increased divergence between rich and poor countries – signs of the failure of developing countries to catch on to global markets, but also signs of a failure of development cooperation in the past.

One cannot speak anymore about poverty reduction without speaking about HIV/AIDS. The scourge of HIV/AIDS demands, more than ever, effective aid. HIV/AIDS is a challenge of a dimension and magnitude, and of a human and political complexity, which is unmatched in history.

The development community, rich and poor countries alike, have set high goals for the next decade (Section 2.5): the MDGs (Millennium Development Goals). However, all existing trends show that these objectives are unlikely to be reached without major (rather: dramatic) changes both in the way development cooperation takes place, and in the context of that cooperation. The context should include better rules for globalization. Development cooperation needs to be more integrated and work as one, rather than involving a disparate group of donors all engaged in their own thing with more attention to flag planting than effective development (as we shall explore later on in this book).

The first decade of the new millennium need not be a lost opportunity for substantial improvement of the fate of the very poor in the world, provided we learn from the past. The MDGs can still be reached, but time is running out.

2.1 POVERTY IN THE WORLD

Why poverty is so close to our hearts and minds is for the philosopher to ponder and analyse. Yet the basic elements of our commitment to poverty reduction seem to be clear. We are concerned about ourselves, but also about our children, whom we wish to see live a life of dignity, free of poverty, with opportunities to grow. We apply what we hope for ourselves also to others. Our commitment to help poor people (when we see them) is presumably closely related to what we hope for ourselves.

We provide help in a direct way or in an indirect way through government intervention, which we support even when we know we will be taxed for that intervention. This solidarity between people to prevent and reduce poverty is well institutionalized within nations. But the borders for this solidarity exceed the borders of a country. The solidarity in a family or within the neighbourhood may be stronger than the solidarity with those we have not met and do not know ourselves and who may live far away. Yet solidarity is not bound by kinship, by personal relations or distance, as is evidenced by the generosity in rich countries towards poor countries. We do donate in response to the plight of poor people in far-away countries when we see them on CNN. People also agree to the institutionalized solidarity with poor people across country boundaries through development cooperation or other means of support, even if this means increased taxes.

The awareness of the plight of poor people in poor countries has grown in the rich countries. There may have been misunderstandings some decades ago about poverty in poor countries. The notion may have existed that it is not a plight to have a small income, if only the sun is shining and the soil is fertile and if one has good company. We know, however, that this romantic image does not apply to the poverty we measure by living on less than a couple of US dollars a day (or the equivalent in local currency). Such incomes are known to imply a life full of hardship and with little dignity.

Living in poverty means to be deprived of adequate food, shelter, education and health and the basic freedom of choice. These deprivations make poverty an intense and painful experience. The reports *Voices of the Poor* (2000, 2000 and 2002)[1] from the World Bank state the following ten dimensions of powerlessness and ill being as experienced by those living in poverty:

- Livelihood and assets are precarious, seasonal and inadequate;
- Places of the poor are isolated, risky, un-serviced and stigmatized;
- The body is hungry, exhausted, sick and poor in appearance;
- Gender relations are troubled and unequal;
- Social relations are discriminating and isolating;
- Security is lacking in the sense of both protection and ease of mind;

- Behaviours of those more powerful are marked by disregard and abuse;
- Institutions are disempowering and excluding;
- Organizations of the poor are weak and disconnected;
- Capabilities are weak because of the lack of information, education, skills and confidence.

In other words – as poor people express it – a life in poverty is a life without human dignity. Yet poverty is an everyday reality for more than half of the world population – or 3 billion people have to live on two dollars a day. A fifth of the world population or 1.2 billion people live on one dollar a day or less. In all developing countries one finds dire poverty (see Figure 2.1).

The largest segment of poor people (more than 40 per cent) still live in South Asia (where substantial and sustained economic growth would be a major boon in poverty reduction worldwide). Sub-Saharan Africa houses the second largest group (more than 20 per cent), together with East Asia and the Pacific (also more than 20 per cent). Figure 2.2 augments this knowledge with the changes in the past decade in poverty numbers by region.

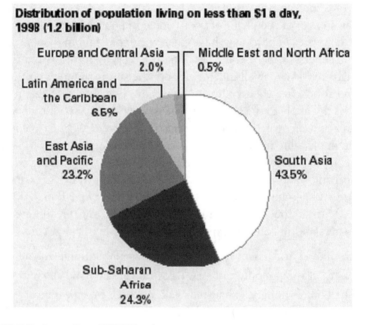

Source: World Development Report 2000/2001, p.4

Figure 2.1 Where the developing world's poor live

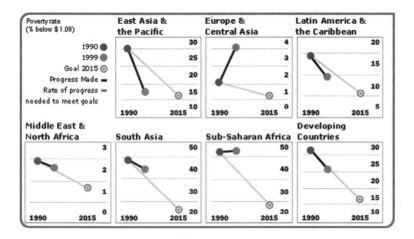

Source: Millennium Development Goals, World Bank, http://www.developmentgoals.org/Poverty.htm

Figure 2.2 Global poverty rates down 20% since 1990, but progress is uneven

The figure shows that the percentage of poor people more or less remained the same in the different regions during the 1980s and 1990s, except for East Asia and the Pacific, where the percentage of 1990 was reduced by half by 1999 and for Europe and Central Asia, where the poverty rate doubled. The figure also lists the aim of the world community for lowering the percentage of poor people by 2015 (derived from the goal of a reduction by half between 1990 and 2015). If one compares the trend of the 1990s with that target, then one sees that there is a major 'challenge' ahead. In particular, poverty in Sub-Saharan countries appears not easily remedied.

Poverty 'is a result of economic, political and social processes that interact with each other and frequently reinforce each other in ways that exacerbate the deprivation in which poor people live' (as the World Development Report 2000/2001, p.1 puts it). Over the years the understanding of the complexity of poverty has deepened. And so has the approach to poverty reduction. For example, in the 1950s and 1960s, the main concern in development cooperation was on income poverty and the main remedy was physical capital investment, which would create a 'rising tide, lifting all boats' (including the poor). Chapter 4 discusses these changes over time in the approach to poverty reduction.

The World Development Report of 2000/2001, entitled 'Attacking poverty', gives a good overview of the changes in thinking about poverty. It makes a distinction between the following dimensions: income poverty, health and education, vulnerability, lack of voice and powerlessness. These dimensions can move in different directions and stress the different ways in which poverty develops itself. The distinction offers tools to measure poverty. Nevertheless the different measurements are all approximations each with their own measurement problems:

- Income poverty: measures monetary income or consumption. The weakness of this measurement is that the estimates are based on household expenditures rather than individual income, thus ignoring the potential of considerable inequality within a household.
- Health and education: the absence of health and education are considered to be good indicators of poverty. There are problems with trying to assess these factors statistically, however; for example, the fact that enrolment numbers for education do not say anything about attendance or completion, or that child mortality rates are mostly estimates based on extrapolated trends and models.
- Vulnerability: the risk that one will experience poverty in health or income over time. Vulnerability is difficult to measure as a dimension of poverty since it is dynamic and may fluctuate.
- Lack of voice and powerlessness can be measured by participatory methods such as polls, surveys and civil and political liberties.

Poverty in its different dimensions tends to trap people in a vicious cycle, which inhibits them from escaping poverty. Factors which create this vicious circle and which are targeted by development organizations such as the World Bank are, among others: HIV/AIDS, corruption, debt, lack of education and training, shortage of energy, and an environment that is polluted or tormented by natural disasters etc.

The deepening in our understanding of poverty has resulted in some 800 indicators (as are used in the report 'World Development Indicators, 2003'; see World Bank website), covering a whole range of aspects of poverty and of development. Both the World Bank and UNDP (the Human Development Report) have provided the analytical work, which has been of great assistance in helping to understand poverty.

The moral case for development cooperation aimed at poverty reduction is particularly strong in view of the present distribution of income in the world. The 1 billion people in the richest countries have about 70 times as much to spend as the 1.2 billion people living in desperate poverty.

There is not only a moral outcry for development cooperation to help poor countries improve the fate of their poor people. Nobel prize winner Jan Tinbergen was one of the first to emphasize that development cooperation results in a win-win situation. Next to the altruistic or moral case for development cooperation stands the economic benefit for both the donor and the receiver as an important factor for investments in development cooperation. A healthy global economy is in the best interests of all, since this increases both demand and production, in this way stimulating the economy and improving the living conditions of people around the world. His emphasis is an echo of earlier thinking by John Maynard Keynes, the famous economist, who was one of the founding fathers of the World Bank.

Tinbergen also often referred to the importance of combating poverty worldwide in order to come closer to world peace. Great differences in income between countries may give rise to tensions and can be an important factor in the emergence of conflict. September 11, 2001 may well have underlined this argument. The hijackers of the planes that struck the Twin Towers and the Pentagon clearly felt themselves to be part of a movement which appeals worldwide to the downtrodden and poor. Poverty reduction worldwide may not be the only answer to Al Qaeda, but it should definitely be part of that answer.

2.2 DEVELOPMENT AID AND OTHER TRANSFERS

The figure of 0.7 per cent of GNP has become a rallying point for the size of the contribution of rich countries to development cooperation. Rich countries have in the past often indicated that they indeed intend to adhere to this figure as their goal. For poor countries it has been seen as part of the development contract between rich and poor nations. But in reality the generosity of the developed world is closer to 0.2 per cent of their incomes.

But still, development cooperation has achieved the substantial magnitude of around US $50–60 billion a year transferred from rich to poor countries. However only a minor part of the US $50 billion (we shall use this number as the benchmark figure derived from the volume of around 2000, see Table 2.1) goes directly to poor people in poor countries as cash transfers or transfers of goods. Cash transfers or transfers of goods directly to poor people happen as a rule only with emergency and humanitarian aid. For the international community, the emergency and humanitarian aid in the form of food, medicine, shelter and clothing are the exception, mostly reserved for refugees, and for relief after natural disasters like drought, floods, earthquakes or during or after civic conflicts.

The US $50 billion a year, which the rich countries donate, would be a drop in a bucket if it were given as humanitarian aid. It would amount to a bit more than ten cents a day for each of the very poor of the world. Rather the international community aims at helping poor countries to help themselves by providing the tools for fishing rather than the fish. The $50 billion is used to support poor countries in their efforts to improve the lives of their people, to make sure that in 10–15 years time we are no longer speaking about 1.2 billion very poor people, but maybe half that number or less.

The US $50 billion a year of official development assistance (ODA) is not the only flow of capital from rich to poor countries. Table 2.1 gives an impression of the net flows over the period 1997–2003.

Table 2.1 Net capital flows to developing countries

$ billions

	1997	2001	2002	2003e
Net equity flows	193.7	179.4	152.0	149.5
Net FDI inflows	171.1	175.0	147.1	135.2
Net portfolio equity inflows	22.6	4.4	4.9	14.3
Net debt flows	105.3	−1.2	7.3	44.3
Official creditors	13.2	26.9	4.1	−6.3
World Bank (IDA+IBRD)	9.2	7.5	−0.2	−1.9
IMF	3.4	19.5	14.0	8.0
Others	0.6	−0.1	−9.7	−12.4
Private creditors	92.2	−28.1	3.2	50.6
Memo items:				
ODA	48.5	52.3	58.3	na
Bilateral aid grants (excluding technical cooperation grants)	25.3	27.9	31.2	34.3
Net private flows (debt + equity)	285.8	151.3	155.3	200.2
Net official flows (aid + debt)	38.4	54.8	35.3	28.0
Workers' remittances	66.1	77.0	88.1	93.0

Note: na = not yet available
Source: Global Development Finance, 2004, p.197–8

The table is set up from two different perspectives:

- Whether the capital flow refers to equity or to credit/debt;
- The type of flow distinguished by bilateral grants, private flows, official flows and workers' remittances.

The Development Assistance Committee (DAC) of the OECD is the international forum for defining aid, which identifies two categories of aid: Official Development Assistance (ODA) and Official Aid (OA). ODA consists of loans and grants provided by the donor countries' governments to developing countries and territories, which are on a list, called 'Part I' of the DAC list of recipients. The Part I list contains poorer countries. OA is intended for countries in Part II of the DAC list of recipients, which, among others, consists of countries in Eastern and Western Europe, the Russian Federation, Israel etc.

The US $50 billion of ODA refers to the (net) official flow, which includes grants as well as credit (net flows to developing countries). Notice that the ODA flow in the period 1997–2003 has been around US $50–60 billion.

The table also shows the position of the World Bank (and that of its sister, the IMF) as official creditors. For example in 2001 the total of ODA (aid plus debt) of US $57.5 billion consisted of $29.5 billion in aid (grants) and (net) $28 billion in the form of loans. The World Bank was responsible for providing (net) $7.5 billion in loans. In other words: the giant World Bank is a major player in poverty reduction, even if it accounted for about 15 per cent of net ODA. However, its gross lending volume was for example in the fiscal year 1999 of the magnitude of US $29 billion.

There are further points, which put the efforts of the international community of rich countries to help to reduce poverty in poor countries through ODA in perspective:

- For developing countries the flow of remittances of workers exceeds that of ODA. At the same time one should realize that worker remittances are not spread in the same way as ODA (ODA is nominally based on the highest incidence of poverty). Table 2.1 indicates an amount of US $88 billion in 2002. Note that this is only the amount transferred through official channels. The IMF and World Bank estimate that the total amount transferred through official and unofficial channels is around US $200 billion (see further Section 10.4). It appears to be also a growing amount, reaching an estimated $93 billion in 2003 (World Bank, Global Development Finance 2004)
- The net private capital flows have become the most important flow of capital to developing countries with a magnitude which is in 2003 at least 5 times that of official ODA. Private capital flows are heavily concentrated in a few countries: 68 per cent in 10 countries in 2003 (World Bank, Global Development Finance 2004).

In other words: ODA is no more than 10 per cent of the total of resource transfers to developing countries.

A way to put the generosity of rich countries in perspective is by comparing the ODA flow to the annual income in rich countries, which was in 2003 around US $25 trillion. ODA then totals 0.2 per cent of the gross national income of the rich world (this in contrast to the 0.7 per cent goal mentioned above). It brings that US $50 billion to the poor and middle-income countries with a combined GNP of 6 trillion (5 trillion for the middle-income and 1 trillion for the poor countries). So we are speaking about a transfer that contributes less than 1 per cent to the incomes of the poor and middle-income countries.

The amount of ODA (Official Development Assistance) has decreased over the 1990s as Figure 2.3 indicates. Among the countries that decreased their expenditures on ODA, Australia shows the biggest drop from 0.46 per cent of

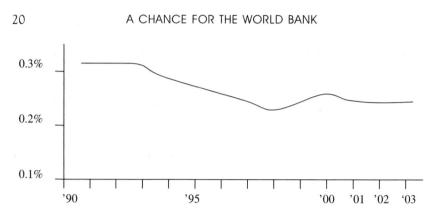

Source: UN Statistics Division, OECD website

Figure 2.3 ODA over time (% of GNI of rich countries)

its GNI in 1988 to 0.25 per cent in 2001. The US fell from an already low percentage of 0.21 in 1988 to 0.10 per cent in 2001, while countries such as Ireland increased this percentage from 0.20 in 1988 to 0.33 in 2001 and Spain climbed its way from 0.07 per cent in 1988 to 0.30 per cent in 2001, this way ending up higher than the US. Maybe (hopefully) 2001 marks an all time low in ODA. From 2001 to 2002 the ODA volume increased in real terms by 4.9 per cent.

Donor countries have expressed, through United Nations, their commitment to increasing their official development assistance (ODA) to developing countries at the International Conference on Financing for Development held in Monterrey, Mexico, in March 2002. According to OECD estimates, fulfilling these promises would raise ODA in real terms by 31 per cent (about US $16 billion) and the ODA/GNI ratio to 0.26 per cent by 2006 – still well below the ratio of 0.33 per cent consistently achieved until 1992, but a major extension of their generosity today (2005).

Why the goal of 0.7 per cent of GNI for development cooperation is not realized is anybody's guess. Maybe it is because there is no political basis, as many people in rich countries may have serious doubts about the way in which this solidarity at present is exercised, is implemented. They may doubt the effectiveness of development cooperation. On the other hand, perhaps they are simply shortsighted and egoistic.

ODA is dwarfed by the flows in the private sector, through 'foreign direct investment' (FDI) and through remittances of individuals working in rich countries to family and friends in their country of origin. The private flows, however, cannot replace ODA, as they go to different countries from those which need and get ODA.

Let us just mention the present efforts for ODA in rich countries. Denmark, Luxembourg, the Netherlands, Norway and Sweden are still the only countries to meet the United Nations ODA target of 0.7 per cent of GNI. Three other countries have given a firm date to reach the 0.7 per cent target: Belgium by 2010; Ireland by 2007; and France to reach 0.5 per cent by 2007 and 0.7 per cent by 2012. The UK has promised to raise its annual budget for development assistance (ODA) by 9.2 per cent a year between 2004 and 2007, which would make it number seven in terms of GDP per capita.

The USA increased its ODA by 11.6 per cent in real terms in 2002 to $12.9 billion, representing 0.12 per cent of its GNI. This increase was mainly due to additional and emergency funds in response to the September 11, 2001 terrorist attacks as well as new aid initiatives, especially in relation to health and humanitarian aid.

Japan was in the 1990s for a while the largest donor. Yet its generosity is often questioned as it provides a substantial part in loans. The net flows from Japan to developing countries are therefore much smaller than the gross flows.

Further information on ODA flows can be found on the website of the organisation for Economic Co-operation (OECD) at http://www.oecd.org/

Too often ODA is given to developing countries in the form of goods (e.g. school benches) or services (e.g. consultants). This is called 'tied aid'. Tying 'aid' reduces substantially the value of that aid for the receiving party, which would be able to use the money better.[2] According to the World Bank's Global Monitoring Report 2004, the proportion of aid provided in cash is falling (while it should be rising; see Chapter 11, p. 6); it fell from 60 per cent in 1981 to 30 per cent in 2002. Tying aid can come in many forms. To quote the WDR 2000–2001 (Chapter 11): 'In 1998 almost a quarter of official development assistance was tied, meaning that the procurement contracts were limited to the donor country or group of countries. Driven by domestic political interests, this practice goes against the very free-market principles that most donors are trying to encourage in developing countries and results in inefficient use of aid. It has been estimated that tying aid reduces its value by 15–30 per cent. The practice should be ended as quickly as possible, and contracts should go to the best bids.'

Apart from demanding that the goods are purchased in the donor country, aid can also be tied when donors impose conditions, which decreases the value of the investment. A bizarre example is found in Senegal for schools built with Japanese funds. The schools have to be earthquake proof, although the chance of an earthquake hitting Senegal is about as remote as that of a meteorite hitting the planet.

In conclusion: the concern of rich countries about poverty in poor countries is real and well exemplified in the flow of official development assistance. The magnitude of this flow is however meagre compared to the incomes in the rich countries and is dwarfed by the transfers of funds through remittances and foreign domestic investment.

2.3 MORE AWARENESS IS NEEDED

Public support in the developed countries for the principle of providing aid to developing countries is evident. The percentage of the population that supports aid has been high and stable for two decades now, ranging from 70 per cent in France to 95 per cent in Ireland. Despite this support, public awareness and understanding of development policies and issues remains limited. To give an example, when Europeans are asked what percentage of their national income is spent on development cooperation one third said: 'do not know' and another third estimates these investments to be between 1 and 5 or 5 and 10 per cent of their GNI. Only a small percentage is aware that this number is less than 1 per cent of the national income, and that even the highest scoring countries spend under 0.8 per cent of their national income on development cooperation (OECD, Public Opinion Research, 2003).

This lack of awareness and understanding reduces the significance of the public's support, and is combined with criticism of the effectiveness of development cooperation and concern about the legitimacy of the development cooperation policies. Another way of saying this is that the institutionalized generosity of the rich world is in danger because it lacks accountability. It is of the first importance to increase awareness about development cooperation. Active and open communication about development cooperation is needed which appeals to the basic concepts of that cooperation, in particular poverty reduction. Denmark is a good example of active communication with its inhabitants about development cooperation. In 2001, 90 per cent of the population knew that DANIDA is the agency for development cooperation and more than 50 per cent of the population estimated the right percentage for ODA (Official Development Assistance).

2.4 POVERTY AND GLOBALIZATION

Globalization is defined here as the increased access to information worldwide, the reduction in time needed for access to information, and the reduction of costs of mobility over large distances. The economist might say that we define globalization in terms of the reduction in the transaction costs for information and for mobility. These cost reductions have contributed to rising expectations. Box 2.1 gives an example of its impact.

This is globalization at work, where tastes and expectations around the world are no longer anchored in 'keeping up with the Joneses', the comparison with the next-door neighbours, not even with the standards and customs in the village or the region, but with those of the world. 'Happy with what you have' is not the basic attitude of most people in the world. They aspire to

Box 2.1: Globalization at Work

A still young woman comes to complain to me about her 12-year-old son, who is running around in the playground of a school I am visiting in Nov. 2001, some 30 miles north of Bamako, the capital of Mali. The boy wears the latest fashion baggy pants, quite at odds with the traditional wear of his mother. 'They cost me a month's income', she complains, 'but he had to have them, since everyone was getting them'. The power of the hidden persuaders (in this case transmitted through TV) permeates even to this rural village in Mali. The boy and his classmates derive their aspirations for fashion from the world, not just their own environment.

more, and not just for goods and services from their own soil, but for whatever is available in the wider world. Rural Mali is no exception to this rule.

If we stop and consider for a moment, it is clear that our economic dynamics are based on aspiring for more, on wanting to improve our living conditions. This does not only relate to mental living conditions (like the feeling of safety) but also to material living conditions. We all may have our philosophical reservations on the driving force of material living conditions, exerted by market economies, we may even add the notion that people should be concerned more about the substance of life, and yet, it is there as a reality, as a real driving force. 'Happy with what you have' may always have been the privilege of a few, in rich and poor countries alike.

Increased communication reduces physical and psychological distances. In this way, globalization also makes poverty at a large distance more visible in rich countries: that is one side of the medal of globalization. At the same time, the existing means of communication have contributed to rising expectations of poor people, as the example of Mali shows. This is the other side of the medal. In the global village we are all neighbours.

Increased expectations on the one hand and increased solidarity or at least awareness on the other: these are two sides of one medal, which ought to create convergence. More generally, one expects on the surface that globalization should be an equalizing, converging force between nations. It should provide, as it were, a coil between nations that keeps them together and brings them closer. If they grow too far apart, the coil comes under stress and pulls the countries back together, reducing the divide: once one country outgrows the other economically, the second will inevitably be pulled back because of lower wage costs. The coil – of course – only exists if the countries are tied through open markets with each other (and the image is highly simplistic).

However, the recent history of poor countries (except East Asia) and the rich countries can be better compared to that of the increasing divide between separating planets travelling their own course. The wage cost difference between the poor and the rich countries has indeed massively attracted investments towards the poor countries in the 1990s. But this has not been enough; and quite often, efforts to bend the course of divergence around into one of convergence are focused on a small number of selected countries (except for East Asia): globalization is overwhelmingly accompanied by divergence.

This divergence is the reason why development assistance in general – and more particularly the World Bank – has been attacked by the anti-globalization movement. Often the Bank is under attack for being one of the most evil forces of globalization, because it propagates the opening up of markets for goods and services as well as the opening up of financial markets and, in that way, may bring countries into a downward spiral, worsening the fate of the poor rather than helping to reduce poverty.

The agencies of development cooperation like those of the Governments of rich countries, of the UN, but also including the World Bank certainly have a lot to explain about their limited effectiveness in helping poor countries. In this book, I will defend their approach: to help developing countries to be more part of the world economy. This was in principle the right one. There was in fact little alternative. However, the lessons learned from the past need to be applied. Among them (but this is definitely not the only one) is the late recognition of the importance of good governance, which has hampered the effectiveness of aid.

Why there is little alternative can well be illustrated with the example of Box 2.1 on expectations. These expectations are global in the sense that they are based on the global availability of goods and services. It is clear that these aspirations cannot be satisfied with goods and services that are locally produced. Some products have to be imported. And then the simple albeit dismal equation of globalization enters: one has to export as much (in value) as one wants to import.

The principle of free trade originates from the fact that trade enabled people to obtain food and materials that they could not produce for themselves. Countries specialize in producing the goods that they can produce most efficiently in comparison to others, and countries trade their surpluses of those goods for the products they cannot produce, or are relatively less efficient at producing.

Not only is export an imperative for the aspirations which lead to imports, free trade can also be a tremendous boost for the exports of developing countries as a wealth creator. Many of the rich countries have benefited from 'export-led growth'. Developing countries often have the comparative advantage of being low-wage countries creating substantial comparative advantages for their export position. Free trade has also the advantage of integrating economies, so that developing countries can have access to the knowledge and the technologies of the developed world. This – in itself – can accelerate the pace of development.

What went wrong when development assistance started to focus in the 1980s and 1990s on free trade (in line with the increased attention among rich countries to freeing up trade)? With the advantage of hindsight (it is easy to judge with hindsight!) the effectiveness of development assistance has been handicapped by ignoring the adjustment processes, the social consequences of changes, the quality of governance and institutions and the prevalence of the rule of law in the aid-receiving countries.

Good governance has become a key word for development. Figure 2.4 depicts the characteristics of good governance as recognized by the UN.

Good governance has eight major characteristics. It is participatory, consensus oriented, accountable, transparent, responsive, effective and efficient, equitable and inclusive and follows the rule of law. It assures that corruption is minimized, the views of minorities are taken into account and that the voices of the most vulnerable in society are heard in decision-making. It is also responsive to the present and future needs of society. In the absence of good governance, development aid will be less effective. How much less effective may depend on the specific circumstances.

Ignoring 'good governance' as an essential element of effective development cooperation is not the only reason for the divergence between rich and poor countries. There is also the tendency of developed countries to protect their

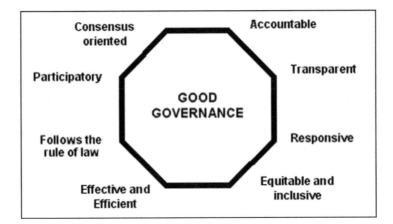

Source: http://www.unescap.org/huset/gg/governance.htm

Figure 2.4 Characteristics of good governance

trade against the main export products of developing countries, creating in this way unfair competition instead of free trade.

The failure of development cooperation in the past is not only visible in the divergence between rich and poor countries and the relatively small reduction in poverty. It is also apparent in the debt crisis. The debt crisis was without doubt the expression of a crisis in development cooperation. The naked fact is that by the end of the 1980s, there was a debt crisis. Developing countries were unable to pay back the loans they had received in the 1960s, 1970s and 1980s on highly favourable ('concessional') terms (low interest, long duration). Table 2.2 presents the classification of countries by indebtedness.

It is clear that the debt crisis has in particular hit the low-income countries. This is tantamount to saying that the loans granted in the 1970s and 1980s did not contribute enough to make it possible to pay these loans back out of the newly acquired growth (see also Section 3.3 on debt reduction). The debt crisis also begs the question why the major development agency, namely the World Bank, should give loans (however 'concessional', meaning with very low interest) to poor countries rather than grants (see Section 4.6).

The development crisis was not only apparent in the debt levels of countries; it was also visible in human development. One way of measuring the level of human development is by the Human Development Index (HDI). The HDI measures average achievement in three basic dimensions of human development, namely a long and healthy life, knowledge, as well as standard of living. It was created to emphasize that people and their lives should be the ultimate criteria for assessing the development of a country, not economic growth or interest rates (see: www.undp.org). To give an indication of the ranking of countries according to the HDI, Table 2.3 gives an overview of the ten countries highest on the HDI of 2000 and the ten lowest countries.

It is clear that the countries that are low on the list of human development have made very little progress in the past decades in human development.

A new setback for development came in the 1980s and 1990s in the form of HIV/AIDS. HIV/AIDS is a scourge the impact of which can hardly be overestimated. Late in 2002, UNAIDS reported that in Southern Africa national adult HIV prevalence rates had risen higher than was thought possible, exceeding 30 per cent in four countries. Table 2.4 illustrates the magnitude of the epidemic.

Fields in Southern Africa are lying fallow because there is no one to work them. 30 per cent of the adult population is infected with HIV/AIDS. Whoever is not sick is tending the sick and dying or taking care of the orphans. Food can no longer be produced. We encounter for perhaps the first time in world history a food shortage and famine which is induced or at least magnified by incapacitation due to illness. Even the chronicles of the Black Death epidemic

Table 2.2 Classification of countries by levels of external indebtedness and income
(138 economies in World Bank Debtor Reporting System)

Severely Indebted low-income	Severely Indebted middle-income	Moderately Indebted low-income	Moderately Indebted middle-income	Less Indebted low-income	Less Indebted middle-income
Angola	Argentina	Bhutan	Bulgaria	Armenia	Albania
Benin	Belize	Cambodia	Bolivia	Azerbaijan	Algeria
Burkina Faso[a]	Brazil	Cameroon	Chile	Bangladesh	Barbados
Burundi	Ecuador	Ghana	Colombia	Equatorial Guinea	Belarus
Central African Republic	Gabon	Haiti	Croatia	Eritrea	Bosnia and Herzegovina
Chad	Guyana	Kenya	Dominica	Georgia	Botswana
Comoros	Jordan	Mali	Estonia	India	Cape Verde
Congo, Dem. Rep. of	Lebanon	Mongolia	Grenada	Lesotho	China
Congo, Rep. of	Panama	Papua New Guinea	Honduras	Mozambique	Costa Rica
Côte d'Ivoire	Peru	Senegal	Hungary	Nepal	Czech Republic
Ethiopia	Syrian Arab Republic	Tanzania	Jamaica	Solomon Islands	Djibouti
Gambia, The	Uruguay	Togo	Kazakhstan	Ukraine	Dominican Republic
Guinea	Yugoslavia, Fed. Rep. of	Uganda	Latvia	Vietnam	Egypt, Arab Rep. of
Guinea-Bissau		Uzbekistan	Malaysia	Yemen, Republic of	El Salvador
Indonesia		Zimbabwe	Philippines		Fiji
Kyrgyz Republic			Russian Federation		Guatemala
Laos			Samoa		Iran, Islamic Rep. of
Liberia			Slovak Republic		Lithuania
Madagascar			St. Kitts and Nevis		Macedonia, FYR
Malawi			St. Vincent and the Grenadines		Maldives
Mauritania[a]			Thailand		Malta
Moldova			Tunisia		Mauritius
Myanmar			Turkey		Mexico
Nicaragua			Turkmenistan		Morocco
Niger					Oman
Nigeria					Paraguay
Pakistan					Poland
Rwanda					Romania
São Tomé and Principe					Seychelles
Sierra Leone					South Africa
Somalia					Sri Lanka
Sudan					St. Lucia
Tajikistan					Swaziland
Zambia					Tonga
					Trinidad and Tobago
					Vanuatu
					Venezuela

a. Enhanced HIPC assistance will be accounted for in *Global Development Finance 2004*.

Income and indebtedness classification criteria

Income classification	Indistinctness classification		
	PV/XGS higher than 220 per cent or PV/GNI higher than 80 per cent	PV/XGS less than 220 per cent but higher than 132 per cent or PV/GNI less than 80 per cent but higher than 48 per cent	PV/XGS less than 132 per cent and PV/GNI less than 48 per cent
Low-income: GNI per capita less than $745	Severely indebted low-income countries	Moderately indebted low-income countries	Les indebted low-income countries
Middle-income: GNI per capita between $746 and $9,205	Severely indebted middle-income countries	Moderately indebted middle-income countries	Less indebted middle-income countries

Note: PV/XGS is present value of debt service to exports of goods and services. PV/GNI is present value of debt service to gross national income.

Source: Global Development Finance 2003, Appendix, p.235

in the thirteenth century in Europe do not mention – to the best of my knowledge – such a disaster.

2.5 THE OBJECTIVES OF DEVELOPMENT ASSISTANCE; MILLENNIUM DEVELOPMENT GOALS

Development is, in the words of another Nobel Prize winner, Amartya Sen, 'the expansion of capabilities, increasing the possibilities for more people to realize their potentials as human beings through the expansion of their capabilities for functioning' (Sen, 1990, p. 308).

Table 2.3 Human Development

Ten countries highest on the HDI	Ten countries lowest on the HDI
1 Norway 0.942	164 Mali 0.386
2 Sweden 0.941	165 Central African Republic 0.375
3 Canada 0.940	166 Chad 0.365
4 Belgium 0.939	167 Guinea-Bissau 0.349
5 Australia 0.939	168 Ethiopia 0.327
6 United States 0.939	169 Burkina Faso 0.325
7 Iceland 0.936	170 Mozambique 0.322
8 Netherlands 0.935	171 Burundi 0.313
9 Japan 0.933	172 Niger 0.277
10 Finland 0.931	173 Sierra Leone 0.275

Source: Human Development Report, 2004

Table 2.4 Global summary of the HIV/AIDS epidemic December 2002

Number of people living with HIV/AIDS Total	42 million	
	Adults	38.6 million
	Women	19.2 million
	Children under 15 years	3.2 million
People newly infected with HIV in 2002 Total	5 million	
	Adults	4.2 million
	Women	2 million
	Children under 15 years	800 000
AIDS deaths in 2002	Total	3.1 million
	Adults	2.5 million
	Women	1.2 million
	Children under 15 years	610 000

Source: Aids Epidemic Update December 2002, UNAIDS/WHO

Development cooperation was brought into life in Bretton Woods at the end of the Second World War. The direct objective was to stabilize the economic situation in order to prevent another economic crisis like that of the 1930s. Initially the focus was on Europe, but slowly the objective turned to the developing countries in Africa, Asia, the Pacific and South America in order to reduce poverty and to enable the poor to change their situation themselves and to rebuild their own economy. Development organizations offer a hand in taking this first step, which is often difficult, or even experienced to be impossible, without financial or political aid from outside.

At this moment the Millennium Development Goals (MDGs) are the best formulation of what the different nations in the world agree to be the objectives of development assistance. The 188 Heads of State belonging to the United Nations who signed the declaration stated 'We, Heads of State and Government, have gathered at United Nations Headquarters in New York from 6 to 8 September 2000, at the dawn of a new millennium, to reaffirm our faith in the organization and its charter as indispensable foundations of a more peaceful, prosperous and just world.' They accepted a resolution that describes the Millennium Development Goals. These are the following eight objectives (which are divided into several sub-objectives, see: www.un.org/millenniumgoals/):

- Eradicate extreme poverty and hunger: reduce the proportion of people living on less than $1 a day to half the 1990 level by 2015 – from 29 per cent of all people in low and middle-income economies to 14.5 per cent.
- Achieve universal primary education: in 2015 all children everywhere should be able to complete a full course of primary schooling.

- Promote gender equality and empower women. Eliminate gender disparity in primary and secondary education, preferably by 2005, and in all levels of education no later than 2015.
- Reduce by two thirds, between 1990 and 2015, the under-five mortality rate.
- Reduce by three quarters, between 1990 and 2015, the maternal mortality rate.
- Combat HIV/AIDS, malaria and other diseases.
- Ensure environmental sustainability.
- Develop a global partnership for development.

Are these MDGs another set of promises made by the world, only to see some decades later that few if any have been achieved? It certainly looks as if it will not be an easy ride, according to the World Development Report of the World Bank of 2004, which gives a detailed overview of the likely prospects for the realization of the MDGs *if the present trends continue*. Figure 2.5 details where we stand on the MDGs worldwide.

Combining Figure 2.5 with the information of the World Development Report 2004 leads us to the following conclusions for the realism of the MDGs worldwide:

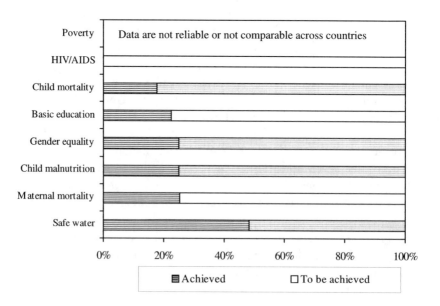

Source: UNDP, 2002

Figure 2.5 MDGs: where we stand

- The poverty goal is likely to be achieved mainly thanks to the impact of the high poverty reduction in China.
- The access-to-safe-water goal is 'on track'.
- All other goals are not on 'track'.

But what are the prospects for reaching the MDGs in individual countries? Figure 2.6 presents those prospects for two of the MDGs: school completion and child mortality.

From this figure it is clear that only very few of the developing countries are able to achieve these central MDGs for education and child mortality.

Let us explore the practical context for a single one of the MDGs, namely the MDG to reduce child mortality by half by 2015:

- On the one hand the urgency is clear. The death of babies and young children is a tragedy beyond comprehension. The sorrow of and shock to the parents and family is no smaller when you are poor. At the same time, the goal looks at first view quite feasible if one compares the situation in developing countries with that in rich countries. In developing countries the present level of child mortality is abysmally high with 1 in 10 children dying before the age of five. The MDG set as a goal that child mortality should be reduced to 1 in 20 by 2015. The rich countries (as well as Cuba, which is the exception to the poor countries) have been able to reduce the suffering of children dying by informing the parents about nutrition and (clean) water, by measles injections and by the proper care when the child develops diarrhea, to 1 in 200. So even 1 in 20 is a goal that is not only minimal, if 1 in 200 can be reached, but it also looks – at first sight – to be quite feasible.
- On the other hand, it turns out that in the recent past any reduction in child mortality has been very difficult to achieve and slow to come. If we extrapolate past trends it becomes obvious that a major challenge is ahead. In 2003 at least 80 of the developing countries were not 'on track' to reduce the level of child mortality by half by 2015.

'Business as usual' would also fail to deliver the education goal ('all kids in quality schools' in at least 80 countries. There is an overlap between the 80 which will fail to reach universal primary education and the 80 which will fail to reach the reduction in child mortality, but it is far from a complete overlap, as is shown in Figure 2.6.

In other words: the heads of state showed substantial courage in signing up to the Millennium Declaration, because they knew that reaching the MDGs was an unusually large challenge. The challenge could only be met if certain changes were to take place in developing countries. These changes would

(Child malnutrition)

PRIMARY SCHOOL COMPLETION

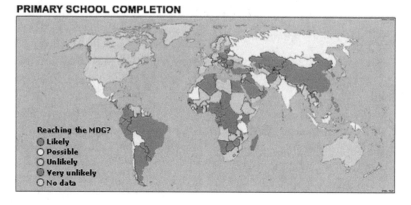

Realising the MDG ?

CHILD MORTALITY

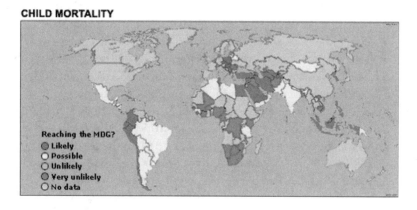

Source: UN, MDG Website

Figure 2.6 Realising the MDGs

require considerable political courage, and well-increased room for manoeuvre to put them into practice as well as improvements in governance, public service delivery and poverty reduction. But the developed countries were also brave in signing the Millennium Declaration because it it was clear, in addition, that much had to change in the way in which the donors and the international organizations work and in particular work together. The developed world needed indeed, among other things, to be willing both to cast aside its 'flag planting' mentality and to be more generous (in order to reach a level of ODA of 0.7 per cent of the rich world's GDP). The conclusion was positive and upbeat. It could be done.

Can development assistance indeed contribute to reaching these goals, even though it has not up to now shown too much effectiveness (at least not until approximately 1990–1995)? Certainly the organizations of development cooperation have to learn from the failures of the 1960s, 1970s and 1980s. The 1990s showed a number of successes, not only in East Asia, but also, for example, in Uganda and Mozambique. It is easy to make the case that the MDGs are indeed realistic goals. Yet much has to happen to make the first decade of the twenty-first century a success for development assistance in the sense of realizing the MDGs.

3

Globalization Does Not Automatically Lead to Convergence

The world is becoming more and more a global village due to interconnectedness. Information and money flow in nanoseconds around the globe, people travel easily from continent to continent and goods or services are as available in a far-away country as in the country of origin.

The degree of interconnectedness has been rising constantly throughout the ages, but it has shown an exponential increase in the past decades. We question ourselves: can this go on? Have we reached the boundaries of the possible or are there still great leaps ahead with, for example, personalized visual connections? Agencies of development cooperation (and among them the World Bank) have not just surfed on the waves of globalization. They have actually contributed in word and deed to globalization, in the sense of contributing to connectedness. They believed that more interconnectedness would increase the speed of poverty reduction and would contribute to convergence. Looking back now to past decades, this belief was insufficiently founded. Too little attention was given to the circumstances under which globalization took place and the ways in which the interconnectedness increased.

Globalization has turned out to be a force that can initiate and stimulate development, but can also cause poverty and divergence. In the last five decades poverty has been reduced. In the last decade alone the average proportion of people living on less than $1 per day decreased from 32 per cent in 1990 to 25 per cent in 1999, but we cannot know whether a higher speed of reduction would have been achieved with a different organization of the global economy during this period of rapid globalization. The organization of the world economy, including the mandate for and organization of the World Bank, is the main thrust of this book.

Figure 2.2 showed the change during the 1990s in the percentages of people living under extreme poverty, per region. Another way of looking at the changes in world (in)equality is by comparing the annual income growth rates of countries over time. These are shown in Table 3.1 for the 1980s and 1990s.

Table 3.1 Global real GDP growth, 1981–2004

GDP in 1995 prices and exchange rates, average annual growth (%)

	Average		1998	1999	2000	2001	2002	2003e	2004f
	1981–90	1991–2000							
World	3.1	2.7	2.1	3.0	4.0	1.4	1.8	2.6	3.7
High-income	3.2	2.5	2.2	3.1	3.8	1.0	1.4	2.1	3.3
Industrial countries	3.1	2.5	2.2	3.0	3.6	1.1	1.4	2.0	3.3
European Union (15)	2.4	2.1	2.9	2.8	3.7	1.7	1.1	0.7	1.9
Japan	4.1	1.5	-1.2	0.2	2.8	0.4	-0.3	2.7	3.1
United States	3.2	3.2	4.2	4.4	3.7	0.5	2.2	3.2	4.6
Other high-income	4.9	5.6	1.0	4.5	7.6	-1.0	2.3	2.6	5.0
Asian NIEs	7.3	6.1	0.9	5.1	7.6	-1.5	3.0	2.7	5.6
Developing countries	2.6	3.1	1.7	2.9	5.2	3.0	3.4	4.8	5.4
Excluding China	2.1	2.2	0.6	2.1	4.7	2.0	2.4	3.8	4.7
Excluding Central Europe and CIS	3.0	4.6	2.2	2.6	5.0	2.7	3.3	4.6	5.5
Severely indebted	1.5	3.3	-0.7	0.0	3.3	0.8	0.2	2.4	4.2
Moderately indebted	2.8	0.8	-1.8	1.9	6.2	1.8	3.6	4.5	5.2
Less indebted	3.1	4.6	5.1	5.1	5.8	4.7	4.9	6.1	6.0
Middle-income countries	2.2	3.1	1.9	2.6	5.4	2.6	3.3	4.6	5.2
Upper-middle-income countries	0.9	3.1	1.9	0.8	4.1	0.6	-0.1	2.0	4.0
Lower-middle-income countries	3.4	3.2	2.0	4.2	6.6	4.2	5.9	6.5	6.1
Low-income countries	4.3	3.1	0.4	4.3	4.2	4.5	4.1	5.4	6.1

East Asia and Pacific	7.3	7.7	0.6	5.6	7.2	5.6	6.7	7.7	7.4
China	9.3	10.1	7.8	7.1	8.0	7.5	8.0	9.1	—
Indonesia	6.4	4.2	-13.0	0.3	5.3	3.4	3.7	4.0	—
Europe and Central Asia	1.8	-1.5	-0.2	2.9	6.8	2.4	4.6	5.5	4.9
Russian Federation	2.0	-3.9	-5.3	6.4	10.0	5.0	4.3	6.8	—
Turkey	5.2	3.6	3.1	-4.7	7.4	-7.5	7.8	5.0	—
Poland	-0.3	3.7	4.8	4.1	4.0	1.0	1.4	4.2	—
Latin America and the Caribbean	1.1	3.3	2.0	0.1	3.7	0.3	-0.6	1.3	3.8
Brazil	1.5	2.7	0.1	0.8	4.4	1.4	1.9	-0.2	—
Mexico	1.8	3.5	4.9	3.7	6.6	-0.3	1.0	1.2	—
Argentina	-1.5	4.5	3.9	-3.4	-0.8	-4.4	-10.9	7.6	—
Middle East and North Africa	1.6	3.3	3.5	1.9	4.4	3.5	3.3	5.1	3.7
Saudi Arabia	-1.7	2.3	1.7	-1.8	4.9	1.2	1.0	4.8	—
Iran, Islamic Rep. of	2.7	4.2	2.0	2.5	5.9	4.8	6.7	6.2	—
Egypt, Arab Rep. of	5.5	4.3	4.5	6.3	5.1	3.5	3.0	3.1	—
South Asia	5.6	5.2	5.4	6.4	4.2	4.7	4.3	6.5	7.2
India	5.8	5.5	6.0	7.1	3.9	5.2	4.6	6.8	—
Sub-Saharan Africa	1.7	2.2	2.2	2.4	3.1	3.1	3.3	2.4	3.4
South Africa	1.3	1.7	0.8	2.0	3.5	2.7	3.6	1.9	—
Nigeria	1.1	2.7	1.9	1.1	4.2	2.2	1.8	3.0	—

Note: not available: *e* = estimate: *f* = forecast.

Source: Global Development Finance, 2004, p.185

The table shows that there was a slight divergence between the total of the rich countries and the total of the poor countries in the 1980s, but that the 1990s showed some convergence. This does not apply to the poorest countries (low-income): their economic growth rates were also higher in the 1980s than those in the rich countries (high-income). In fact, they lost some of their edge over rich countries in the 1990s. Also, the convergence in the 1990s is only slight. Note also that we are speaking in Table 3.1 of total income growth, not in terms of income per capita. Since population growth in developing countries still exceeds that of the rich world, the total picture of the 1980s and 1990s is one of a divergence between rich and poor countries.

Overall, the high expectations of globalization in the 1980s and 1990s with respect to their effect on poverty have not been realized. Indeed, over the whole time period of fast globalization (from 1970 onwards) the divergence between the rich and the poor countries has increased. The average income in the richest 20 countries is now (2004) 37 times the average wage in the 20 poorest countries. This is double the ratio of 1970 (World Development Report, 2003, p. 183). This increase in divergence is acknowledged by the rich countries and was part of an intensive discussion among heads of state in Monterrey in 2002. From this discussion the so-called 'Monterrey Consensus' emerged. This is a commitment to closing the gap in development, to speed up poverty reduction and the reduction the gap between rich and poor countries through higher growth in poor countries (see also Section 4.6). To quote: 'Specifically, the Monterrey Consensus links aid effectiveness with developing country ownership of good policies and sound governance. Furthermore, it recognizes that developed countries have a responsibility to increase aid, ease debt burdens, and reduce barriers to trade. The new compact reflects hard-won lessons of development experience' (World Bank web site).

Those are the words. However, it needs to happen, it needs to be implemented. Trade barriers for example, including the agricultural subsidies in rich countries, still need to be reduced more substantially (although there are some positive signs). We have to see the money of the 24 per cent increase in official development aid from $50 billion to $62 billion. On the one hand we see, for example, progress in the UK, on the other we notice that much of the US increase is aimed at specific purposes (like Afghanistan or Iraq), not augmenting the ODA efforts of the start of this century. The harmonization of aid still has to take place. On this front there seems to be more of a retreat than progress.

This chapter focuses on the misconceptions that led to the high expectations about the impact of globalization on convergence in the world. These are the misconceptions that need to be addressed for development assistance to become more successful.

A first misconception is that it is easier to grow fast if the country is poor (Section 3.1). The basic mistake made in this position is not to see that there are underlying reasons for a country being poor and that those very reasons (a lack of institutions, a lack of a history of working together) make it very difficult to generate the necessary economic growth for a substantial reduction of poverty. What could be accomplished in China in economic growth may not be feasible in Ethiopia or Bolivia.

A second misconception is that the pace of divergence has decreased with increased globalization. It is the opposite: a comparison between 2000 shows that in particular the poorer countries had more trouble in growing in the later period than in the former (Section 3.2), even though the 1980s and 1990s were the first period since 1950 when developing countries on average grew faster in per capita income than rich countries. Here we also focus on human development. Progress in human development might well be a precursor to progress in per capita income some years later.

A third misconception is that the divergence was the result of insufficient room for market forces in developing countries. The case can easily be made that it has been the opposite. Indeed, many developing countries may have suffered in the 1970s in their social and economic development from a communist style organization of economic life. But the fast switch in the 1980s from these regimes to an organization of the economy based on undiluted market forces may have been a drag on development, rather than a support (Section 3.3). Markets need institutions, and institutions are not built up overnight. The speed of change was too fast to realize the intended results.

A fourth misconception is that the focus of trade liberalization has been too much on the trade restrictions in developing countries and too little on those in the rich countries. Poor countries are heavily dependent on agriculture. Trade was liberalized in poor countries while the rich countries maintained or increased their agricultural subsidies and import restrictions on imports for poor countries. As a result trade liberalization has not contributed to convergence (Section 3.4). It is only recently that this focus has (fortunately) changed.

A fifth misconception puts also the spotlight on the rich world. Corruption and civic conflicts in poor countries are in part due to the interaction between poor and rich countries. Corruption is to a certain extent induced, by the involvement of foreign firms with considerable financial interest. Civic conflict is often induced or increased by foreign involvement (remember the Sierra Leone civil war in the 1990s which was fuelled by diamond merchants). This is the subject of Section 3.5.

A sixth misconception is that higher education would build the leadership for developing countries while in practice we see a considerable 'brain drain'

(Section 3.6). We also realize that the emphasis of development cooperation, which was rightly placed on 'education for all', has unfortunately contributed to a neglect of the quality of higher education.

This chapter concludes with a number of observations on requirements for a more equitable globalization (Section 3.7).

3.1 BOOTSTRAP LIFTING: NO EASY CHALLENGE

Convergence would require the economies of poorer countries to grow substantially faster than those of rich countries. But reality does not come close to this requirement, if we leave China aside. Instead, it shows an opposite trend, as Table 3.1 shows for the period 1980–2000.

This is contrary to expectations. Simple reasoning would state that it should not be a real effort for poor countries to grow faster as other countries have reached income levels far above those of developing countries. Also, the low wages of developing countries should attract all kinds of productive activities, which could strengthen their income generating capacities.

'Lift yourself by your bootstraps': that used to be the command to developing countries. If only the challenge of convergence could be met that simply! Yes, some countries did move ahead quickly and converged (e.g. Ireland and Portugal in Europe, and China and Thailand in East Asia). Yet the general tendency throughout the past century has been one of *divergence*.

As Pritchett[1] concludes: 'One overwhelming feature of the period of modern economic growth is massive divergence of absolute and relative incomes across countries.' He shows that between 1970 and 1985 the ratio of per capita incomes between the richest and poorest countries increased sixfold. The standard deviation of per capita incomes increased between 60 per cent and 100 per cent, and the average income gap between the richest and the poorest countries grew almost ninefold (from $1,500 to over $12,000). Between 1960 and 1990, income grew 2.6 per cent per year on average in the Organization for Economic Cooperation and Development (OECD) countries and 1.8 per cent in other countries. Among the poor countries, 43 per cent have grown slower than the slowest growing OECD country and 70 per cent have grown at a slower rate than the median for OECD countries. It will be clear that the required increase in growth for developing countries is as good as impossible to achieve. Apparently, the initial income effect (i.e. the lower the income in a country, the easier it grows) is more than offset by the 'first mover advantages' of the developed countries (i.e. once you know the 'trick' you can move ahead faster).

There may be a tendency for more rapid growth rates when the initial income is lower, but this is not enough for absolute convergence when 'conditioning variables', as Pritchett calls them, are themselves a function of income. This means that even strong conditional convergence can predict absolute divergence, stressing the importance of sustainable development and sensitivity to the different dimensions of poverty. In other words: one still assumes that it is easier for a country to grow economically when it is poor, but this has only happened in practice as an exception. This reveals that there are inherent problems (conditioning variables) that prevent the lift-off. Development cooperation should therefore be aimed at resolving these inherent problems.

Among these problems may be the poverty trap. The poor will not be able to invest in themselves or provide their children with opportunities to escape poverty. This will generate a new wave of poor people as a result. This implies the necessity of sustained financial support for primary education over a longer period for the full range of education expenditures (not just buildings).

Under conditioning variables one may also rank institutions (like those needed to implement the rule of law, including a well functioning police and judiciary). These are not easily achieved in a very poor country, where salaries for policemen and judges may be too low for reasonable subsistence.

According to Pritchett, these factors also underline the vulnerability of the progress made by many of the developing countries. The question is how this vulnerability can best be changed into structural growth, and improved general living conditions. The more general conclusion is that globalization has not 'automatically' created convergence, but rather the contrary, because 'bootstrap lifting' proved to be a misconception. One may go one step further: 'bootstrap lifting' became more difficult under globalization for many reasons:

- The opening up was one-sided (much opening up for the exports of rich countries to poor countries, but little the other way around).
- The influence of multinationals in developing countries became more strongly felt and more dominating (as much in the extractive industries as in other kinds of foreign direct investment). This might have slowed down the process of improvement of governance due to induced corruption.
- People in poor countries became more aware of the conditions in rich countries, reducing their commitment to engaging in the local situation, along with an increased connection with the international labour market (see also Section 3.6 on the role of higher education).

3.2 GLOBALIZATION AND DIVERGENCE

Xavier Sala-i-Martin presents a very detailed and thorough account of divergence between the countries of the world in his 2002 publication 'The World Distribution of Income' (NBER Working Paper 8933, Cambridge,

Massachusetts): he completes the picture by focusing subsequently on the distribution within countries and concludes more optimistically than the World Bank publications do, namely that overall global income inequality decreased in the 1980s and 1990s despite a divergence in the incomes between countries. This paradox is easily explained. Some of the poorer countries that are on a convergence path with the rich countries are huge, in terms of the size of their population (notably China). It is good to keep this nuance in mind when we focus on the rising inequalities *between* countries.

The views of development economists on the policies that serve developing countries have changed over time. In the 1950s and 1960s the economies of developing countries were believed to function differently from those of developed countries: there were the different 'stages' of economic growth (as was advanced by the American economic historian Walt Whitman Rostow in his 1960 book *The Stages of Economic Development, A Non-Communist Manifesto*,' (Cambridge University Press). Rostow argues that to achieve 'modernity' all countries have to pass through the same stages. This led to a distinction between the type of economic policies to be applied, depending on the 'stage' of economic growth (see also Chapter 4).

Currently, the paradigm of the global economy dominates all countries; whatever their level of income, they all have – more or less – to engage in the same policies, with a strong emphasis on the role of the market. This emphasis on the market (or maybe better: the way this emphasis is translated) is the point of debate between, on the one hand, the agencies involved in development cooperation, like the World Bank or the IMF and, on the other hand, the anti-globalists (see also Section 3.7).

There is, in fact, a wide consensus that the new economic policies of the last two decades have boosted economic growth rates in low and middle-income countries (a statement even confirmed by most critics of globalization), despite the continued divergence. In the 1980s developing countries were in economic growth 0.5 per cent on average per year behind the high income countries, while over the whole period of 1960–1990 the difference was on average 0.8 per cent per year in favour of rich countries; and in the 1990s they 'outgrew' those countries by 0.8 per cent (see Table 3.1). In other words: there are signs that the divergence is turning around into convergence, if it were not for the substantial difference in population growth, which effectively has meant that the divergence in per capita incomes still continues.

The real debate focuses on the relation between the current rules of the organization of the world economy and divergence. Can the rules of the game of globalization be changed so that globalization can be accompanied by (faster) convergence?

There is no easy way to measure the effect of globalization on divergence, since we cannot measure how the situation would have been if these policies had not been applied; we cannot assess the counterfactual or '*anti-monde*'. Nevertheless, a considerable amount of research has been done with the aim of measuring whether the situation in developing countries has improved since the start of the latest wave of globalization, in around 1980. This is the wave characterized by its focus on the market mechanism (in line with Thatcherism in Europe and Reaganism in the US).

An example of such research is the scorecard on globalization for the period 1980–2000 produced by the Centre for Economic and Policy Research (CEPR, 2001, see: http://www.cepr.net/globalization/scorecard_on_globalization.htm). The scorecard records the difference in absolute and relative growth during the last twenty years. This is the period of the opening up of the economies of developing countries (as opposed to the more inward-looking economic policies of the 1960s to the 1980s). The research compares countries by looking at a number of the main economic and social indicators, such as growth of income per person, mortality among infants, children and adults, as well as literacy and education. For each indicator the countries were divided into five groups. For example, in the case of per capita GDP, countries were divided according to per capita GDP. So Group 1 was characterized by per capita GDP levels between $375 and $1,121, Group 2 between $1.122 and $1825, Group 3 between $1,826 and $3,364, etc.

The group that was at level *x* in 1960 is compared with the group of countries that was at the same level in 1980. Note that the inclusion of the less prosperous 1970s makes sure that the benchmark is not set too high for the period 1980–2000. The main findings are as follows:

- *Economic growth.* Per capita growth is considerably slower in the second period; the poorest group (per capita GDP between $375 and $1,121) went from a per capita GDP growth rate of 1.9 per cent annually in 1960–1980, to a negative growth of –0.5 per cent per year in 1980–2000. The growth rate of the middle group (per capita GDP between $1,826 and $3,364) decreased from an annual percentage of 3.6 to less than 1 per cent. The other three groups also showed substantial declines in growth.
- *Life expectancy.* Economic growth and life expectancy are related to one another. It is therefore not surprising that the progress of life expectancy was reduced for four out of the five groups which were distinguished. Only the highest age group (69–76 years) had an increase, from 0.15 to 0.19 per cent. The group of 44–53 years experienced the biggest decline from 0.56 per cent to less than 0.18 per cent. In addition, while both men and women saw the growth rate of their life expectancy halt, the percentages for women slowed down faster than those of men, especially in the group of

44–53 years. While life expectancy grew 0.54 per cent in 1960–1980, it grew by only 0.2 per cent in the period 1980–2000. The data for adult mortality in general shows that four out of ten groups show better outcomes for the second period, the top two groups improved significantly, as well as the worst performing group, while for the groups second and third from the bottom the growth rate fell by 65 and 60 per cent respectively.

- *Infant and child mortality.* In the case of infant and child mortality, growth slowed down for all groups. This slowdown was the smallest for the best performing group while, for example, the growth of the middle group of countries for child mortality (80–151 deaths per thousand live births) dropped in growth by 20 per cent compared to the first 20 years.

- *Education and literacy.* Countries in most groups performed worse than in the first 20 years. However, this decrease was not as large as for economic growth and health. On average, the better performing countries saw a more rapid improvement in the second period, while the speed of improvement in the middle and poorer performing countries slowed down in the same period. In all countries except the better performing ones the growth of school enrolment was slower, literacy rates and public spending on education lower. The results of the last indicator in fact worsened for all countries, including even the better performing countries. The growth in the literacy rate of the two groups of worst performing countries slowed down from 1.1 per cent to 0.8 per cent, while the middle group improved from 0.9 per cent to 1.1 per cent in 1980–2000. Finally, the growth of enrolment in primary education slowed down for the worst performing group from 1.9 per cent to just over 1.0 per cent in 1980–2000. The rates of enrolment growth for secondary education remained constant for the worst performing countries, while the growth decreased for the other countries. The largest drop was for the middle group, which experienced a slowdown in growth from 1.7 per cent to 0.7 per cent. The enrolment rates for tertiary education worsened for the three lowest groups, while the second-highest performing group only had a small increase, from 0.76 per cent to 0.85 per cent.

These findings show that there was growth for the separate indicators, but this growth slowed down rather than increased during the period 1980–2000 for countries in the same situation, especially in the worst performing countries. In the few cases that growth increased during the last twenty years, it was mainly concentrated in the best performing countries.

The findings do not prove that globalization has aggravated the general situation, but they do show that during the economic reforms of the last two decades the improvement of the economic and social situation in general advanced at a slower pace for the low to middle-income countries than had been the case in the same fields during the 1960s and 1970s. As a result, divergence has grown in the past two decades.

These observations are an important caveat to the general finding that in the 1990s (on average) developing countries grew faster than rich countries – for the first time since ODA started. This faster growth is fully concentrated among the 'best performers'. The results emphasize in particular that 'bootstrap lifting' for the poorest countries has become more difficult with increased globalization.

3.3 THE FAILURE OF THE WASHINGTON CONSENSUS

The 'Washington Consensus' has been an essential part of globalization in the period up to around 1997/1998. And although the period of the use of the Washington Consensus as development paradigm may now have passed, it is still important to discuss what happened and what can be learned. The Washington Consensus was the development paradigm of the World Bank and the International Monetary Fund in the 1980s and 1990s. In one sentence (for a more elaborate overview: see Section 6.2): the Washington Consensus aims at using the forces of the free market to reduce poverty and create convergence between poor and rich countries. While in theory the Washington Consensus approach held many promises, in practice it failed because of an unsophisticated and one-sided approach, as is evidenced by the slow pace of poverty reduction and the divergence between rich and poor countries in the relevant period. In the analysis of many it shows that in the past in the application of the Washington Consensus many mistakes were made, notably:

- There was too little attention to the preconditions of good governance that are needed to make market forces work.
- There was also too little attention to the pace of economic policy reforms such as, for example, import tariff reduction and the opening up of capital markets.

The fast pace of economic policy reforms has often reduced their effectiveness or even led to results which were opposite to earlier expectations or to projections based on the best macro and micro economic models. For example, the reduction of import tariffs has hurt infant industries. Industries that are still young and unable to protect themselves against the influence of more developed and efficient competitors require some protection in their infancy. The competitors could 'kill' them by a short-term price war. Protection of these industries allows the products to become settled in the developing countries, thus reducing imports. It allows developing countries to grow an industry that is able to compete with its competitors in developed countries. Yet the debate between developing countries and the Bretton Woods institutions on the merits of this 'infant industry' argument was in the past too often and too easily decided in favour of the Washington Consensus: abolish the trade tariffs as part of a Structural Adjustment Program.

Structural Adjustment Programs (SAPs) used to be the centerpiece of the Washington Consensus and one of the most heavily criticized policies of the World Bank. SAPs used to be the preconditions that developing countries had to conform to in order to qualify for World Bank or IMF loans, whether these were for new programs or for refinancing of old debts. The goal of SAPs was – in general terms – to improve the micro and macro economic environment, so that economic growth would be spurred (a precondition for poverty reduction). Privatization and liberalization of markets used to be general ingredients of this approach. SAPs attempted to make the market of developing countries as attractive as possible for FDI (Foreign Direct Investment), often requiring countries to devalue their currencies against the dollar, lift import and export restrictions, balance their budgets (and not overspend), and remove price controls and state subsidies. Devaluation makes their goods cheaper for foreigners to buy and theoretically makes foreign imports more expensive. It is easy to comprehend the economic rationale behind the SAPs: this opening up makes the economy of the country more competitive.

Of course, one realizes that the short-term effects of opening up are often traumatic for the people in a country. It is giving up an old way of life for a new one, with no way back. Even in successful countries, the effects of opening up are felt to be painful (as in China or Hungary). This may also have to do with the speed of adjustment. Adjustment speeds were high in most developing countries. For example, tariff barriers were halved in developing countries in the 1990s. It was this high speed of adjustment that often gave rise to chaotic developments. While rich countries consider room for manoeuvre and a limited speed of adjustment as a given fact of life in policy-making (compare for example the discussion in France and Germany in the late 1990s and early parts of the twenty-first century on the much needed revision of the pension system, in order to deal with the aging of the population), they often denied developing countries such 'luxury'.

The lessons to be learnt from the past are clear: adjustment needs to be placed within the framework of its social consequences. For example, adjustment needs to be accompanied by the introduction and expansion of safety nets. Also, it has become clear that the social sectors can be sectors of investment rather than sectors of 'wasteful' spending of tax money. In particular, education and health need to be viewed as an investment sector, which will predate investments in physical assets. The importance of social safety nets came through loud and clear in the East Asia crisis. For example, in Korea expenditures for safety nets went up from 0.6 per cent of GDP in 1997 to 2 per cent in 1999.[2] The overall experience of Korea is one of quick recovery. The social cohesion brought about by the recognition of the social processes may have contributed.

Of equal importance is that major elements of the process of development were overlooked in the past SAP approach. In particular it was overlooked that markets need reliable institutions to function, like banks, like a banking system which guarantees that your savings are indeed safe, like a functioning system of justice to enable you to sue if your rights have been trampled on.

The institutions needed to sustain world competitiveness were often not yet present at the time of the introduction of the SAPs and could not be built overnight. Institution building is a gradual process. In the past, many mistakes have been made in developing countries where demanded changes far exceeded the capacity to develop the required institutions.

Often, SAPs turned out to be ineffective. However, there are also many places where countries did indeed open up successfully. The long-run effects of successful opening up have proved to be beneficial, time and again, as the 2002 report of the World Bank on Globalization (Globalization, Growth and Poverty) shows. But note that this applies to those countries that could manage the jump. In this respect, the report starts with a tautology: it considers countries to be globalized if they are heavily integrated into world trade. This is tantamount to saying that they have been successful. The real question is a different one, namely how to gain access to world trade. It is by now clear that the right policy includes attention to the social consequences and to institution building, and that the outright elimination or substantial reduction of trade restrictions in the developing country is in itself not a sufficient condition.

Opening up has also been a cause for concern in rich countries. This concern was originally focused on the loss in rich countries of lower skilled jobs to developing countries. The first years of the twenty-first century, however have seen a dramatic increase in the transfer of middle or higher skilled jobs from rich countries to poorer countries, in particular to India and China. In some countries, notably the USA, this has led to fierce pleas for economic protection. This must sound quite ironic to developing countries, which have been led to believe (for example in the Uruguay trade round in the 1980s) that they had to gain from worldwide competition and therefore had to open up. The protectionist view in the rich world is tantamount to seducing the poor world to go by car, but when they have learned how to drive to cut off the gas supply.

There has been also a concern in rich countries that capital mobility may lead to tax competition. Tax competition is expected by some observers to result in tax rates that cannot sustain a welfare state. This could eventually lead to 'social dumping' and could result in reduced bargaining power for states and for labour. Moreover, the international financial market would decrease the autonomy of the individual state or government to set macro policy. These concerns about a race to the bottom, however, are not based on experience so far. For example, highly globalized economies, like Ireland, continue to maintain a welfare state with high levels of taxation. There is no link to be found between globalization and lower wages, child labour or harm to the environment. On the contrary, the industries which are the most polluting, with the worst labour standards and which use child labour, are to be found in countries with a low degree of globalization (World Bank, Report on Globalization 2002), where globalization is defined by integration in the world economy measured by, for example, the ratio of trade (imports and exports) to GDP.

For the world at large, developing and developed countries alike, it is easy to demonstrate that by far the best course is to lower trade barriers further and to allow the maximum opening up in capital markets. Protectionism in rich or in poor countries goes against the interest of poverty reduction, against the interests of economic growth. But the pace with which trade barriers are eliminated and capital markets are opened up should be well chosen. It should be sustainable in any one country and should be accompanied by growth of employment and exports. There are many examples of countries where such an approach of gradualism succeeded, and they should not be ignored. One such country is (mentioned here once again) Ireland. On the one hand it opened its capital markets quite quickly. On the other it has benefited greatly from the trade barriers of the EU in order to increase its agricultural production and export.

It should be realized that reduction of trade barriers and open capital markets will have the side effect of new and more severe volatilities in economic development, as we have seen in the rapid increase in the succession of financial crises. With every crisis we thought we had not only weathered the storm, but also mastered the dynamics behind it, only to see a new crisis emerging faster than before. However much it is regrettable to say so, it is quite likely that we will have a new and severe world crisis in this first decade of the twenty-first century. An important factor for crisis is the speed with which huge amounts of financial capital can be moved across the globe. While tremendously beneficial for world economic growth, the downsides should be clearly envisaged and, if possible, dealt with. This double-edged sword of globalization has been clearly visible in, for example, New Zealand, Romania, South Africa and Turkey, where large capital inflows, a huge boon to the economy for job creation and for individual incomes, were quickly reversed, bringing these countries to the brink of, or sending them into, crisis.

The debt crisis (continuing on Section 2.4) is related to the Washington Consensus. In the period of rapid globalization a debt crisis of an unprecedented magnitude and spread has occurred. Never before have so many countries been burdened by so much debt. There is also irony here. The origins of this crisis are found not in a cowardly, but rather a courageous stand of the World Bank at the time of the oil crises of the 1970s and early 1980s. These left developing countries with huge bills to pay for oil imports, which could not be matched with export earnings. The then President of the World Bank, Robert McNamara, looked for ways to help and was able to raise the money needed to give developing countries the necessary loans. And here the Washington Consensus sneaked in. The loans were given on conditions of economic reforms, which were believed to promote economic growth to levels that would enable the countries to repay the loans. Unfortunately this did not happen and the debt crisis became a fact.

The debts of many poor countries were so big that many became faced with 'reverse flows': they paid more back in debt than they received in new loans or in aid. This is demonstrated in Figure 3.1. This is also visible in the negative net flows of the World Bank in 2002 and 2003 in Table 2.1.

The transfers of the IBRD (International Bank for Reconstruction and Development) of other multilateral concessional and of bilateral concessional as well as private lenders became negative sometimes as early as 1985. Debt relief became the only chance for the heavily indebted countries to reduce

US$ billions

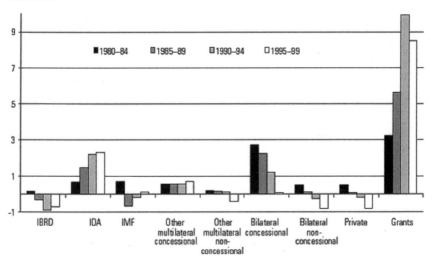

Source: *Global Development Finance, 1999*

Figure 3.1 Change in net transfers to HIPCs

their deficits. Launched in 1996 by the World Bank and the International Monetary Fund, the Heavily Indebted Poor Countries Initiative (HIPC) is the first comprehensive debt relief plan integrating all bilateral, multilateral and private creditors in one framework. The initiative aims to reduce the amount of debt owed by eligible countries in order to prevent them from defaulting on their own outstanding loans.

Along with debt relief another major innovation in development cooperation took place. Donors became united around 1998 on the need for a common approach to the development of a country. This would be the country-owned Poverty Reduction Strategy, laid down in a Poverty Reduction Strategy Paper (PRSP). This document would be the basis for determining eligibility for debt relief, describing a country's macroeconomic, structural and social policies and programs to promote growth and reduce poverty, as well as associated external financing needs. The PRSP is to be prepared by the government of the country through a participatory process. This process involves civil society and development partners, including the World Bank and the IMF. In practice the first PRSPs were far cries from this process objective: they were often written by a small group of local and external consultants without the required, broader discussion. The PRSP, the ratio of a country's debt to the value of its exports, and its commitment to follow economic policy prescriptions dictated by the World Bank and the IMF were the determining factors for debt relief.

A report of the Operations Evaluation Department of the World Bank (OED, 24 February 2003; see World Bank web site) states that the HIPC is but a small part of the development assistance effort. However, the reduction of unmanageable debt is a precondition for many developing countries to be able to invest in development. HIPC is considered to have opened up the processes around debt regimes. It is the task of the donor countries to help the HIPC countries to improve their exports, to build the required institutional capacities and to provide sufficient resources for them to meet the development priorities for HIPC (e.g. freeing up more resources for increased social expenditures). For this reason, the HIPC debt relief should in truth be additional to other aid flows. The start of the HIPC initiative happened to coincide with a sharp decline in global net resource transfers. As a result, the HIPC countries receive an increasing share of the (unfortunately decreasing) amount of aid resources, but in absolute terms they are not or only to a limited extent receiving additional funds. Thus the objectives and the expectations about the effectiveness of the HIPC have increased over the past few years, but the means to realize these objectives and expectations have stayed the same.

The OED report closes with the remark that debt relief is no panacea, and that for true sustainable debt and poverty reduction, the governments of the HIPC countries need to work to improve exports and promote broad-based growth and human capital development. In order to make the HIPC initiatives as effective as possible OED formulated four recommendations:

1. Clarify objectives and make sure the design is consistent with these objectives. Communicate these objectives and the accomplishments clearly to the public.
2. Improve the transparency of the methodology and economic models for the debt projections and the realism of the growth forecasts.
3. Maintain the standards for policy performance.
4. There ought to be a bigger focus on pro-poor growth (i.e. the kind of economic growth which helps the poor most) in order to provide a better balance among development priorities. This would entail more emphasis on social expenditures.

To conclude: there is but one recipe for successful participation in the globalizing world and that is development from within. Creating good governance and the rule of all rules, creating trust among the people, creating a solid social system that benefits the poor, based on a solid tax base. On a billboard in the middle of Accra (Ghana's capital) there is the text: 'VAT [value added taxation] helping build a better Ghana. File your VAT returns promptly.' In the background one sees a group of merrily laughing Ghanaians. It is the spirit of taking responsibility for the financing of, for example, education, which appeals and which can ultimately be the only successful method. Development from within means also the creation over time of the means to engage in the world economy.

3.4 The Trade Playing Field is Not Level

The playing field is not level since rich nations compete unfairly in agriculture, whereas developing countries are very dependent on agriculture. Most developing countries are strongly agriculturally based in their production structure and face a tremendous, unnecessary and unfair hurdle in accessing the markets of rich countries. The hurdle is twofold:

- Rich countries subsidize their farmers by as much as $1 billion a day in the year 2004 (or seven times as much as these nations devote to resource transfers to poor countries).
- Rich nations impose high tariffs (on average no less than 15 per cent in 2004) on agricultural imports from poor countries.

Worldwide trade negotiations take place under the guidance of the World Trade Organization. They culminate in 'rounds' where all trade negotiations are brought together into one basket, such as in Punta del Este, Uruguay in 1986. A new round was announced in November 2002 in Doha, with the common knowledge that the Uruguay trade round had not contributed much to improving the trade position of poor countries. The World Bank and developing countries together invested a lot in the preparation of the Doha trade round, for which the proposals had to be submitted by the end of March 2003. In March 2003, however, it became clear that the reduction of trade barriers was not taking place as fast as had been hoped for. The agricultural tariffs were the topic of especially intense debate. There are some positive signs that the Doha trade round may have been beneficial for developing countries. But it remains quite uncertain whether the rich countries will indeed take the round seriously as a means to create a level playing field, even given the positive outcomes of the Geneva meeting of August 2004.

The fierceness of the debate on agricultural protection in rich countries had already been expected, since during the run-up to Doha the French had made it clear that they would not easily agree to a change in the agricultural subsidization policy of the European Union, the Common Agricultural Policy (CAP). Their suggestion that developing countries should also entertain the notion of a similar subsidization policy must have been based on 'misunderstandings'. These countries simply do not have the tax revenues for such a policy on a level similar to the CAP or the policies of other rich countries. In addition, it disregards the history of globalization in which the International Monetary Fund often imposed the condition that developing countries cut their agricultural subsidies as a means to reduce their budget deficits.

The EU sometimes defends its position by claiming that agriculture is the lifeblood of any society and safeguards food security. Both arguments have more populist appeal than substance. To connect the lifeblood of a society with agriculture does injustice to the fact that the societies of rich countries have remained vibrant, despite a tremendous decrease in the number of farmers and in the contribution of agriculture to GDP. Of course, farming has helped to maintain an attractive landscape in many countries. But that function is not inherently related to the subsidies on the products, and could also be maintained by direct provision of landscape maintenance. At the same time, the subsidies in the Netherlands, for example, which grows largely only the subsidized products, have led to much less diversity in agricultural production. And in some cases it has led to a boring landscape with one sugar beet field after another, while the costs of imported sugar might be less than 60 per cent of the costs of sugar from this beet.

Food security is an equally spurious argument. A territory the size of Europe can always be autarkic, if it needs to be (even when we know that before the Second World War Europe was a net food importer). But when would this really be needed? Can one imagine a world situation so terrible that Europe (or for that matter the US or Japan) would not want to import any food from other countries?

There are some positive signs as well, however. The EU has engaged in the 'Everything But Arms' initiative with the 49 poorest countries. This initiative is an amendment to the EU's Generalized Scheme of Preferences (GSP) and gives – with phase-in periods for sugar, rice and bananas – tariff-free and quota-free access to farm products from these countries. In practice this means that:

- Customs duties on fresh bananas have been reduced by 20 per cent per year starting on 1 January 2002 and will be totally eliminated by 1 January 2006, at the latest.
- Customs duties on rice will be reduced by 20 per cent on 1 September 2009, at the latest.
- Finally, the customs duties on sugar will be reduced from 20 per cent on 1 July 2006, by 50 per cent on 1 July 2007, by 80 per cent on 1 July 2008, and totally eliminated on 1 July 2009, at the latest.

As far as the last two products are concerned, in order to compensate for this lag time the EU will provide immediate access to its territory, as of 2002, by creating a quota free of tariffs for sugar and for rice, initially based on the Least Developed Countries' best export figures over the last few years, plus 15 per cent. These quotas will increase by 15 per cent per year during the transition period. This transition period must make it possible to adapt these three products' common market organization. Imports of rice, bananas and sugar will be carefully monitored in order to apply safeguards, if necessary, in case of substantial growth. The novelty of the 'Everything But Arms' (EBA) initiative is that it opens up the European farm product markets, particularly those covered by the CAP, and enables the adaptation of European producers in these three sectors. But let us not be too optimistic about the impact of EBA. The small print reduces its effectiveness considerably. For example, the EU will for the time being allow no more than 1 per cent of its total sugar use to be imported from developing countries.

Another example is the Africa Growth and Opportunity Act, signed by the US, which allows duty and quota-free access to the US market for thousands of products made in the 38 eligible countries. The US is now the biggest importer of African goods, and US imports covered under the Africa Growth and Opportunity Act (AGOA) totalled US $8.2 billion in 2001. But these swallows do not yet predict the arrival of an early spring. Spring will not arrive until the rich countries have by and large abandoned their subsidies. Moreover, a World Bank evaluation of AGOA shows that the gains for poorer countries have been minimal.[3]

Joe Stiglitz[4] described the recent development in aid and trade as dominated by the slogan: 'trade, not aid' while in reality, as developing countries took steps to open their markets, they found '… themselves confronting significant trade barriers (anti-dumping, high tariffs in sectors of natural comparative advantage, like agriculture or clothing) – leaving them, in effect, with neither aid nor trade' (p.438), because aid per developing country resident decreased by roughly one third in the 1990s.

The World Bank calculates that developing countries lose at least US $200 billion a year due to the trade restrictions facing their merchandise, exports and services, together with the effect of contingent protection (anti-dumping, safeguards and subsidies). Free access would increase their exports to rich countries by 11 per cent (for Sub-Saharan Africa even 14 per cent; see World Bank web site).

These examples show the negative effects of protectionism in rich countries on the opportunities for trade of developing countries, but what about intellectual property? Intellectual property rights need to be acknowledged in order to generate the investments needed for scientific and technological progress. This is unless, of course, a utopian situation were to emerge whereby international public resources could be used to provide financing for the international public good of scientific progress, discoveries meanwhile remaining equally efficient under a public system as under a private one.

There are huge dangers attached to the application of intellectual property rights (IPRs) in a globalized world:

- In medicine, it has now been recognized that using the same price worldwide (which includes the costs of intellectual property rights) bars poor people from access to life-saving medication. There are now many proposals and concrete pilots to deal with this. In the end it means that the price for research leading to the intellectual property has to be paid elsewhere. But given this consequence, would consumers in the rich countries be willing to show such solidarity? The medicines that help to sustain a reasonable quality of life for HIV/AIDS victims have been a case in point. Gradually the climate has evolved in which the price for these medicines in developing countries is indeed below that in the developed world and where the risk of low-priced products from poor countries being smuggled into rich countries has been well taken care of.

- In high-tech in general and particularly in electronics, intellectual property rights may be a force for divergence. Developing countries have different technological development objectives, perspectives and capabilities; these make it hard for them to participate and share the costs of research and development or to buy the rights of more advanced and fast developing technologies. Investing in intellectual property rights only reinforces the asymmetrical access to accumulation of knowledge and can in some cases be considered a measure of protectionism. IPRs reinforce the first mover advantages and weaken the initial income effect as a driver in convergence (see Section 3.1). It is also for this reason that development cooperation should invest in R&D efforts in the developing countries rather than focusing on technology transfer from developed countries.[5]

3.5 WHOSE CORRUPTION?

The effects of corruption in the rich business world are a serious stain on the commitment of the rich countries to help poor countries come clean. While the governments of the same rich countries have – rightly – demanded that poor countries get serious about honest government, they have done precious little on their side of the equation. Box 3.1 gives an indication of the concern in a developing country for this question.

The attitude of donor countries toward the subjects of conflict and corruption has changed during the last few decades. The emphasis on good governance and anti-corruption is the fruit of the demise of the Cold War. Before, in development cooperation, the donor countries felt compelled to let money flow to countries which declared themselves friendly to a bloc (the Communist bloc or the Western bloc) whatever their quality of governance. At the same time the development community had been acutely aware of the need for development from within, starting with the quality of governance.

But it took a while before the issue of 'good governance' took centre stage. I remember discussions in the Dutch Cabinet in which I took part as late as 1995. Any reference that was made to the (often poor) quality of governance in developing countries was hotly counter-argued by the minister of development cooperation. It was World Bank President Jim Wolfensohn who made corruption a central issue in his 1996 speech at the Annual Meeting of the World Bank, which brings together all the shareholders of the Bank. The groundwork had by then been prepared. Extensive studies had clearly shown how heavy a burden corruption is on the poor, and how forcefully corruption acts as sand in the wheels as opposed to greasing the machine. Subsequently in 1997 the OECD (*Organization of Economic Cooperation and Development*) launched a convention outlawing bribery by multinationals or officials abroad. This was the much needed counterpart to the action within developing countries, making sure that 'induced' corruption by multinationals would be stopped as much as was possible.

Box 3.1: Two to Tango

'It takes two to tango,' says Moyane Malek, Lesotho's natural resources minister. If the developed world cannot bring to justice multinationals which bribe abroad, it is hard to sustain the argument that leaders of developing countries should heed the hectoring of the IMF and the World Bank and donor governments about 'good governance' and fighting corruption. – Corruption is a dance of the corrupted and the corruptor. In a globalized world, with steadily rising international trade, the tango is increasingly an international one.

In order to give more practical efficacy to the anti-bribery initiatives by the OECD, Transparency International and Social Accountability International initiated the formulation of the *Business Principles for Countering Bribery*. These guidelines were developed in cooperation with companies, academia, trade unions and other non-governmental bodies. The resulting program, presented in late 2002, gives guidelines for anti-bribery efforts, such as values, policies, processes, training and guidance. However, there is no official policing of the OECD convention and hence companies are still at liberty to corrupt or not to corrupt.

Since the convention came into effect in February 1999, the 35 signatory countries have been engaged to make the bribery of foreign public officials illegal. But law-making for corporate responsibility has been slow and tortuous. Apart from US cases brought under the 1997 Foreign Corrupt Practices Act, we are still waiting for the first fines or prison sentences, in the knowledge that there is still a substantial amount of corruption induced by multinationals, even though many companies have changed their ways and are attempting to refrain as much as possible from paying bribes. Meanwhile, scandals in the rich world, like the Enron, the WorldCom and the AHOLD scandals have focused attention once again in rich countries on the rules of proper behaviour in business.

The quest for good governance is a difficult one. It requires a step-by-step process of putting the conditions in place that will support honesty in a certain area. This starts with information for citizens, knowledge of the reality, good and reliable data and access to these data (see Section 8.1). These data may show, for example, to villagers that the amount of money allocated to their school is much higher than the actual amount they receive. Or it may show that the number of teachers is actually much lower than the one that appears on the salary sheets (because people in power give positions to friends, a practice known in Latin America as a 'caramelo', a 'sweet').

This increased need and demand for transparency and attention to corruption is evidenced by the following example. When Bechtel, one of the world's largest engineering-construction firms, won the Iraq War contracts for infrastructure reconstruction, it hit the news as a bombshell and the case was publicly discussed as a possible example of corruption. The initial contract was estimated to be $680 million over 18 months, but the experts expected this amount to grow by as much as $100 million. Bechtel also advises both the federal agencies that provide loans and insurance to American companies overseas. In addition Daniel Chao, Bechtel's senior vice-president, is a member of the advisory board of the US export-import bank. According to activist groups this conflict of interests will hurt the Iraqis, and will lead to increased costs.

Organizations such as Transparency International work to collect and analyse data on corruption, its sources and its consequences in order to prevent and reduce corruption. Transparency International has made a Corruption

Perception Index (CPI), which is published every year and gives insight into the causes and consequences of corruption. 'The CPI aggregates the perceptions of well-informed people with regard to the extent of corruption, defined as the misuse of public power for private benefit. The extent of corruption reflects the frequency of corrupt payments, the value of bribes paid and the resulting obstacle imposed on businesses.'[6]

While in-depth diagnostic surveys examine corruption in just one country, perception surveys examine the problem across a large number of countries and can thus show where corruption problems are perceived to be higher and where they are perceived to be lower around the world. Figure 3.2 gives an overview of perceived corruption in 1998.

The result does not come as surprise: corruption is more likely to be felt when per capita income levels in the country are lower. Anti-corruption policies should not only be pursued more vigorously by these countries and by multinationals. Donors too, including the World Bank, should adjust those policies that might indirectly contribute to corruption. An example of such a policy has recently been reported by the OED, which wrote a review of the World Bank's mining, oil and gas projects. The OED reports, based on its experiences in Chile, Ecuador, Ghana, Kazakhstan, Papua New Guinea and Tanzania from 1993–2000, that the World Bank should renew its lending policies to these industries to avoid corruption and mismanagement. This renewal is necessary because the current policies of the World Bank towards extractive industries are reported to be damaging. It devotes 'minimal attention' to environmental issues, which has frequently led to social conflicts with affected communities and has caused degraded environments. The Bank should therefore not support extractive industry in countries where the government is unable to manage large investments in these industries. Also, the World Bank should encourage borrowers to invest in regulating the environmental impacts, to provide local compensation when necessary and to involve the local communities in decision-making.

An increasing number of internationally operating companies acknowledge the importance of Corporate Social Responsibility (CSR). This acknowledgement tends to be based on morality, a feeling of responsibility, combined with the pressure of the more socially and environmentally conscious consumers and investors. More and more companies adapt a code of conduct or align themselves with organizations such as CSR Europe, which is a business-driven membership network. CSR Europe's mission is to help companies achieve profitability, sustainable growth and human progress by placing corporate social responsibility in the mainstream of business practice. Nevertheless, most of these organizations are in favor of self-regulation and protest against strict regulation, claiming that such regulation will limit the feeling of responsibility

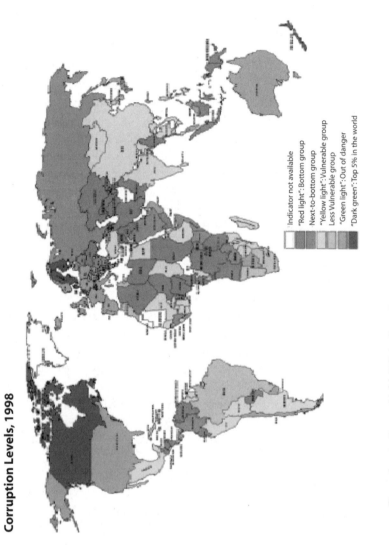

Corruption Levels, 1998

Indicator not available
"Red light": Bottom group
Next-to-bottom group
"Yellow light":Vulnerable group
Less Vulnerable group
"Green light":Out of danger
"Dark green":Top 5% in the world

Figure 3.2 Map of Corruption Levels, 1998

Source: WB, Youth for Good Governance, Distance Learning Program, Module V, Seeing Corruption

and effectiveness in CSR. As the definition of Corporate Social Responsibility by the European Commission explains, it is 'essentially a concept whereby companies decide *voluntarily* to contribute to a better society and a cleaner environment.'[7] At the same time, companies feel obliged to maximize 'shareholders' value', while social and environmental values do not count in the calculation of a company's profitability other than through the image of the company (see Chapter 8).

The multinational character of many internationally operating companies enables them to escape the legislation of the countries in which they operate. Cases such as that of Cape PLC in South Africa, in which the claim of Northern Province and Northern Cape communities that they had been victims of asbestosis was finally decided at the House of Lords in London, are still exceptional. This civil lawsuit case, which was moved from South Africa to London, was a culmination of a joint partnership among democratic South Africa's socio-political players. A case such as this, in which companies are sued in their own country for crimes committed in a developing country with less legislation on this point could create precedents and the beginning of new legislation.

An ambitious UN convention against corruption was organized in Vienna in August 2003, with the objective of setting global standards. 'The draft text covers the gamut of international corruption issues, envisaging requirements for governments to prevent or criminalize areas from the bribery of appointed and elected officials, to onward funding of political parties, trading in influence, accounting fraud and banking secrecy.'[8] However, there are discussions on the scope of the convention, since it will be difficult for countries with different legal traditions and political structures to agree on a common denominator.

3.5a CIVIC CONFLICT

The extreme case of an induced breakdown of governance is when foreign interference leads to civic conflict. Civic conflicts are nowadays more prevalent than they were 10 or 20 years ago. The last decade has seen a disturbing escalation in violence, with at least 20 major conflicts in Africa affecting some 200 million people. Conflicts increasingly rage across borders. Conflict not only impedes development in the countries directly affected, but it also has negative external effects for the African region as a whole. The numerous examples include Sierra Leone and the Darfur region in Sudan.

There are two types of foreign interference that may lead to conflict or to an aggravation of conflict: the pushing of arms sales and the direct business between multinationals and armed rebels (as was the case in Sierra Leone where diamond trade fuelled the war). Box 3.2 gives an example of an arms-push, which fortunately has not yet led to a conflict.

Paul Collier and Anke Hoeffler have used the data from arms races in other areas to show the determinants of the ratio of military spending to GDP, which is better known as the defense-burden.[9] Countries spend on average 3.4 per cent of GDP on military expenses. However, this average is the result of enormous variations, from 0.1 per cent of GDP to 46 per cent of GDP. This study is the first integrated empirical analysis of developed and developing country behaviour to incorporate both external and internal threats. The explanatory factors include political, social, geographic, historical and especially economic factors next to the enhanced political power of the military in non-democratic regimes, and the financial resources available to the government. Internal threat cannot be omitted, and is in fact a more influential determinant than the threat of international wars, since the rate of occurrence of civil war is now ten times higher than that of international wars.

Collier and Hoeffler furthermore find that economic factors are particularly important, since 'the risk of civil war is higher if the level of per capita income is low, if the growth rate of the previous period is low or when the country is dependent on primary commodity exports.' Ethnic dominance is an important social factor which doubles the risk of a civil war, and geography and history can increase the risk of civil war through a dispersed population and a recent occurrence of war. Furthermore, countries can be influenced by the expenditures of neighbours on the military, for other reasons than direct military threat. One explanation is that in the absence of clear indicators for military need, governments base their judgement on the behaviour of their neighbours, causing a multiplier effect.

Moreover, the data show that military spending does not decrease the risk of civil war, and is thus a 'public bad': 'if they (governments) fail to recognize the arms race multiplier effects, they substantially exaggerate the contribution of an increase in the military budget to external security.' Collier and Hoeffler also claim that regional cooperation on reduction of trade restrictions offers less scope for mutual benefit than cooperation on mutual reduction in military spending. Military spending reduction agreements are rare however, since the low observability of military expenditures creates a prisoner's dilemma.

Armed conflicts in developing countries are one of the greatest impediments to progress in poverty reduction. Paul Collier sums up the background for such conflicts in two simple phrases:

- 'The rage of the rich' meaning that rich parts of the country (like for example Katanga in Congo) want to become independent, so that they do not have to share their wealth.
- 'Not by grievance but by greed' meaning that the control over the income from natural resources is the driving force behind many of the ethnic conflicts.

Box 3.2: Should Chile Buy Fighter Airplanes?

Chile's ex-minister of education, Arellano, is quite pessimistic about the chances of stopping the purchase of fighter jets by the Chilean Government in March 2001. Paul Collier has prepared a careful analysis of the tremendous effects of snowball spending on weapons in the region which would be triggered by this purchase. Neighbouring countries (some of which, like Peru, are still in a dormant territorial conflict with Chile) will feel forced to react by buying equipment to detect and attack the fighters (radar and anti-aircraft artillery). They might also feel obliged to buy fighter jets themselves, leading to a chain reaction. This information is quietly shared with the top decision-makers in the Bank and in Chile. But the die is already cast. The iron gridlock of on the one hand the Chilean military that wants to buy and on the other the US interests who want to sell is not to be broken. The Chilean military has been able to save up for this purchase. They have a considerable war chest: 10 per cent of all proceeds from the export of copper are earmarked for the military. The military also has strong political influence. When Pinochet transferred power to a civilian government, this was under the condition that four of the senators would always come from the military. Rumour has it that the military has made it quite clear that they will not condone a trial of Pinochet if they do not get the jets. Case closed. The jets are bought and we keep our fingers crossed that the predicted arms race will not take place.

In these situations arms are the oil that fuels the fire. Indeed, the rich nations realize that arms should not be sold to countries in conflict. Yet the problem is broader. Arms, which are available worldwide, find their way to conflict areas. Arms are a problem in themselves.

Conflicts are often associated with the nature and location of natural resources (see Table 3.2). In this regard, Addison, Le Billon and Murshed identify two main types of resources:[10]

> Point resources such as minerals are non-renewable, geographically concentrated and their extraction requires little labour input. The second type of resources are diffuse resources such as soils and water. These are renewable and geographically spread and they are used in the production of stocks and livestock, usually mobilizing huge amounts of labour. Countries that are abundant in point resources are more likely to experience conflict than countries that only possess diffuse resources, especially when the latter also undertake land reform as in North East Asia.

Globalization has been accompanied by an increased interference between rich and poor countries, by more readily and easy access to arms worldwide, and by higher levels of induced corruption when trade relations increase. The

Table 3.2 Conflicts in Africa and the role of natural resources

Country	Date of armed conflict	Deaths	Point resources	Diffuse resources
Algeria	1992–	70,000	Oil, gas	
Angola	1975–	500,000	Oil, diamonds	Timber, ivory
Cameroon/Nigeria	1997	<1,000	Oil	
Chad	1980–94	300,000	Oil, uranium	
Congo-Brazzaville	1993,1997	9,000	Oil	
DRC/Zaire	1993–	200,000	Gold, diamonds	Timber, ivory
Kenya	1991–	2,000		Cattle
Liberia	1989-96	175,000	Iron, diamonds	Timber, drugs
Mozambique	1976-95	1,000,000		Shrimps, ivory, timber
Rwanda	1990–	650,000		Coffee
Senegal	1997–	<1,000		Drugs
Sierra Leone	1991–99	80,000	Diamonds	Timber
Somalia	1988–	n.a.		Bananas, camels
South Africa	1990s	200,000		Drugs
Sudan	1983–	1,600,000	Oil	Cattle, timber
Western Sahara	1976–	n.a.	Phosphates	

Source: Addison, Le Billon and Murshed (see footnote 10, chapter 3)

onus is on the rich countries to make sure that these side effects of globalization, which impact negatively on the development of poor countries, are brought under control.

In the face of such a clear analysis of a major reason for human suffering and for poverty (namely civil war) as that presented by Collier and Hoeffler, it is important that international policy is formulated which might counteract the size and number of civil conflicts. Transparency in the form of a worldwide mandate for the IMF (or an equivalent organization) to investigate military expenditures would be one answer. It would at least help to create the information needed to act upon. Another, more rigorous answer might be a worldwide moratorium on weapon sales. Increased restraints on the part of the rich countries in arms sales would also be helpful.

3.6 TERTIARY EDUCATION AND DIVERGENCE

In general, tertiary education propagates human talent throughout societies, providing the basis for sustainable economic growth and broad social development. The test of its impact is the capacity of society to capture international knowledge for local use, to contribute to that knowledge and then to participate in the globalized society on an equal knowledge footing.

Knowledge has become the main factor of production in the developed world. Education has become the main vehicle towards a knowledge society with a special role for tertiary education and research.[11]

The influence of knowledge as a factor in income differences is exemplified in Figure 3.3.

One of the important preconditions for effective development and good governance is the provision of high-quality higher education with equality in the access to that education. In that way the leadership for the country is prepared, both for the public as for the private sector.

The situation in developing countries is clearly different. Quality and participation rates in higher education are low, financing is inadequate and management is too bureaucratic. Changing such a situation means facing many difficulties, as an OED report on tertiary education projects commissioned by the World Bank illustrates: [12]

- While more than three-quarters of tertiary education projects in middle-income countries – particularly in East Asia – had satisfactory outcome ratings, those in low-income countries, especially in Africa, performed poorly.
- These completed projects rarely addressed the goal of improved access for poor and disadvantaged students and provided little evidence that those students benefited.

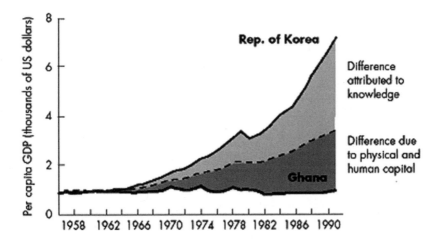

Source: World Bank (1999c): Constructing Knowledge Societies

Figure 3.3 Knowledge as a factor in income differences between countries: Ghana and the Republic of Korea, 1956–90

- Most of the projects met input and output targets, but data on education and labour outcomes were rarely collected, weakening the ability to link Bank-financed projects to economic growth and poverty reduction.

The World Bank has invested in higher education since 1963. Tertiary education in the poorer countries, however, has not sufficiently played its role as knowledge builder and contributor to social cohesion and democracy. In 2003, a World Bank report 'Constructing Knowledge Societies' was published, which concludes that the World Bank should increase its spending on higher education. Next to increased spending, the OED reports that the effects of the World Bank's investments have not yet been sufficiently measured. To improve the effectiveness of its investments, the World Bank should adjust its higher education policies in the following way:

- Guarantee an upward quality spiral.
- Improve the relevance of the programs.
- Provide a long-term financing basis, including the use of private financing embedded in a strategy of equality of opportunity.
- Maximize the use of proven successes of ICT applications in tertiary education.

But even if this were accomplished, one would meet another roadblock along the road to stronger capacity: the so-called brain drain. The international market for well-trained graduates exerts an often irresistible pull on graduates from developing countries, who feel forced to leave home because of poor conditions and a shortage of opportunities. The effect of the brain drain was first noticed in the 1960s. How big the impact of the present size of the brain drain is on the economies of developing countries is anybody's guess, because of the lack of reliable data. We only know that it is sizeable.

Moreover we know that the brain drain is not going to go away any time soon. Developed countries increasingly rely on graduates from developing countries. The best examples of this are doctors and nurses. The recruitment campaigns of developed countries in, for example, Africa have made it even harder for the developing countries to keep their graduates. In the meantime it has become clear that the brain drain is going to affect the chances of attaining the Millennium Development Goals for health and education.

Brain drain not only represents a lost opportunity, but also a lost investment when people educated in their own country emigrate without paying back the investment the government made in their education. Another important consequence of the brain drain is that there are fewer skilled people. Their absence causes the level of education to go down. The remittances of trained staff that have left the country may be large, but they are presumably far too small to generate a sufficient rate of return for the investment made within the country.

What are the numbers we are dealing with when looking at the migration of higher-educated persons? The immigration flow of people with no more than primary education into the US is much smaller (500,000 individuals out of 7 million immigrants) than the largest group, which consists of immigrants with no more than secondary education from other North American countries, primarily Mexico (3.7 million out of 7 million immigrants). The second largest group consists of immigrants from Asia and the Pacific with tertiary education. Of the 128,000 immigrants from Africa, 95,000 are highly educated, and 75 per cent of Indian immigrants have tertiary education. In general (except for Central America and Mexico), highly educated persons have the highest emigration rates from developing countries. The country with the highest emigration rates for highly educated persons is Guyana, where 70 per cent of all persons with tertiary education leave to the US (see Table 3.3).[13]

These figures for the US are not an exception. The attractiveness of Europe for well-trained staff is presumably not much less than that of the US.

In summary: there are few developing countries where higher education plays its proper role of providing the leadership for the country. In part this is the result of local circumstances. But it is also the result of an absence of organized concern for high quality tertiary education on the part of the partners in development cooperation, including an absence of concern for the brain drain from poor to rich countries.

3.7 EQUITABLE GLOBALIZATION

In the debate about globalization, the definition of globalization is often so value-laden that it prevents a fruitful discussion and creates a crude division between 'globalists' and 'anti-globalists'. In this division the 'globalists' are often defined as those who strongly believe that in the end 'globalization' in the sense of countries joining international trade will lead to a better economy and convergence. The 'anti-globalists' on the other hand are often presented as those who are against the extension of neoliberalism and the new neo-liberal world order.

In reality it appears as if there is in fact a substantial agreement between 'globalists' and 'anti-globalists', namely that the development cooperation practices of the past should be changed. Also, there is agreement that the framework or context for development cooperation should be changed, so as to include the lessons of the past. The disagreements may be more visible when we try to formulate the implementation of this broad agreement – when

Table 3.3

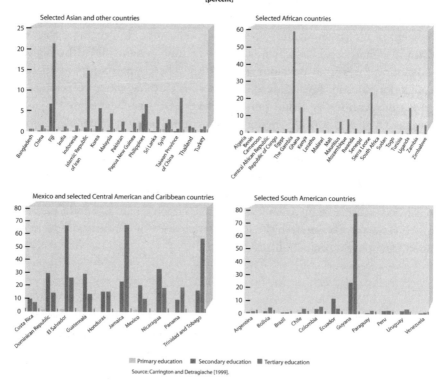

Migration rates to the United States in 1990, by educational category
[percent]

■ Primary education   ■ Secondary education   ■ Tertiary education
Source: Carrington and Detragiache [1999].

Source: Carrington and Detragiache (1999)

we work out the details. Then we will notice that among the globalists and anti-globalists large differences exist in background and principles. Porto Allegre was the place where the first World Social Forum took place in 2003. This forum is a good example of the diversity among anti-globalists. Among them are groups that favour more institutional and government intervention, groups that favour restrictions on trade, while others demand changes in the multilateral institutions such as the IMF and the World Bank. Others oppose biotechnology or focus on the improvement of working conditions or of health in the developing world.

One finds among the 'anti-globalists' few people who are anti-globalization, if it means that people's aspirations and tastes should be curtailed, or even worse, that their access to information should be restricted. A minority of the anti-globalists disputes the role societies attribute to markets; they acknowledge that they are anti-capitalist, which means that they go against the belief and conviction that markets are better instruments for economic order than state planning to provide wealth for people. But what concerns many anti-globalists is the way the market is organized. This is a notion that is very much underlined in this book.

Free markets have many advantages. However, the use of markets in allocating goods and services should not turn into an idolization of markets. Markets are useful instruments, not goals in themselves. Markets can only function with a lot of government control (because the individual entrepreneur will seek monopoly positions, because information is essential, etc.) and they need to be accompanied by an organization for public goods and for social protection by the state or local governments.

For this reason, the concern about globalization and its effects on the poor are well-founded, and equally so for those who believe in markets and free access to information. The World Bank mostly takes the right course in setting the rules for development assistance and globalization, yet it might be more adamant in helping to improve the 'rules of the game' of globalization, which are at present too much skewed to benefit richer nations.

To sum up: there are at least four areas of concern with the ways in which globalization is taking place in our time:

First of all, the rules around trade in particular favour the rich countries disproportionately. They shield their markets from imports of agricultural products from poor economies (through subsidies and tariffs), while at the same time they have easy access to poor countries for their exports (often manufactured goods).

Second, under the rules of the game, I also include the way in which the rich countries and their companies enforce anti-corruption policies. Globalization has increased the role of multinationals, located in the rich countries. While on the one hand rich and poor countries alike agree that good governance is key to development, there is still no effective policing of the anti-corruption policies of foreign companies.

Third, I would also argue for a more restrictive weapons-sales policy. The joint interests of the military in developing countries and the weapons industry in the developed world is part of a weapons race which, albeit on a lower level than during the Cold War, still devours too many resources.

Fourth, the brain drain of talent from poor to rich countries needs urgently to be reversed.

PART II

THE WORLD BANK: A CLOSE ENCOUNTER

4

Shifts in Development Paradigms

'Everyone wants development, but no one is willing to change' is one of the quips of development thinking. It is illustrative of the difficulty we have in coming to grips with the ingredients that are necessary to have rapid economic growth associated with poverty reduction and greater opportunities for education and health for major parts of the population ('development'). The thinking of development economists on these ingredients has decidedly changed in recent decades. The lower half of Figure 4.1 illustrates the major changes in development thinking in the period after the Second World War.

The upper half of Figure 4.1 illustrates the different types of capital involved in development that we have come to distinguish. The notion of physical capital has been around for ages. In the economic analysis of economic growth, physical capital was the only type of capital that was explicitly recognized until the 1970s. Human capital had not yet been 'discovered' in economic growth analysis. Of course, we knew that well-educated people could be a tremendous asset for adding value to the economy, but until the beginning of the 1970s, this had not been empirically tested, nor had it been explicitly introduced in development thinking. Natural capital (the wealth of the natural resources) is recognized and known, but empirical analyses do not show a strong impact of natural wealth on economic growth. This lack of correlation is easily exemplified: the oil-rich countries of the Arab peninsula have benefited enormously from their natural resources, but other equally oil-rich countries like Nigeria and Venezuela have made little or no progress. In the 1990s, social capital was advanced as a major factor in economic growth with some empirical evidence supporting this hypothesis.[1] Social capital is defined as the networks people have, the interconnectedness of society and the trust people have in each other. It stands for the feeling that a society that has a sense of working together will have more economic growth and a more equal income distribution.

The understanding of the ingredients that are necessary for rapid development can easily be translated into the main instruments of development cooperation, or aid to developing countries. Economic growth is still the

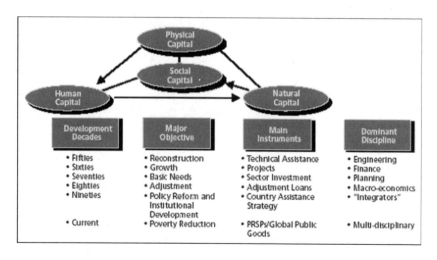

Source: OED report, the Monterrey Challenge, p. 4

Figure 4.1 Reconceptualization of the development agenda: a World Bank view

centerpiece of development, even though development is a broader concept, focused among other things on poverty reduction. But the latter cannot be accomplished without economic growth. At the same time, not all growth necessarily leads to poverty reduction of an equal size.

In their focus on poverty reduction, institutions of development cooperation such as the World Bank use increasingly the 'usual' socio-economic analysis: i.e. an analysis which is applied equally to rich as to poor countries. The time for development economics as a separate discipline (in the sense of a different approach and analysis for developing as opposed to developed countries) is over. This is the result of a convergence in thinking over the past 50 years. Hence mainstream economic analysis is the backbone of the approach to development. Rostow's (1960) suggestion of separate stages of development (see Section 3.2) has quietly been set aside.

In addition, the socio-economic and political contexts are to be taken into account. Tools are used such as:

1. Dialogue with the developing country: a developing country no longer gets a 'present' from development cooperation without prior dialogue in which the two parties exchange views on what the country needs and what the development institution can offer. Moreover, the dialogue has to lead to an agreement. Admittedly: it is not a dialogue between equal partners, even if the development agencies do their utmost to put the developing country in the position of equality.

2. Country ownership: no development institution expects to 'buy' good policies from a country without a full commitment of that country's political leadership to engage in the required changes.

3. Cultural sensitivity: this is perhaps the least easily acquired by the development institutions, which tend to treat policy changes as 'technical', while they in fact need to be deeply rooted in the culture of the country.

4. Good governance: good governance is now widely recognized as a prerequisite for changes towards 'good policies' – that is, policies that lead to economic growth. In particular, corruption stands in the way of the kinds of economic growth that could alleviate the fate of poor people in the country. The most obvious requirement of good governance is that donor money is used for its proper purpose (and does not end up in the hands of middlemen or in Swiss bank accounts).

This approach to development is relatively new. In the past, development policies applied often a different framework, with other objectives, instruments and disciplines, as Figure 4.1 indicates. Perhaps the most important shift in development policies has been the shift of attention from physical capital (roads, bridges, dams) to human capital, social capital and natural capital. We also see this shift in the developed world, as expressed by the election slogan of Prime Minister Blair in 1997, 'Education, education, education', or by the European Union's emphasis on the knowledge economy (compare this also with the Lisbon declaration of 2001). But equally important is the shift over time in the emphasis on the political framework of development cooperation. While originating as a 'technical', purely economic-analytical topic, development cooperation has matured into a framework in which cultural, social and political aspects are well taken into account.

4.1 1945–EARLY 1950S: RECONSTRUCTION AND INVESTMENT

Development assistance after the Second World War unfolded with the urgency of postwar reconstruction. The ravages of the Second World War would have been sufficient reason to engage in a grand scheme for reconstruction, but there was more. There was a preparedness for broad-based international cooperation, because of the failure of the free, unguided market to address the problems of the Great Depression of the 1930s. At that time, economists like Keynes had already pleaded for international cooperation. Yet other economists, like Von Hayek carried the day by alleging that international cooperation was not needed: the market would resolve all. With hindsight, it is obvious that more was needed. The laissez-faire, laissez-aller policies of the thirties brought about a disastrous and prolonged depression and – in its aftermath – the Second World War.

It was in this context that the Bretton Woods conference of 1944 took place. There was considerable support for international agreements as a means to further economic cooperation and growth worldwide. This gave life to the World Bank and the IMF. The Bretton Woods institutions were set up to help first and foremost in the reconstruction of Europe, to secure stable trade and prices and to prevent another economic and political escalation, as happened during and after the Great Depression. Technical assistance was the most important tool in reconstructing the bombed infrastructure in Europe. The Bretton Woods conference agreed on fixed exchange rates and closed capital markets.

At that time there were few developing countries. The developing countries of today were then still mostly colonies. However, already at the inception of the Bretton Woods institutions the notion was included that developing countries should partake in these institutions and should benefit from them in the same way as the developed world did.

4.2 1950s–1960s: Foreign Exchange

These are the golden years of development. The rich world enjoys an unprecedented economic boom. The colonial powers, in part through conviction, in part through the growing insurgence in their colonies and with the pressure of the US, transfer power, as in India (1949), Indonesia (1949), Congo (1960) or Uganda (1962). Most of the new countries inherited from their colonial masters a well trained, albeit small elite, a strong education system (for only a small group) and a reasonable legal and institutional infrastructure. The newly created developing countries grow fast (economically), often with strong leadership that transcends the national borders, such as that of Nyerere in Tanzania.

Economists – in rich and poor countries alike – work with a relatively simple concept of the economy, in which the main ingredient for economic growth is investment in physical capital (machinery, buildings, infrastructure). It is in this context that the developing countries aim for economic growth through planned investment, where the planning is often captured in five-year plans. The developed world is supporting development in poor countries through foreign exchange, because that is regarded as the missing factor: development economists argue that developing countries cannot yet earn enough foreign exchange through exports to make the necessary investments in infrastructure (roads, dams and machinery). Also, local savings are insufficient – even if high in the international metric – to make those investments for growth, while capital markets are national, and private banks cannot finance such investments either.

Foreign direct investment (private firms of the rich world investing in poor countries) exists, but is at a low level, simply because of the uncertainties of reclaiming the investments.

In retrospect, the generosity of the developed world was at its peak in these years and developing countries fared well, with an overall spirit of optimism on growth and poverty reduction. The UN named this decade 'the development decade'.

However, lurking in the background is the Cold War, which creates an atmosphere of building camps around the globe. Potentially powerful and capable leaders in developing countries are shunned by the Western camp if they wish to keep an open mind about political systems, i.e. whether they should be more or less centrally controlled. President Nyerere of Tanzania is a case in point. He gradually fell out of favour with the West when he tried to follow an independent course.

4.3 1970S: OIL PRICE HIKES AND CONFUSION

The economic growth of the 1950s and 1960s cannot be sustained in the 1970s. The 1960s have shown a high rate of economic growth. However, the international community feels that developing countries have been less successful in promoting human capital development and employment. They also notice that income inequality within the developing countries has been rising rather than declining, contrary to what people in both developing and developed countries had hoped for. Also poverty is on the rise (in terms of absolute numbers). These are the reasons that the UN 'development decade' of the 1960s ends in frustration and disappointment. Towards the end of that decade the donor community shows, as a result, a sagging morale.

In the 1970s, the policy lines of the 1960s are pursued in development cooperation, albeit with greater attention to human development and income inequality. Attempts are made to bring donors to the table and to have them reconfirm their commitments to more support for poor countries, with little success. The effect of the Cold War is felt more strongly than before in development cooperation. For example, when Salvator Allende becomes president of Chile, donor support for the country virtually ceases to exist, due to US pressure.

What really impacts upon the world, however, is the quadrupling of oil prices in 1973 and a further doubling of that price in 1979. Developing countries sink in the flood of oil prices, as they are (net) importers of oil with a substantial part of export earnings devoted to the payment for oil imports. Many of the large investment projects of the 1960s turn out to be unsustainable. The first signs of the impact of the breakdown of governance on economic development become visible. Once-renowned universities in developing countries show signs of a quality collapse.

In many respects it is a time of confusion in development cooperation. Eyes remain closed to the governance issues, which in turn seriously hinder the adaptation process in developing countries to the oil price shocks. Added to this, the existing structure of planned investment and state control also leads to inflexibility.

The developed world slightly adapts its development paradigm, by adding substantial extra loans to the package of development aid with the rationale that the oil price shocks have badly bled the developing countries and that a blood transfusion of loans is necessary. This means also a new life for the IMF. The IMF was largely set up to address the problems that might arise from the adoption of fixed exchange rates in 1945; fixed exchange rates might result in balance of payment deficits, which could not be undone by devaluations. The system of fixed exchange rates was abolished in 1973; however, the IMF stayed in place, now focusing on oil-importing countries with short-run balance of payment problems and gradually focusing on countries in crisis.

4.4 1980s: Free Markets

The 1980s are the period of the upsurge of free market thinking in the world. President Reagan in the US and Prime Minister Thatcher in the UK set the tone worldwide, in a period of deep stagnation both in the developed and in the developing world. Economic growth in the developing countries is urgently needed for repayments on the loans made in the 1970s (and to pay for higher oil prices). However, the economic machinery of developing countries has virtually ground to a halt with little ability to pay for the debts incurred. The debt crisis is born.

Official development assistance is no longer increasing. The developed world is too busy with its own problems: reducing budget deficits, bringing inflation in check and freeing up 'supply powers' through economic liberalization. This is also applied as the recipe for poor, debt-laden countries: free up economic dynamism, while reducing government deficits as well as inflation. The 'Washington Consensus' is born, with the IMF emphasizing limited government deficits and inflation, and the World Bank 'helping' developing countries in structural adjustment, for example through trade liberalization. 'Helping' means: offering new loans on the condition of structural adjustment.

There is a keen awareness now that new loans might not be the answer. Rather, debt relief or even bankruptcy might be a better solution. However, the developed world shies away from radical solutions and opts for pushing the problem into the future, only to realize that by the end of the 1980s the developing countries have paid more to the developed world than they have received in aid, and that the debt crisis has become structural. The 1980s are once again a period of divergence, within developing countries and between the rich and the poor world, with rising poverty.

4.5 THE 1990S: THE END OF THE COLD WAR; GOVERNANCE

The decrease in the amount of development aid, which started in the 1980s, continues in the 1990s (see also Figure 2.3). The end of the Cold War in 1989 decreases the sense of urgency over supporting those countries that previously needed to be 'protected' by the West against the influence of the communist states, countries that in turn the communist world was attempting to 'protect' against westernization.

At the same time, 'governance' is no longer a forbidden word. In the Cold War era, governance hardly played a role in considering the aid-worthiness of a country. It was political correctness that counted, with the result that billions of aid dollars given to pro-Western governments disappeared to Swiss bank accounts. The aid to Zaire under Mobutu is a case in point. The introduction of 'good governance' in the allocation of development aid may have increased the effectiveness of development cooperation by a factor of ten, as Craig Burnside and David Dollar[2] calculate. Still, their figures are puzzling. Does it really take about $3,000 in development aid to lift one person permanently out of poverty? In that case, one might as well put the money into a bank and transfer the interest income directly to the poor person (as this would have the same effect). In any case, as the Global Monitoring Report of the World Bank, 2004 (Chapter 11, p. 4) shows, aid *reduces* growth in countries with 'bad' policies and contributes to growth in countries with 'good' policies.

The 1990s show a continuation of the market liberalization line in development cooperation. The miracle of the Asian Tigers, which experience fast economic growth after market liberalization, is considered to be proof of the effectiveness of the market in promoting development.

Civil society is a new force in the development paradigm at this time. It can contribute to transparency and to democratization, and help to place more emphasis within countries on poverty reduction, as well as contribute to more ownership for policy restructuring.

As a result of the liberalization of capital markets, the 1990s show a tremendous growth in foreign direct investment (FDI). FDI is possibly the strongest factor in contributing to development in developing countries in the 1990s. By the end of the decade, FDI has reached a level of at least five times the flow of Official Development Assistance to poor and middle-income countries. It remains quite stable under highly unstable general economic circumstances.

The liberalization of financial markets, however, have led at the same time to a rapid succession of financial crises, of a kind that have not been seen since the Great Depression. Mexico, Argentina and other countries are hit (sometimes more than once) by a financial crisis, culminating in the East Asia crisis in 1997.

4.6 THE START OF A NEW MILLENNIUM

The new millennium starts on an upbeat note with the Millennium Declaration (2000) heralded and signed by the heads of state of 188 countries (see Section 2.5). The Monterrey Consensus (2002) emerges (mentioned in Section 2.2). There is the New Partnership in African Development (NEPAD) in 2002. NEPAD pledges to attack corruption in Africa and takes responsibility for improving solid and economic policies. A new attitude towards the creation of a better banking system in East Asia increased this spirit of optimism. The banking system in East Asia had become laden with bad debts by the end of the second millennium. The open acknowledgement of existing problems is seen as the first step to resolving the problems. It looks as if the new millennium is going to bring the ultimate success for development cooperation, applying the hard-won lessons of the past and effectively bringing the poor countries gradually into the world of the 'haves'.

September 11, 2001, however, marks a turning point. The planes not only crashed into the World Trade buildings and the Pentagon. They also seem to have destroyed for some of the major world powers the confidence in peaceful solutions to the growing tension between the Muslim fundamentalist world and the values of the Western world. The Cold War was succeeded – after an interbellum of less than a decade – by the war on terrorism.

This era might re-introduce the danger of concentrating on 'friends' instead of on good governance (as in the 1970s and 1980s), which in turn would lead to a simplified view of 'good' and 'bad' countries and a decreased attention to the effectiveness of development cooperation. Developing countries' room for manoeuvre in the area of policy changes might become smaller, slowing down the development process.

Paradoxically, September 11, 2001, was followed by two major conferences on development cooperation: the Monterrey Conference (2002) and the Johannesburg Conference on Sustainable Development (also 2002). In particular, the Monterrey Consensus seemed to support and accelerate the development process, in part in response to September 11: major nations (including the US) pledged to increase ODA. The 'Monterrey Consensus' emerged.

In his introductory remarks Horst Köhler, then the Managing Director of the IMF (and now President of Germany), summarized the Monterrey Consensus (2002) as a global statement that 'we need to work on a better globalization – one that provides opportunities for all and one in which risks are contained.' The Monterrey Consensus stressed that aid effectiveness is linked to the measure in which countries themselves take responsibility for their own economic and social development. This requires growth by further integration and a new partnership between the developed and the developing countries, which is characterized by capacity building and country ownership of good governance and the rule of law. It also recognizes that when poor countries are ready to live up to these responsibilities, the international community should provide faster, stronger and more comprehensive support.

What is missing is the clear dedication to a change in the rules of the game of globalization (see summary of Chapter 3): improved access of developing countries to the markets of rich countries and better protection for induced corruption. In other words: 'Monterrey' could have paid more attention to the *context* of development cooperation.

'Monterrey' shied away from the discussion on 'loans versus grants' as means to support developing countries. At the setting up of the Bretton Woods institutions, the agreement was that loans should also be used by the World Bank and IMF for the poorest countries, albeit on 'concessional terms'. These terms imply, in the case of IDA loans (loans to the poorest countries, see Section 5.1), that approximately 70 per cent is in fact a grant. In the 1990s this system became heavily debated. The liberalization of capital markets made the loans by the Bretton Woods institutions all of a sudden an instrument comparable to the loans of private banks. The Meltzer Report (named after its chairperson Allan H. Meltzer, 2000, see www.house.gov/jec/imf/Meltzer.htm), prepared for the US Congress, proposed to abolish loans by the Bretton Woods institutions as a means of development assistance. In Chapter 10 we will propose that indeed grants, if sustainably supplied, might well improve the quality of development cooperation.

The Monterrey Consensus does capture the current approach to development cooperation. Hanna and Picciotto formulated this approach as follows: 'Monterrey combines a *results-orientation*; domestic *ownership* of improved policies; *partnership* between governments, the private sector and the civil society; and a *long-term, holistic* approach that recognizes the interaction between development sectors and themes.'[3] The principles of effective aid issued by the Development Assistance Committee (DAC) of the Organization for Economic Cooperation and Development (OECD) embody these tenets.[4] The same principles animate the Comprehensive Development Framework (CDF) and the Poverty Reduction Strategy Program (PRSP) endorsed by the Development Committee of World Bank governors. They also underlie the United Nations Development Assistance Framework (UNDAF) used to improve coherence among the activities of United Nations specialized agencies at the country level.

The difference between the 'old' and the 'new' paradigm is presented in Figure 4.2 in terms of their evaluation methodologies.

There is optimism that the new paradigm can help to spur the achievement of the MDGs. As was discussed in Section 2.5, the Millennium Development

Evaluation methodologies are being adapted to reflect dominant paradigms of development policy	
Dominant concepts of development	**Characteristics of development evaluation**
Project focus	Project evaluation
Investment-driven growth	Cost-benefit analysis
BEFORE	
Import substitution	Shadow pricing
Central planning	Self-evaluation
Conditionality	Macro-standards
Country focus	Portfolio evaluation
Structural adjustment	Policy evaluation
NOW	
Outward-oriented policies	Risk analysis
Decentralized decisionmaking	Participatory evaluation

Source: adapted from OED

Figure 4.2 Monterrey evaluation framework

Goals pose significant challenges for development cooperation. Growth of per capita incomes in developing countries would have to reach twice the levels achieved in the 1990s for the period 2000–2015 in order to reach the MDGs' income and poverty reduction objective, and only 33 developing countries are on track to meet this goal (OED, 2002, see World Bank web site). A study by Buckley underlines the importance of ownership of improved policies.[5] Countries with such 'good' policies achieved GNP per capita growth three times as high as the rate of countries that had not yet achieved durable adjustment and six times higher than countries that have oscillated between weak and strong policy environments. Unfortunately the OED study of 43 adjusting countries over the period 1975–1996 showed that only 12 per cent of the countries demonstrated the capacity and the commitment to achieve durable and major improvements in their policy regimes.

The new paradigm stresses the importance of partnering. However, the wording of the commitment is far too soft. What is required is a clear road map towards full integration and harmonization of all development aid, replacing the present (2004) inclination of donors to put 'flag planting' above development effectiveness.

5

Decision-Making at the World Bank

In July 2004, the World Bank celebrated its 60th anniversary. Its origins lie in Bretton Woods (New Hampshire, US) where, during the Second World War, eminent economists and civil servants met to discuss the rebuilding of Europe after the war. From these discussions the so-called Bretton Woods institutions emerged. There are three of them. There are the two 'sisters', the World Bank and the IMF (the International Monetary Fund). But the World Trade Organization (WTO) is also often included, because it has its roots (and was proposed) at the Bretton Wood conferences, but did not come into its present form until 1995 via an earlier appearance as GATT.

The World Bank's mission is to reduce poverty in developing countries, while the IMF is entrusted with the role of a worldwide central bank and the WTO with the task of bringing about free trade.

The 50th anniversary of the World Bank in 1994 was met with sharp criticism. The movement '50 years is enough' alleged that during the past 50 years, World Bank policies have not been effective in reducing poverty. It furthermore stated that the World Bank 'has been promoting and financing inequitable and unsustainable development overseas that *creates* (rather than reduces) poverty while destroying the environment. [It is] also profoundly undemocratic in that [it has] consistently denied citizens information about, and involvement in, major decisions affecting their respective societies.' (see www.globaljusticeecology.org). The World Bank is not the only target of this criticism: often the IMF is even more harshly depicted as the villain of development cooperation.

These arguments of the '50 years is enough' movement may sound extreme. However, they are widely shared among NGOs, politicians, scholars and students from outside the Bank and among action groups, sometimes in more and sometimes in less extreme terms. Such criticisms may also be heard within the Bank (as well as in the IMF).

In this chapter we discuss the World Bank's history and decision-making structure, while Chapter 6 gives an overview of its current organizational structure and culture, taking Jim Wolfensohn's appointment in 1996 as President of the World Bank as a starting point. In this chapter we consider first the present financial structure of the Bank (who owns it, who provides the money and how the money is provided – Section 5.1), while subsequently putting that against the background of the founding of the Bank (Section 5.2). The Bank is supervised and directed by its Governors. These are the representatives of the owners of the Bank, who mostly act through the Development Committee, a group of 24 ministers representing the full board of Governors (all owners). These meet twice a year as Section 5.3 describes, while the Board of Governors is presented in Section 5.4. This formal structure might give the impression of balance in the positions of countries. In the informal structure, however, the power balance is quite unequal: it is highly slanted towards US dominance (Section 5.5). The influence of developing countries is discussed in Section 5.6. Keynes, one of the founding fathers of the Bank, believed that the position of the developing countries (as clients) was overemphasized in the structure of the Bank. Anti- and other globalists believe that there is an under-representation of developing countries in decision-making in the Bank, because they are the targets. Does this mean that maybe there is actually a nice balance?

5.1 SIXTY YEARS OF THE WORLD BANK

Today the World Bank is, like the IMF and the WTO, often viewed as part of the UN structure, which is what we have as 'world governance'. Figure 5.1 gives an overview of this structure. The governance structure of the three Bretton Woods institutions deviates quite substantially from that of UN organizations (see also Section 7.1). Currently, the World Bank has 184 member countries (the owners of the Bank) and consists of five development institutions: the *International Bank for Reconstruction and Development* (IBRD), the *International Development Association* (IDA), the *International Finance Cooperation* (IFC), the *Multilateral Investment Guarantee Agency* (MIGA) and the *International Centre for Settlement of Investment Disputes* (ICSID). The Bank only deals with Governments as clients. The Bank is prohibited from dealing directly with private clients or public clients other than Governments.

The main goal of the World Bank is poverty alleviation, which is formulated as follows in its mission statement:

> *To fight poverty with passion and professionalism for lasting results.*
> *To help people help themselves and their environment by providing resources, sharing knowledge, building capacity and forging partnerships in the public and private sectors.*

To be an excellent institution able to attract, excite and nurture diverse and committed staff with exceptional skills who know how to listen and learn.

The staff is recruited through worldwide competition. Recruitment is not subject (as in UN organizations) to quota (even though the Bank always will try to have a balance in the staff composition between countries and regions). Everything is done in the work environment to live up to the core values.

As mentioned before: between the many agencies with the objective of poverty reduction the World Bank functions in many respects as the throbbing heart of development cooperation. A significant proportion of the US $50 billion (which includes humanitarian aid) flow through the World Bank in the form of loans, making it financially the largest single partner to deal with the full set of policy issues. Bilateral aid, like that of the Japanese, the US, or the European Union, is in total substantial, but the World Bank is a bigger provider than any single bilateral. Other United Nations organizations, like the World Health Organization (WHO) may be larger in staff (15,000 versus the 8,000 of the World Bank), but lack the leverage of financial support to

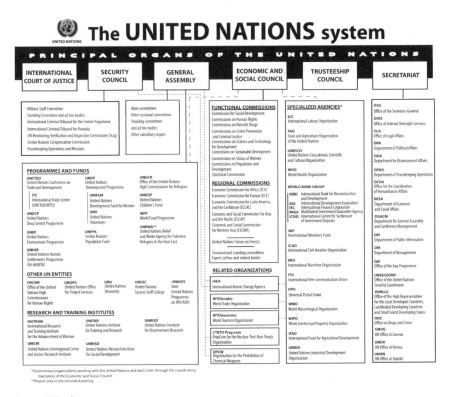

Figure 5.1 The structure of the United Nations system

countries. They also may be less effective in a country because they focus solely on one of the policy areas of the country (like health) and have no means to work with the country across the board.

At the political level, as represented by member states, the Bank has observer status in several UN bodies, including the General Assembly and its Second and Third Committees and ECOSOC, which address issues that bear directly on the work of the Bank, for example, population, poverty, HIV/AIDS, gender issues and women and development, governance and civil society, communications and the environment. In addition, the Bank maintains an active dialogue with individual member states and political groups such as the G–7 and the European Union. At the operational level, the Bank works with other UN Funds and Programs in its project work through policy coordination, project implementation, co-financing and aid coordination (see Section 7.1).

In gauging the relative position of the World Bank, as I did above, one should be aware that the billions of US dollars which flow through the Bank are a mixture of zero-interest and low-interest loans, while most of the flows from other donors (like the bilaterals) are grants (sometimes more and sometimes less tied to specific usage of the grant money, for example for consultants or for goods from the donor country).

IDA and IBRD together are responsible for making the investments of the World Bank: the projects or programs which contribute to poverty reduction and which cannot be financed from countries' own resources. IDA and IBRD operate by giving loans to governments on 'concessional' terms, where concessional means: (far) below market rates. The concessionality of the terms of IDA loans effectively means that 70 per cent of their value can be considered grants.

Governments of developing countries turn to the Bank when they are not able to finance their projects themselves. Moreover, there is also no way to get the money on the private capital market at reasonable interest rates. Private bankers may be willing to jump into a project, but then only with very high interest rates. The high level of interest is due to the risk or uncertainty of recouping the program's costs. As a result, many programs and projects in developing countries would not come to fruition without IDA or IBRD. Of course, developing countries will always first seek the assistance of agencies (like many of the bilaterals) that provide grants.

IDA loans are only available to poor countries (per capita income of less than US $865 in 2004). IDA loans are virtually interest-free and only need to be repaid after a long period (30 years). This is the kind of loan every individual would love. Developing countries are no different. It is the World Bank staff that has to ensure that the loans are made for projects or programs with the highest return to the country, so that they can be paid back easily. Unfortunately, the reality has been different. Many countries did not grow enough (economically) in the 1980s and 1990s to be able to repay their debts (including the IDA debt): the 'debt crisis' was born (see Section 2.4 for more about debt problems).

IDA loans are made out of a pot, which is filled by 'replenishments' and repayments. Every three years the donor countries 'replenish' the IDA pot. The latest (13th) replenishment took place in September 2002 for a period of three years. Starting in the middle of 2002, the replenishment amounted to about US $23 billion over the next three years.

Table 5.1 gives an overview of the 13th replenishment. The US is the largest contributor with 20 per cent of the contributions, followed by Japan (16 per cent), Germany (10.3 per cent), the UK (10.1 per cent), France (6 per cent), Italy (3.8 per cent), Canada (3.75 per cent), Sweden (2.62 per cent) and the Netherlands (2.6 per cent). Note that the contributions of the EU countries together far exceed those of the US.

The 13th replenishment was the first time that the IDA provided borrowers, civil society and the public with the opportunity to attend the replenishment discussions. IDA also released policy papers for publication.

Internally, the Bank allocates the IDA funds to countries according to anticipated 'development effectiveness' and within countries on the basis of the Country Assistance Strategy. The focus on development effectiveness is relatively recent. It is very much related to the conclusion (see also Section 4.5) that aid is only effective under conditions of good governance.

The replenishment process of the IDA is an important governance process for the Bank. Yet this process is highly informal. This is a weak point in the governance of the World Bank. At the same time, it may have an even greater legitimacy than the IBRD governance, because the IDA replenishments get a lot of attention in the parliaments of the donor countries. For example, the 13th replenishment – with at its core the debate about the IDA grants – was widely discussed in the press, at the G–7 and the EU ministerial councils.

Also, it was the IDA replenishments that led to the establishment of the OED (Operations Evaluation Department) and the QAG (Quality Assurance Group). The OED was entrusted with an evaluation of the IDA itself. This process has contributed to trust in IDA as a donor agency and partly explains why the IDA was able to raise its replenishment in September 2002 by an astonishing 18 per cent, while at the same time the UN family was struggling to keep its financing stable.

In contrast to the IDA, the IBRD is almost organized as a Bank, with shareholders who have paid in capital. The IBRD is the Bank's wing for middle-income countries. Almost all countries (with the exception of Cuba and North Korea) are shareholders. The US is the largest single shareholder with 16.4 per cent of total subscriptions, followed by Japan (7.9 per cent), Germany (4.5 per cent), the UK (4.3 per cent), and France (4.3 per cent). It should be noted that the 15 EU countries (before the enlargement of May 2004) have a total of 18.6 per cent. The Europeans could easily outvote the US if they were willing to work together. But this is seldom the case. As a rule they vote entirely separately, thereby giving the lead to the US.

5.2 How the World Bank was Established

Getting the world's major powers to agree on the creation of a 'throbbing heart' for development cooperation is an astonishing feat in itself. It could only happen in a period when there was a desperate need for new steps for joint action on the world level. The end of the Second World War was such a period. Joint action was needed to make Western Europe rise from the ashes. The Allied Forces disagreed, however, on the way this should be done, and in particular on the nature of the resurgence of Germany. Should Germany be dismantled, so that it would never be able to become a military power again, as Josef Stalin had it with some sympathy from the Americans (President Roosevelt and his secretary of the Treasury, Morgenthau), or was there room for a German resurgence as a united, industrial power, as Churchill advanced (see: Michael Beschloss, *The Conquerors,* Simon and Schuster, 2002)? The British and the Americans did, in any case, agree that there should be a World Bank and an International Monetary Fund (as well as the first notions of a trade organization) and gathered a large number of countries at the Bretton Woods Conference in 1944 which joined in on the Anglo-American consent. The Russians followed suit.

It is not unusual in history that the same inventive notion occurs to different people around the same time, but it still remains a special moment when the invention is created. Harry Dexter White (1893–1948), the chief economic adviser to US Treasury Secretary Henry Morgenthau, was the 'inventor' of the notion of an International Monetary Fund and a World Bank in the summer of 1941. These institutions would be created to function as instruments to bring about a healthy world economy, with robust trading partners for the US.

On the other side of the Atlantic, the famous economist and adviser to the British Treasury, John Maynard Keynes (1883–1946), had developed – completely independently from White – a similar plan for global economic cooperation with a 'central bank' for the nations of the world. Keynes, with his book *The General Theory of Employment, Interest and Money*, was one of the most influential economists of the time.

Although there was agreement on the general outline, White and Keynes disagreed entirely when it came to concrete elaboration. When White managed to have the US Congress discuss a draft in October 1944 and US Foreign Secretary Morgenthau published a summary on October 8th, Keynes reacted as if he had

Table 5.1: Contributions to the Thirteenth Replenishment

Contributing Members	Basic contributions (%)	Supplemental SDR Million	Incentive SDR Million	Contributors SDR Million	Total Rates SDR Million	Exchange NC (NC/SDR)**	IDA13 Million
Argentina a'	0.05%	5.00			5.00	1.26451	6.32
Australia	1.46%	146.01			146.00302	2.46552	360.00
Austria	0.73%	78.16			78.16	1.43546	112.19
Bahamas, The	0.009%	0.90			0.90	1.25339	1.13
Barbados	0.002%	0.20			0.20	2.51723	0.50
Belgian	1.55%	155.31			155.31	1.43546	222.50
Brazil a'	0.61%	61.12			61.12	3.04319	186.01
Canada	3.75%	375.75	27.05		402.80	1.95189	690.40
Czech Rep.	0.05%	5.01			5.01	49.04147	245.70
Denmark	1.58%	158.32			158.32	10.69731	1,693.56
Finland	0.60%	60.12			60.12	1.43546	86.30
France	6.00%	601.20			601.20	1.43546	863.00
Germany	10.30%	1,032.23			1,032.23	1.43546	1,481.72
Greece	0.12%	11.59			11.59	1.43545	16.64
Hungary	0.06%	5.95			5.95		5.95
Iceland	0.04%	4.01			4.01	126.13175	505.54
Ireland	0.18%	18.04	16.80		34.83	1.43546	50.00
Israel	0.10%	10.02			10.02	5.31981	53.30
Italy	3.30%	380.76			380.76	1.43546	546.57
Japan	16.00%	1,603.29			1,603.29	154.58522	247,844,40
Korea	0.91%	91.18			91.18	1644.84532	149,980.29
Kuwait	0.14%	14.03			14.03	0.38833	5.45

(Table continued)

(Table 5.1 continud)

Contributing Members	Basic contributions (%)	Supplemental SDR Million	Incentive SDR Million	Contributors SDR Million	Total Rates SDR Million	Exchange NC (NC/SDR)**	IDA13 Million
Luxembourg	0.10%	10.02			10.02	1.43546	14.38
Mexico a' b'	0.05%	5.01			5.01		5.01
Netherlands	2.60%	260.52			260.52	1.43546	373.97
New Zealand	0.12%	12.02			12.02	3.03567	36.40
Norway	1.52%	152.30	21.14 a'		173.44	11.49853	1,751.27
Poland a'	0.03%	3.01			3.01	5.19579	15.62
Portugal	0.20%	20.04			20.04	1.43546	23.77
Russia b'	0.08%	8.00	12.00		20.00		20.00
Saudi Arabia c'	0.39%	39.53			39.53	1.26502	50.00
Singapore a'	0.28%	28.06			28.06	2.27261	63.76
Slovak Republic a'	0.19%	1.32			1.32	61.38745	81.85
South Africa	0.08%	8.02			8.02	10.36396	83.09
Spain	1.80%	180.36			180.36	1.43546	258.90
Sweden	2.62%	262.52			262.52	13.29035	3,489.04
Switzerland	2.43%	243.49			243.49	2.17960	530.70
Turkey a'	0.09%	9.02			9.02		9.02
United Kingdom	10.14%	1,016.21			1,016.21	0.38564	900.00
United States	20.12%	2,015.78		237.15	2,252.93	1.26502	2,850.00
Venezuela a' b'	0.03%	3.01			301		1.01
Sub-total	90.75%	9,096.43	55.85	237.15	9,389.43		
Supplemental contributions with attribution d'	0.56%	55.85	55.85				

Supplemental contributions without attribution	3.43%	343.83			343.88
Unallocated gap	5.23%	523.85			286.70
Total donor contributions	100.00%	10,020.00	55.85	237.15	10,020.00
Memo item:					
Contribution from IDA12 array-aver for long-term cost of grants θ		100.00			100.00

a' Not yet in a position to commit, figure is indicative.

b' Contributions of countries with inflation rates greater than 10% per annum during 1998–2000 will be determinated in SDR_T.

c' Assuming contributions denominated in US dollars.

d' Supplemental contributions through accelerated encashments and or additional contributions.

e' Supplemental contribution through accelerated encashments and/or additional contributions to finance potential additional needs of up to SDR 2.0 billion. Does not count towards filling the unallocated gap.

f' Preliminary indications have been received from some donors of willingness to provide up to GBP 100 million (SDR, 112.9 million) dependent on the design and funding requirements of the scheme which may be agreed during the mid-term review.

** Exchange rate arranging period: April 1 to September 30, 2001.

Note: Details do not add up due to rounding.

Source: IDA–13, *Supporting Poverty Reduction Strategies*, 25 July 2002. *http://siteresources.worldbank.org/IDA/Resources/FinaltextIDA13Report.pdf*

been bitten by a snake. 'God knows what you think of it when you see it, for it is an extremely odd document.' His main objection was that the governance of the Bank was inadequate and gave far too much room for clients in the decision-making process and too little power to those who provided the funds.

'To all appearances the scheme makes no difference whatever between creditor and debtor countries' .... 'There is no sort of linking up between the responsibility for overseas investment and the possession of a favourable balance of trade. Indeed, everything is done to dissociate these ideas as much as possible' ... 'Having put these lunatic robes on his [White's] Frankenstein, he then proceeds at various stages to introduce jokers, which might actually cause the scheme to work out in practice in a way exactly the opposite of what it appears to be on the surface.'[1]

Keynes was not convinced that something so ill-conceived as a functional organization might be effective. Unfortunately, neither Keynes nor White witnessed the true functioning of the Bretton Woods institutions, since they both died of heart attacks in 1946 and 1948, respectively.

Keynes might still make that same observation today, if he were alive, as the organization of the institutions has remained a relatively constant factor and is decidedly peculiar. At the same time, the debate has gone in a different direction, namely to give a greater role to the developing countries within the Bank. Anti-globalists and others object to the limited degree of democracy in the decision-making of the Bank, meaning that the representation of developing countries should be increased.

In its modus operandi, the Bank (as well as the IMF) went through many transformations. A major transformation was the early shift in focus away from Western Europe towards developing countries. When the US $12 billion Marshall plan was introduced in 1947, the Bank – with a lending volume of less than half a billion dollars at that time – became virtually irrelevant for Western Europe's reconstruction, although it remained engaged with projects and programs in Europe over a long period. This era came to an end when Portugal 'graduated' in 1994 (graduated means: having exceeded the threshold of an annual income of US $5185 per capita, at 2004 values, and having access to the international capital market with a stable foreign capital exchange).

Developing countries in Africa, Asia, and Latin America – which had always been part of the mandate of the Bank – became early on the focus of the Bank's work. Chile was the first of the developing countries to apply for a loan in 1947 (US $40 million). This request was strongly supported by the US. But it is an illustration of the philosophy at the Bank at that time that the request was viewed with great suspicion by the then Bank President Meyer. Apparently he was still not too sure where the focus of the Bank should be.

A second major transformation was the shift under President McNamara (1968–1981) away from loans for investments in infrastructure, like factories, equipment, dams and roads, to a focus on the broader support for development projects, including projects in human development, and programs which included substantial financial support for economic transformation. This second transformation went along with the (re-)discovery that it was not the lack of foreign exchange or domestic savings which stood in the way of profitable investments, but rather a business and investment climate in which the return of profitable investments could not always be secured because of a lack of governance: the lack of a legal framework and the enforcement thereof. Another important change took place during the presidency of J. Wolfensohn (see Chapter 6). This is the change towards the new development paradigm of 'development from within' (see Section 4.6 on the Monterrey Consensus).

5.3 THE DEVELOPMENT COMMITTEE

Each member country of the Bank appoints a 'Governor'. The shareholders of the World Bank, represented by these 'Governors of the Bank' (mostly ministers of finance or central bank presidents, with some ministers for development cooperation from European Union countries), meet once a year at the Annual Meeting. This is a huge jamboree, which is mostly used to meet informally to conclude and sign contracts with the private sector. The Annual Meeting is the place for the President of the Bank to be accountable to all the shareholders and to map out the strategy for the upcoming year. President Wolfensohn's speeches at the Annual Meetings have been instrumental in shaping and communicating the changes in the philosophy of development cooperation.

The Development Committee (the group of 24 ministers who act more or less as a board of supervisors for the Bank) represents a selection of the Bank's governors. This acts as a forum of the World Bank and the International Monetary Fund that facilitates intergovernmental consensus-building on development issues. The Committee's mandate is to advise the Boards of Governors of the Bank and the Fund on critical development issues and on the financial resources required to promote economic development in developing countries. Over the years, the Committee has interpreted this mandate to include trade and global environmental issues in addition to traditional development matters.

The Development Committee meets twice a year: in the spring in tandem with the International Monetary and Financial Committee, and in the fall before the Bank-Fund Annual Meetings. The agenda for the meetings is based on issues recommended by the Chairman, the President of the Bank, the Managing Director of the Fund, and the Executive Boards of the Bank and Fund. Given the Committee's focus, the President of the Bank has a special responsibility to propose topics that he believes require the attention of the ministers. The (2003) Chairman is Minister Trevor Manuel, Minister of Finance of South Africa. The Executive Secretary is Thomas A. Bernes. Figure 5.2 gives an overview of the Development Committee.

The figure shows how the development committee represents the full membership of the Bank. Each minister represents a constituency, which may include several countries, a 'voting group'. For example, the Netherlands represents a total of 12 countries (developed and developing countries), like Armenia, Israel, Romania and the Ukraine. Large countries (the US, Japan, Germany, the UK, France, Russia, China, but also Saudi Arabia) represent themselves.

Box 5.1 gives an impression of the substance of a Development Committee's meeting and the way such a meeting is prepared.

The meetings of the Development Committee of the years around 2000 were associated with major, and sometimes violent demonstrations, with large perimeters established around the World Bank and IMF buildings and thousands of police officers deployed. On September 7th, 2001, the estimate was that 40,000 demonstrators (of which 20,000 would be US trade union members), including some hundreds of violent anarchists, would demonstrate.

Box 5.2 shows the aftermath: September 11 has entirely changed the scenario.

The Development Committee moves very slowly in promoting effective development cooperation. If the World Bank is blamed for changing its ways too slowly, then it should be clear that the Bank itself is handicapped by a lack of room for manoeuvre.

Critics of the World Bank often believe that the problem of the limited room for manoeuvre of the World Bank is not too much involvement from governments of developing and developed countries through the Development Committee, but rather that there is too little democracy. An example is found in the writings of the New Economics Foundation (NEF), a UK-based organization, which states in the paper 'It's Democracy, Stupid!' (see www.jubilee2000.org) that none of the globalization-related problems (unpredictable and turbulent global economy, environmental issues, inequality etc.) can be solved without accountable and representative institutions for global governance. It argues that the most powerful institutions that shape the global economy, like the World Bank, IMF and WTO, are not democratic or inclusive enough and that they separate the economic issues from the social, political and security concerns. Democracy is considered to be an efficient method in the global economy, since it allows competition between ideas, criticism and review from within the system. In addition to democracy, these institutions also need to relate policies to and create policies for the economic, social, political, and security concerns simultaneously, instead of separately as the official functions of the World Bank, IMF and Security Council. These factors strongly influence each other, and when considered as separate they cannot be dealt with effectively.

Valerie AMOS Secretary of State for International Development, Department for International Development United Kingdom	United Kingdom
Ibrahim AL-ASSAF Minister of Finance and National Economy Saudi Arabia	Saudi Arabia
Mr. BOEDIONO Minister of Finance Indonesia	Brunei Darussalam, Fiji, Indonesia, Laos People's Democratic Republic, Malaysia, Myanmar, Nepal, Singapore, Thailand, Tonga, Vietnam
Development Committee Member to be notified	Benin, Burkina Faso, Cameroon, Cape Verde, Central African Republic, Chad, Comoros, Côte d'Ivoire, Democratic Republic of Congo, Djibouti, Equatorial Guinea, Gabon, Guinea, Guinea-Bissau, Madagascar, Mali, Mauritania, Mauritius, Niger, Republic of Congo, Rwanda, São Tomé and Principe, Senegal, Somalia (informally), Togo
Peter COSTELLO Treasurer of the Commonwealth of Australia Australia	Australia, Cambodia, Kiribati, Republic of Korea, Marshall Islands, Federated States of Micronesia, Mongolia, New Zealand, Papua New Guinea, Republic of Palau, Samoa, Solomon Islands, Vanuatu
Joseph DEISS Federal Councillor, Minister of Foreign Affairs Switzerland	Azerbaijan, Serbia and Montenegro, Kyrgyz Republic, Poland, Switzerland, Tajikistan, Turkmenistan, Uzbekistan
Hans HOOGERVORST Minister of Finance Netherlands	Armenia, Bosnia and Herzegovina, Bulgaria, Croatia, Cyprus, Georgia, Israel, former Yugoslav Republic of Macedonia, Moldova, Netherlands, Romania, Ukraine

Famara L. JATTA Secretary of State for Finance and Economic Affairs The Gambia	Angola, Botswana, Burundi, Eritrea, Ethiopia, The Gambia, Kenya, Lesotho, Liberia, Malawi, Mozambique, Namibia, Nigeria, Seychelles, Sierra Leone, South Africa, Sudan, Swaziland, Tanzania, Uganda, Zambia, Zimbabwe
Renqing JIN Minister of Finance China	China
Aleksei L. KUDRIN Deputy Chairman of the Government of the Russian Federation and Minister of Finance Russian Federation	Russian Federation
John MANLEY Minister of Finance Canada	Antigua and Barbuda, The Bahamas, Barbados, Belize, Canada, Dominica, Grenada, Guyana, Ireland, Jamaica, St. Kitts and Nevis, St. Lucia, St. Vincent and the Grenadines
Trevor MANUEL (CHAIRMAN) Minister of Finance South Africa	
Francis MER Minister of Economy, Finance and Industry France	France
Per Stig MØLLER Minister of Foreign Affairs Denmark	Denmark, Estonia, Finland, Iceland, Latvia, Lithuania, Norway, Sweden
Fathallah OUALALOU Minister of Economy, Finance and Tourism Morocco	Islamic State of Afghanistan (informally), Algeria, Ghana, Islamic Republic of Iran, Iraq, Morocco, Pakistan, Tunisia
Antonio PALOCCI FILHO Minister of Finance Brazil	Brazil, Colombia, Dominican Republic, Ecuador, Haiti, Panama, Philippines, Surinam, Trinidad and Tobago

Felipe PEREZ-MARTI Minister of Planning and Development Venezuela	Costa Rica, El Salvador, Guatemala, Honduras, Mexico, Nicaragua, Spain, República Bolivariana de Venezuela
Didier REYNDERS Minister of Finance Belgium	Austria, Belarus,Belgium, Czech Republic, Hungary, Kazakhstan, Luxembourg, Slovak Republic, Slovenia, Turkey
Abdulla Hassan SAIF Minister of Finance and National Economy Bahrain	Bahrain, Arab Republic of Egypt, Jordan, Kuwait, Lebanon, Libya, Maldives, Oman, Qatar, Syrian Arab Republic, United Arab Emirates, Republic of Yemen
Masajuro SHIOKAWA Minister of Finance, Ministry of Finance Japan	Japan
Javier SILVA-RUETE Minister of Economy and Finance Peru	Argentina, Bolivia, Chile, Paraguay, Peru, Uruguay
Jaswant SINGH Minister of Finance India	Bangladesh, Bhutan, India, Sri Lanka
John W. SNOW Secretary of the Treasury United States	United States
Giulio TREMONTI Minister of Economy and Finance Italy	Albania, Greece, Italy, Malta, Portugal, San Marino, Timor Leste
Heidemarie WIECZOREK-ZEUL Federal Minister for Economic Cooperation and Development Germany	Germany

Source: Development Committee Web-site World Bank

Figure 5.2 Board Members of the Development Committee (without alternative
members), and the countries they represent, February 2003

Box 5.1: Corporate Day: Preparing for a Development Committee

September 7, 2001. 'Corporate Day' focuses on the agenda for the Development Committee briefing to be held on September 29. Corporate Day is the monthly full-day (Friday) meeting of senior management of the Bank (some 30–40 people), including JDW (President James David Wolfensohn) and the managing directors. The discussion takes place, blissfully unaware that four days later the world will be irreversibly changed by the terrorist attacks which destroy the Twin Towers of the World Trade Center in New York and leave a gaping hole in the symbol of Fortress America: the Pentagon.

The agenda, which is proposed on Corporate Day for the Development Committee is exemplary for the new approach to development:

- Harmonization (this is almost a regular subject for the agenda, yet very little happens on this front, except by the so-called like-minded, like the UK, the Scandinavian countries and the Netherlands).
- ODA – Official Development Assistance (the constant battle of the developed world to deal with its interest in convergence by transferring money to poor countries; the average GDP contributions to development cooperation is closer to 0.2 per cent than the promised/agreed upon amount of 0.7 per cent).
- Development effectiveness (what works and what does not work, with an emphasis on country ownership and the 'country policy institutional assessment' – CPIA – which indicates the 'quality' of the country's governance).
- Education – gradually the world is awakening to J. K. Galbraith's words 'There is no literate population on this planet that is poor and no illiterate population that is otherwise than poor.' (Galbraith, J.K. 1992. The challenges to the south: seven basic principles', South Letter, Geneva and Dar es Salaam, No. 14, p. 12.).
- Trade – with emphasis on the trade blockages by the rich world's $1 billion a day subsidies for agriculture in the rich world, but also with a focus on the improvement of the position of developing countries in WTO negotiations and on 'behind the borders' constraints in developing countries, like cumbersome customs procedures, lack of cooling storage facilities, etc.

The one topic which might be added to this 'regular' agenda is corruption and in particular the role of the developed world in corruption in developing countries. One can fully agree with Transparency International, the international corruption watchdog when it exhorts: the Bank should do more in the analysis of good practice to combat corruption.

Box 5.2: September 11 Changed the Scenario

September 11, 2001, changed the scenario. The Development Committee met quietly in Washington DC on September 28, without much ado. The ministers did give guidance to development cooperation through the agenda indicated in box 5.1. Yet the communiqué is quite bland. It can be summarized by the statement that the Committee is in favour of development. But on none of the topics is there a serious attempt to quickly change the old ways of working – unharmonized, with little generosity if compared to the GDP of the country, without focusing on effectiveness, with little vigour in pursuing the education agenda, and with very few openings to give developing countries a more fair deal in trade.

Thus this argument comes down to the point that, in the restructuring of the global economy, it is not enough for states to share information among themselves; in order to truly realize more democratic multilateral institutions and more effective development cooperation, 'a new constitutional settlement for the global economy is a matter of survival, … the global architecture must be made of glass and visible to all'. One of the possibilities is to start 'citizens' juries', which are decision-making organs which put people rather than élites at the forefront of the political picture, and which could give constructive feedback to the World Bank. The use of citizens' juries could be the start of a properly weighted system of accountability to the different stakeholders of the World Bank.[2]

In other words, the critics feel that the representation of countries in the governance of the Bank is not sufficiently promoted and that the type of democracy exercised (through elected governments rather than through citizens' juries) is not appropriate or apt.

Members of the Development Committee would disagree strongly with such a view. They are members of mostly elected Governments. Some may not be elected, like, for example, the Government of Saudi Arabia, but are in any case the legitimate governments. They feel that the self-appointed voice of civil society cannot carry the responsibility and accountability that they carry as government officials towards parliaments and citizens. They would also strongly object to a UN-like governance which is dominated by 'circuses' of ministers who assemble once or twice a year to give speeches without many listeners and where the bureaucracy behind the curtains takes over.

How then could the World Bank's room for manoeuvre be improved? It might be useful to have an even more detailed democratic process specifying the goals of poverty reduction (i.e. than was done in the Millennium Development Meeting of the UN in 2000), establishing ownership and commitment, and defining in more detail the performance indicators for the World Bank, while leaving the day-to-day activity to the professionals, on the basis of accountability towards the specified performance indicators.

5.4 EXECUTIVE DIRECTORS

The Board of Executive Directors for each of the 24 constituencies and staff 'live' on the top floors of the main Bank building at 1818 H Street, N.W., Washington, D.C. The Executive Directors are the representatives of the ministers of the Development Committee. Some of them operate with quite a free mandate, while others (for example, the US) operate under direct guidance from their minister (in this case, the Secretary of the Treasury). Box 5.3 presents a typical experience of a Board Meeting.

There are, however, exceptions to this meek attitude. That is when strong political interests of countries come to the surface. It is often the US (see the next section), which demands a certain position and finds in general that its demands are honoured, even if reluctantly.

The Board of the Bank is not like a board of supervisors of a major commercial bank. It is not a parliament. It is the wishy-washy contraption of a more than 60-year-old agreement. It is also a waste of talent and money, without contributing to a democratic form of representation. Many of the Board members are top career economists from ministries of finance or ministries of development. However, in the Board of the Bank they are there to supervise, not to second-guess the work done by the staff of the Bank and – as a result – often put in a position of relative idleness. No wonder that their intellect and energy then will focus outside their duties and indeed they do often attempt to second-guess Bank-staff work.

Yet, however wishy-washy, however frustrating to see so much money wasted with very little effect, however much time the Board takes from management without much return, it is still a lot better than the situation at the UN organizations where most countries have ambassadors with staff (like at the

Box 5.3: A Board Meeting

'Mr Chairperson, from our chair we want to say that we are mildly positive with a number of serious criticisms.' It is almost a liturgy, a Board meeting with most of the 24 Board members responding on a topic, mostly without giving any sign that they have heard what previous speakers have said and with the almost certain reply, that 'Staff thanks the Board and will take the comments and considerations into account.'

UN Headquarters in New York, at WHO or at UNESCO) in the position of 'Board of Executive Directors' with a mixed responsibility for management and supervision.

Is a tremendous level of diplomatic control the necessary price we have to pay for the involvement of many countries in international institutions? Is this necessary to ensure a reasonable degree of democracy in these institutions? Is it the best way to connect the Bank with the capitals of the member countries? I believe that the time is ripe to re-analyse the organization of international institutions, from the perspective of a more modern organizational structure, with a clear distinction between the political role (providing the purpose and the main strategic lines), the supervisory role (checking whether the organization is indeed on track) and the executive or management role (making sure that the strategy is implemented).

What I propose as an ideal, albeit quite radical solution is to undo *all* international organizations from diplomatic control on day-to-day management (which – by the way – stems from a time long past) and to focus the political component on long-run goals with clear performance indicators, including clear guidelines for the accountability of the organization. The organization itself is then endowed with ample room for manoeuvre in order to accomplish the performance goals. But it is also accountable to the political leadership for the implementation of the strategy according to the performance measures put forward.

In such a system there would be little tolerance for the endless speeches of ministers (with very few listeners) as happens at the General Conferences of the UN Organizations; little tolerance for Boards of Ambassadors which wheel and deal (often about positions of staff, or locations of events) and interfere with management decisions. And there would be much stricter control as, at the end of the day, the management decisions would be judged by the political leadership, based on the performance standards that have been laid down.

I fully realize that these proposals may sound quite radical. Yet a globalized world, with more need for international coordination and the involvement of international institutions, demands the more effective functioning of international organizations.

5.5 US Treasury Dominance

The G–7, and in particular the US, play a leading if not dominant or even domineering role within the Development Committee and the Board. There are attempts at counterbalancing this dominant US position by the 'like-minded' donor countries (like the UK, Germany, the Netherlands, Norway and others, which have in practice given substance to untying aid, to donor coordination). The 'like-minded' also attempt to live up to the level of generosity of transferring 0.7 per cent of their GDP to developing countries. This percentage has been reached in the Netherlands and in Norway, but not yet in the UK and Germany, which actually are not even half-way there. The developing countries have a voice in the Development Committee and the Board, both through the constituencies and through the chairs occupied in the Development Committee and in the Board. Their influence in the Bank, however, is stronger through bilateral contacts than through the official 'architecture' or governance of the Bank (see next section). The biggest donor, Japan, is an important player in the Bank, but often allows the US (the majority shareholder) to have its way.

The most amazing and – for a European – the most frustrating experience is to witness how the European countries never seem to be able to use their superiority in the number of votes. It is not exceptional for the European countries to complain about the US dominance, but at the same time they seem to be unwilling to do anything about it.

The dominance of the US sometimes leads to friction between the US Government – the US being the host country to the World Bank, with its main location in Washington DC – and the Bank's management. Sometimes this friction comes close to hostility, as was the case under the Bush (son) administration in 2002, when O'Neill served as Secretary of the Treasury. Box 5.4 gives an example of the obvious hostility.

The George W. Bush administration may have been heavy-handed in trying to influence the Bank, but so was the Clinton administration. Treasury Secretaries Rubin and Summers 'ran' the international financial system. And they were often quite open about it. To their credit, it meant also that the US accepted responsibility and took on leadership. At the same time, it meant that the independence of the Bank (and sometimes the Fund) became affected. Russia is a case in point. The G–7 met in Brussels in 1999 to discuss a US $22.6 billion bailout package. The Bank had heard vaguely that it was supposed to contribute 6 billion to that package, but it had never been asked formally for its position, let alone for its agreement. The then Managing Director, Sven Sandstrom, sat all day and night in his office with a small stand-by crew waiting for a call to discuss the package and the Bank's contribution. The call never came. The G–7, under US leadership, just decided that the Bank should contribute US $6 billion. Jim Wolfensohn had to seek the approval of the Board. He was clear on the history and made no attempt to defend the package. Of course, smart as the Bank is, it stretched the US $6 billion out over time and did not make it easy to disburse money that might end up in the pockets of the oligarchy.

Joe Stiglitz – a constant critic of such US influence – does not agree when Roger Wade says at a conference in Villa Borsig (Germany, close to Berlin)

Box 5.4: A Hostile Host

How little love is lost between President Bush and Wolfensohn (Liberal, presumed Democrat) becomes clear when Bush visits the Bank on July 17, 2002 to advocate more grants for the poorest countries ('50 per cent of the money of development banks should go to grants'). He quips that he is delighted to give this speech at the Bank with Wolfensohn among his audience, as 'Wolfensohn has obviously never heard a speech of mine before.'

on February 20, 2002, that due to the US Treasury, the IMF and the Bank only pursue Anglo-Saxon interests. 'It is a particular interest that is pursued through the Treasury: that of Wall Street.' The US Treasury was not amused about Stiglitz' comments as we see from Box 5.5.

This shows the US influence even in the details of the composition of the staff of the Bank. However, this is in my experience the exception. As a rule the influence of the US is more geared toward the general strategy of the Bank. A particularly disturbing element here is how the US dominance in the World Bank governance has forced the hugely important issue of female health to the sideline (or out of the playing field). Whether 9 billion people can

Box 5.5: US Pressure

Jim Wolfensohn on his side is adamant to me about Joe Stiglitz: 'He needs to be controlled.' It is at the end of a Sunday night dinner at his house in Kalorama, the embassy neighbourhood of Washington, in late 1999. In the middle of the dinner he gets an urgent call. It is Larry Summers. Wolfensohn emerges ash-grey after the call and finds it hard to return to his previous jovial mood: the message was that Stiglitz should leave the Bank. It is only three months later in early 2000 when indeed Joe resigns from the Bank.

Once Joe Stiglitz has left the Bank, the Summers prosecution of Joe continues. Joe is the leading speaker of the Annual Bank Conference on Development Economics (ABCDE) meeting on Tuesday, April 17, just after the Spring Meeting of April 15 and 16, 2000. In a speech during the ritual dinner of the Development Committee on Sunday, April 16 Summers criticizes the 'soft bank' in strong terms. Then, when they leave the room to go down with the elevator, Summers sees the poster of the ABCDE meeting and flies into a rage. 'Stiglitz is twice on your programs and Sachs once. Do you lack all judgement?' The next day the posters are removed. The Conference takes place as planned and is on all accounts a great success, except that the opening address is not from Wolfensohn himself, but from Mats Karlsson for him.

decently live on this planet by the year 2050 was the question in Johannesburg, August 2002. The answer was, if not an outright no, then at best a very hesitant yes. It could be done, provided we all change our ways drastically today (of which there are very few indications). Little or no attention was paid to the question of where the numbers came from. What were the assumptions behind the projections showing that India will continue to grow in population by 50 per cent, or half a billion people, in the next decade, that the population of Indonesia will increase by 50 per cent (or one hundred million), that the US will grow substantially (another one hundred million), and China will 'only' grow by 20 per cent (still two hundred million)?

It was only at the margin in Johannesburg that the question was asked whether these are wanted children, or, in contrast, whether they are born because parents do not have the information or the means to practise birth control. If that question were asked, then the answer would be that, if enabled to choose, parents would opt – worldwide, but in particular in lower income-countries – for fewer children, creating a better life for themselves, their children and the world at large.

It is the US which has moved the parental right to a choice of the number of children to the margin, by pulling the plug on the action program of the international conference on population and development (agreed on in 1984) in November 2002 at the Conference of the Economic and Social Convention for Asia and the Pacific, in Bangladesh. The consequences will be more unwanted pregnancies, hidden abortions, and deaths of mothers and children.

The UNFPA document 'State of World Population 2002' (The World Population Report), makes the following observations on female health:

- Poor infants and children are more likely to die than children in better-off families. In some countries, for example, the under-5 mortality rate of the poorest 20 per cent of the population is more than four times that of the richest 20 per cent. Comparing 44 developing countries, the average infant mortality rate in the poorest families is twice as high as in the richest families. The goal of halving infant mortality could be reached in several regions by bringing national averages down to the levels of the richest 20 per cent.

- A woman's lifetime risk of dying due to maternal causes (pregnancy, delivery and related complication) is 1 in 19 in Africa; 1 in 132 in Asia; 1 in 188 in Latin America and only 1 in 2,976 in more-developed countries. The death of a mother will have grave consequences for the family, but also for the community and the economy.

- Health services concerning reproductive health, such as family planning, are directly related to the empowerment of women. They also improve the lives of mother and child and reduce poverty.

One can look critically at the dominance of the US in the World Bank. Yet the US is not a shareholder with an absolute majority, nor is it the dominant contributor to development aid. Hence, it is the inability of other donors than the US to come together and to agree on the most effective development cooperation that allows the US its dominance.

It is the responsibility of the different member countries to prevent US dominance and to work towards a more balanced and representative staff. One would also hope that the President of the Bank would stand up more to US pressure when the US is not in line with the World Bank's mission and approach.

The bit about the divided EU is easily told. At the end of the day, Europeans prefer American dominance to that of any of their European friends. 'Please, not the dominance of France or Germany or the UK (etc.)'. Discussion about a unified EU chair (based on a unified EU development policy) desperately needs to take place. Such a unified voice would give strength to the EU. It would also be a way for Europe to take responsibility for the world's affairs.

But there are strong proponents for maintaining the status quo (like Eveline Herfkens, the ex-minister of development cooperation from the Netherlands, and since 2004 with UNDP). They argue that:

- It would mean that the many European chairs that unite donors and recipients, like the Dutch Chair (a great innovation in the Board) would be abolished; a EU chair would only stand for the EU (like other chairs of large countries).

- It might lead to a reduction of power of the resident Board which might, as a result, strengthen the US Treasury grip on the Bank, because, after all, a EU chair would get its signals from Brussels, reducing the power of the resident Board.

- The nature of a unified EU policy remains unclear, with quite a few EU countries still being outliers in relation to the development paradigm and working in a very old-fashioned mode. Some 'modern' chairs have more to gain from alliances with the Canadians or the Swiss than from a unified European view.

In particular the last argument is dubious. Europe might gain tremendously by seeking to align on modern external relations. The – in terms of development cooperation – more old-fashioned countries should be given a chance to become part of the modern development paradigm.

Wolfensohn was on the ball when under the Clinton Administration, a commission working for the US Congress (Senate) produced a majority report (the Meltzer Report, named after its chairman), which would virtually have killed the World Bank if it had been fully implemented, by privatizing the

IBRD and by turning the IDA into a grant-funding foundation. Wolfensohn adequately defended the effectiveness of the Bank, and its work through both the IBRD and the IDA. The one surprise in this affair was Jeff Sachs, the maverick ex-Harvard economist with a not always too successful track record of advice in Russia and Latin America,[3] but also a committed supporter of more aid for development, in particular for health. When asked why he supported the majority report of the Meltzer Commission, he said to the participants of the ABCDE Conference on April 19, 2000: 'Bretton Woods institutions bear the brunt of unwillingness of shareholders (in particular the US) to pay for development'.

The Meltzer Report, however, does have quite a bit of merit in the questions it asks on the nature of IDA transfers to developing countries. If a proper financing mechanism of IDA grants could be found for donors (and the UK Treasury Secretary has made proposals in that direction), then grants would be preferable to loans, as I will argue in Chapter 10. The notion that IDA should become a 'foundation' as is suggested in the Meltzer Report, however, does injustice to the well-established consultancy capacity in the Bank.

5.6 DEVELOPING COUNTRIES

Developing countries are represented in the Development Committee as well as in the Board of the World Bank. The majority of the developing countries are represented by medium-sized (in terms of their economies) developed countries. For example the Netherlands, besides itself, represents Armenia, Bosnia and Herzegovina, Bulgaria, Croatia, Cyprus, Georgia, Israel, the former Yugoslav Republic of Macedonia, Moldova, Romania and Ukraine. This is one way in which they can exert influence on the Bank's strategy and its implementation. But the informal channels may be as important.

There are some exceptions, namely the Chairs of developing countries, representing themselves as well as other developing countries (see Figure 5.2), sometimes with a rotating chair.

Developing countries try to coordinate their views on development cooperation in an informal group called the G9. They have a secretariat in Washington that also supports the so-called G24. The Intergovernmental Group of Twenty-Four on International Monetary Affairs (G24) was established in 1971. The member countries are in three regions: Africa, Asia, and Latin America and the Caribbean. Its main objective is to represent the position of developing countries on monetary and development finance issues. The G24 meets twice a year, preceding the Spring and Fall meetings of the International Monetary and Financial Committee (IMFC) and the Joint Development Committee of the World Bank and the International Monetary Fund. The plenary G24 meetings are addressed by the heads of the IMF and the World

Bank Group, as well as by senior officials of the UN system (for more information, see www.g24.org). The G24, the G9 and informal organizations like the World Social Forum contribute greatly to the depth and content of the discussion around the official organizations such as the Bank, and determine in that way the political context in which these organizations operate.

Strong leaders of developing countries do influence the Bank, sometimes even at the cost of diverting the Bank from the 'right' course. President Abdoulaye Wade of Senegal is an example. He feels free to call President Wolfensohn on every possible occasion to plead his cause. Wolfensohn feels obliged to take the calls and does not feel free to argue the case of the Bank in the way it has been prepared by the country director. This is particularly pressing in the case of education. I would argue that some of Wade's policies are hampering Senegal's progress in education and health.

President Wade was elected in April 2000. He was a university professor and the chairman of the professors' union. Since his coming to office, the share of the education budget going to higher education has increased to the detriment of that of primary education, causing primary enrolments to go down from an already low level of 59 per cent in 1999. This is despite the potential risk to his reputation, as he helped to set the stage for speeding up the process of reaching universal primary education. Dakar was the seat of the June 2000 Meeting on Education for All (EFA), with President Wade as its champion. There, the world leaders solemnly pledged to realize EFA by the year 2015. However, the sizeable shift of financial resources away from primary towards higher education will inevitably render the goal of universal primary education in 2015 in Senegal virtually impossible. When I spoke to him in April 2001, he was oblivious of this risk (both a political as well as a serious social risk). He speaks with great commitment about both early childhood education and about higher education. I feel that he should get more feedback from fellow African leaders, from partners in development on his failure to deliver on EFA, particularly as Senegal is so successful in other areas (like in the fight against HIV/AIDS and in macro-economic policy).

The anti-globalists and other critics (see Section 5.3) urge for better representation of developing countries within the Board of the World Bank, because it is their development which is at stake. I would propose a quite different route, namely to rely far more on the developing countries organizing themselves, rather than on formal representation. There are several arguments that go against formal representation, in particular:

1. The argument that Keynes originally advanced, that is, a Bank cannot be led by its clients, but has to be determined by the donors.
2. The obvious limitations to the UN structure of one nation, one vote.

Developing countries could organize themselves in a constructive manner, in which the responsibility for development would be shared in order to have an effective say in the organization and policy-making of the World Bank. An example of good cooperation and a constructive attitude between developing countries is the New Partnership for Africa's Development (NEPAD). The NEPAD is a pledge by African leaders based on a common vision and a firm and shared conviction that they have a pressing duty to eradicate poverty and to place their countries, both individually and collectively, on a path of sustainable growth and development; at the same time they must participate actively in the world economy and world politics as much as possible with a common position. This initiative is thus an effort to change the relationships that underpin Africa's situation and to mobilize the available resources in the war against poverty and underdevelopment.

The World Bank could rely on such initiatives, strengthen them and bring in this way the voice of developing countries to the fore.

6

The Different Faces of the World Bank

When entering office in 1996 as President, Jim Wolfensohn found a Bank that had not yet responded to the opportunity of the fall of the Berlin wall in 1989, or the demise of the Soviet Union in 1992. The Bank was still dug into development cooperation based on Cold War thinking, plodding along with 'successful' loans in collapsing countries. If it had not been for the breath of fresh air brought by Wolfensohn, the Bank would soon have become outdated and irrelevant. In many of the G–7 capitals and in the capitals of other donors, it was by then already clear that development cooperation needed to be based on effectiveness, which meant on governments' ownership of good policies, on honesty and on trust in government, on development from within. Under the new President, the Bank not only followed the emerging thinking, but also quickly took the lead in forging the new development paradigm, forcefully brought to the table in the 'State of the Union' speeches of President Wolfensohn at Annual Meetings. Through these speeches he delivered a program that quickly emerged as a joint program for all partners in development cooperation: inclusion, good governance and partnering as points of departure in development cooperation.

Inclusion is the focus of development for poverty reduction. When this notion was launched, some feared that attention would be diverted from economic growth. Of course, poverty reduction cannot be achieved without economic growth. Yet economic growth is a necessary, rather than a sufficient condition for poverty reduction.

Good governance is the key to development. Corruption makes countries sink into a quagmire. The story goes that when Wolfensohn uttered the word 'corruption' in a meeting of the Bank in 1996, the trusted Chief Council quickly admonished the President, saying that the Bank was apolitical and could not get involved with such highly politicized issues as corruption.

Partnering is the way to coordinate efforts between public agencies, civil society and the World Bank; to join hands in assisting a country to get on its own two feet and walk (or preferably, run).

These notions were the basis for the transformation of the Bank. However, the process of conversion from the 'old' Bank to a 'new' Bank was slow, much slower than planned, but also much slower than necessary. One reason why the process was slowed was the inability to get fresh and renewed leadership which could carry out the transformation with the full trust of Wolfensohn. Fresh blood was a necessary condition for change as it was (and is) viewed as unthinkable that a leadership which has worked for decades with one paradigm (the Washington Consensus) can easily change to another (see introduction to Chapter 4 on the paradigms of country ownership and cultural sensitivity).

It is not that Wolfensohn did not try to bring in new blood. Quickly after entering office, he shed the old group of senior managers in favour of a younger generation of World Bankers. In this first move, it remained an insiders-only job, much to his regret. Then gradually, fresh blood was introduced in senior management from the outside, like Joe Stiglitz (who won the Nobel Prize for economics after he had left), Jules Muis (who left to become the Director General of Internal Audit for the European Commission), Ko-Yung Tung (who had headed the global practice of O'Melveny & Meyers, a New York law firm), Jean Michel Severino (who had been Director of Development in the French Ministry of Cooperation and Development, and who was the Vice President (VP) for both Asia and the Pacific for too short a period), and many others. Yet, as far as I can keep track, they were all gone within four years, so that all of the present operational Vice-Presidents are still old Bank hands with at least twenty years of experience in the Bank Group (including IFC). This is top staff, consisting of highly motivated professionals, but it does lack the infusion of new blood. In other words: rejuvenation through interchange with the outside world has not been successful in the Bank.

The layer of the Managing Directors directly under the President is a special case. There was a time when there was only one Managing Director (until 1998). Since 2000, there have been four: all four new to the Bank (which shows). On the one hand, this is a successful infusion of new blood. On the other hand, there is the drawback that they are all newcomers to the Bank and have little or no knowledge of the day-to-day processes, even though they are learning fast. There is, of course, constant change at the top of the organization, and it was not unexpected when Mamphela Ramphele left as a Managing Director in early 2004.

It was not only 'new blood' that hampered the transition from the old to the new Bank. There was also a lack of management of the process. Changes were sprung on staff, rather than being carefully planned and carried out within a serious time line. Springing changes on staff occurred in virtually all areas, but most notably in the engagement with civil society and the private sector (see also Chapter 8). For a professional used to dealing with civil society like myself, the mood-swings of the Bank became too serious to be amusing any longer. At first, there was no engagement and 'serious' organizations, like Oxfam or World Vision, were not even allowed entrance to the Bank. Then, in 1998, the mood swung to the other extreme of full openness and just about anyone who called himself/herself an NGO would be invited. Senior managers of the Bank, often appearing three or four at a time, would debate with a heterogeneous group of representatives of civil society any odd subject. NGOs had a particular interest in engaging Bank staff in debate on the social impact of structural adjustment, the safeguards against environmental damage by country projects financed by the Bank and high-profile cases of political debate, like the Chad–Cameroon pipeline and the China migration project. Gradually, the dialogue with NGOs is finding a consistent and effective path with a close dialogue on specific items of joint interest (like on 'education for all' between the education unit of the Bank and NGOs) on a basis of continuity, mutual respect and complementarity, which involves the international level, but first and foremost, the country level.

Another decisive innovation that Wolfensohn brought: the decentralization of the Bank was better managed. In 1996, the World Bank was in danger of becoming irrelevant, because of its feudal structure of experts from Washington, flying in to countries and quickly returning home again. The decentralization, which moved 40 per cent of the Bank's 8,000 staff members into the countries for which they work, has added value by making them better informed about the countries concerned, thus enabling a better and culturally more sensitive analysis. However, the 40 per cent includes the 2,500 'local staff', which do not have the same impact and status as the international staff. Decentralization of the international staff needs to be a point of continued attention in order for the World Bank to be the 'listening' Bank it professes to be.

Presidents of the World Bank can have a tremendous impact on the Bank, going beyond the impact of a CEO of any organization that works in a market. For example, however highly lauded, the impact of Jack Welsh on General Electric has been less than that of World Bank Presidents, like McNamara or Wolfensohn, on their institution. McNamara (President from 1968–1976) is a case in point. He changed the Bank almost single-handedly. Jochen Kraske[1] describes 'McNamara's Bank' as follows:

> He dominated the Bank, its staff, its board of directors, and almost any other audience that needed to be controlled in the pursuit of his mission. He relied on his ability to work hard and to absorb huge amounts of written material on every relevant subject. He was always better prepared than anybody else and quicker on his feet than those with whom he dealt.

McNamara changed the Bank quickly, shifting the focus from physical investment projects towards general economic policy and towards human capital development.

It is remarkable how well President Wolfensohn fits into the above quotation about McNamara. He will undoubtedly be viewed in the future as one of the great presidents, even if his agenda is as yet unfinished, even if there still is at the Bank a general feeling of poor management, of poor and erratic planning (although improving), even if the Bank still lacks a well laid out budget allocation for more than one year, even if it is without a wise but stern minister of finance who questions existing work and expenditures to make room for new directions ('old for new'), even if it was in 2003 still without a business model for the financing of operational staff in a way which reflects its priorities, namely the need for donor coordination or for partnering for the involvement of local expertise. (Such activities are at present carried out in the Bank staff's own leisure time.)

In other words, there is still a substantial change agenda ahead for the new President of the World Bank for the period after President Wolfensohn decides to leave the Bank (expected in 2005). Note that the preceding chapters have pointed out that this includes not only change within the Bank, but in particular change in the context of development cooperation, in the rules of the game of globalization.

The World Bank today shows many different faces, which are the result of its history and its different presidents. The faces of the World Bank include:

- The university Bank. In many respects the World Bank is comparable to an American or Anglo-Saxon university in its organizational culture (Section 6.1). The research side of the Bank is one of its strongest traits.
- The Washington Consensus Bank. The Bank has repeatedly and openly departed from the Washington Consensus. The Washington Consensus has been sworn off. And yet: unfortunately, still too much of the thinking in the hearts and minds of the Bank's staff follows the Washington Consensus. This implies a tendency for a quite rigid schedule for economic liberalization, without enough attention to context or the transitions from the old to the new (Section 6.2; this section continues where Section 3.3 left off).
- The external relations Bank. The image of the Bank among a major constituency committed to development (namely youngsters) is disastrous, despite all efforts to improve public relations (Section 6.3).
- The matrix Bank. The organization of the Bank is highly complex (Section 6.4).
- The scaling-up Bank. Large-scale programs, rather than projects, should have a central place at the Bank; yet these are not easily achieved (Section 6.5).

From these faces, an overall image emerges of a Bank that only slowly adapts to the needs of development cooperation. The Bank does not fully take on a role of leadership. This is partly due to the organizational culture. Of course, the internal culture does not stand in isolation. It is heavily influenced by the authorizing environment of the Bank's member states, which are either unwilling or unfitted to adapt to the needs of development cooperation.

Some of the Bank's critics allege that the Bank itself is part of the causes of underdevelopment. That notion should be rejected: all the evidence points in the other direction, namely that the Bank has been helping development. But the Bank can do better, has chances to help countries to realize the MDGs. These 'chances for the World Bank' (as the title of this book puts it) can only be realized through substantial changes within the Bank: shedding the last feathers of the Washington Consensus; and scaling up, accompanied by changes which ensure a better context (better rules for globalization). But the Bank also needs to change faster internally.

6.1 THE UNIVERSITY BANK

I cannot think of any other Bank in which the emphasis on being on top of the latest insights, as well as the academic debate, is so great. There is a strong emphasis on critical thinking, rooted in the latest research. Criteria for promotion still include to a substantial extent the capacity to function in the academic community, in particular the ability to publish in top journals and the engagement in the academic (economics) debate. As a result, top professionals in development thinking who are non-academics will often be at a loss in this university Bank.

Yet, for academically oriented staff the work environment is superb. Most of the professional staff have been top students in their youth, either earning a masters degree or a PhD in economics. Economists still form the largest group of professionals in the Bank.

It is not just a university Bank, it is an American university Bank. For example, it is remarkable that at the 2001 rounds of promotions to level I, one of the highest levels of staff in the Bank, just below senior management (Vice-Presidents), virtually all persons who were promoted had a PhD from an American university. This also applied to those who were not of American origin (the largest part). These people have often gone through a university in their home country, and have continued their education in the US.

One can see the homogeneity of the top grade professionals as both a threat and an advantage. A threat, because it could weaken the capacity for dialogue with counterparts in developing countries. The counterparts in developing countries are often quite suspicious of the example of the US, or reject it outright as irrelevant to their circumstances. Although Bank professionals will generally have a broad international knowledge, the imprint of the US on their experiences is often substantial, just below the surface, or by default. An example: I was in a country where an economist suggested the US model of local school finance (raise taxes based on property values for the financing of schools) to the minister of education. This model is amply debated, even in the US (but the economist was not aware of that), because it might actually be the reason for the substantial inequities in educational achievement in the US. The model definitely does not stand for 'good practice'. It was simply by default that the Bank official suggested the model. The better answer of the Bank official to the counterpart in the developing country when asking about school finance would have been: sorry – this is not my bag of tricks.

The upside of the American top university culture in the Bank is homogeneity and understanding of the rules of interaction, which are the rules of the game in the academic debate. I have always found the climate of the American top universities one of the most attractive in the world to work in. It is based on performance, contribution, openness and frankness with less room for gossip or manipulation than I have found elsewhere.

But the other side of the coin of the academic Bank is a tendency to endless negotiation without clear resolution (as universities often exhibit). And once a resolution is reached, everyone will believe it gives him/her the mandate s/he had before. This has been the main reason why Jim Wolfensohn found it so difficult to translate vision into action. This is why a clear selectivity on what the Bank does (and should not do) never arose. This is why the first important and laudable thrust towards a strategy ended in a good step, but is still not concrete enough to set a course. That is why a 'minister of finance' and a clear priority setting on what to finance never emerged.

However, the academic climate has also generated the backbone of the Bank: a thorough grounding of understanding about what works in development and a credibility in challenging existing constellations on their relevance and function. Trade is a case in point. The Bank was credible when it went all out to challenge the rich countries on their agricultural subsidies and their trade barriers for the import of agricultural products from poor countries. As we saw before, poor countries lose at least $200 billion a year from these restrictions. $360 billion is paid every year for agricultural subsidies in rich countries, more than seven times the amount transferred to poor countries for development cooperation. The credibility was based on the reputation of the staff for top research, which is part of the 'university Bank'.

Could the upsides of the academic climate of the Bank be maintained while avoiding some or most of the downsides? There is ample reason to at least make the maximum attempt, which includes:

- Investing more in a strategy that can be translated into a multi-annual budget. Such a budget would be selective, persistent and continuous, so that staff would know what they are up to and can expect; such a budget, would also keep staff away from an endless negotiation process, which often ends in continuation of the status quo;

- Having a consistent staffing strategy aimed at bringing in the broader (beyond that of the USA and the UK) experience of OECD countries in shaping development. In such a strategy there would be a substantial hiring of PhDs from universities beyond the US (and UK which is a close second to the US in top positions).

The annual World Development Reports are part of the university Bank. The 2000 Report on Poverty was an interesting example of the conflict between the university Bank and the Washington Consensus Bank (see next section). A World Development Report is written by a team and led by a director. The director of a World Development Report has a high standing in the Bank. Ravi Kanbur was the maverick director of the 2000 report. He made a substantial imprint on development thinking through this report by forwarding the notion of empowerment, in addition to opportunity and security, as avenues for poverty reduction.

A draft of the report had been widely circulated outside the Bank, among NGOs and academic institutes, before it was reviewed at the Bank in April 2000. The Bank review turned out to be a tumultuous meeting, presenting sharp disagreements, in particular between Ravi and David Dollar. Dollar felt that the draft report put development thinking on the wrong footing, by emphasizing redistribution, rather than economic growth. 'Economic growth may not be a sufficient, but always is a necessary condition for poverty reduction', while – in his view – economic growth was insufficiently discussed in the report. Moreover, the draft contained quite a few references to, and quotes from virulent Bank critics on, for example, the privatization projects of the Bank. There was, in this review meeting, a strong disagreement with these critics on the facts and the analysis. Ravi felt that the pressure had become too great and decided to quit. In the aftermath, the able team, under Nora Lustig's direction, completed the report.

The quite academic culture of the World Bank should remain the asset it is: providing intellectual leadership. More concentration, however, would be needed to highlight as priorities issues such as those discussed in Chapters 9 and 10:

- Corruption, its origins (as much through international commerce as local), its dynamics as well as its effects. There is quite a bit of work on this issue already (notably by Daniel Kaufmann; see World Bank web site), but more attention to manpower is needed.
- How institutions of high quality develop in countries.

- Transaction costs in development cooperation, the (negative) effects of insufficient coordination and harmonization, and the (negative) effects of untied aid.
- The level playing field in trade. Note that it was the Bank that put this item on the agenda. It was my personal experience that such a shift could indeed be made in the academic climate of the Bank, even if it was hard work to change the direction of focus from the trade restrictions in developing countries towards those in developed countries. The same applies as above for corruption: more work is needed.

The Bank is quite academic, but is it too academic? On balance I would suggest that the academic culture of the Bank is a tremendous asset and that the negatives are far outweighed by the positives. The Bank has been able to set the course in development cooperation through its involvement and productivity in top research.

6.2 THE WASHINGTON CONSENSUS BANK

There is no issue as contentious around the World Bank and the IMF as the Washington Consensus. Those who see the Bretton Woods organizations as the ultimate villains of the destructive forces of capitalism, as well as more moderate critics of these institutions, make the Washington Consensus their focal point. This Consensus was described earlier (Section 3.3) as a set of rules for market liberalization. The Washington Consensus captures most of the basic elements of good policy, like:

- Good housekeeping: public expenditures should not exceed public revenues ('keep budget deficits in check').
- Inflation is a tax on the poorer parts of the population ('refrain from printing more money than can be absorbed by economic traffic, so that the value of the currency is not diluted').
- Inefficiencies in production mean that the price which people have to pay for products is too high ('create or unleash the incentives for efficiency').
- If you let foreign capital in, you have additional resources for growth.

Some will reject these rules outright as 'neoliberalism'. Others, like myself, believe (based on their understanding of how economies work) that market liberalization *can* contribute to development, but that it needs to be embedded in a social and political structure, that it requires good governance and good institutions, and that it needs to happen in small steps. Critics reject the rigidity that is often implied in the Washington Consensus or is used in its implementation. And there is much rigidity. Box 6.1 presents an example of what might be considered a rigid application of the Washington Consensus in the work of the World Bank.

Box 6.1 may seem outdated (it is an example from 1998). But similar examples can be given for each and every subsequent year in which I was with the Bank (until 2003). Rigid market thinking has proved to be difficult to stamp out in the World Bank. And my line of reasoning is precisely on this balance: on the one hand, some of the elements of the Washington Consensus are simply elements of sound economic policy. On the other hand, they need to be applied with a clear eye for the context, for the social and cultural environment and with an open-minded analysis of the consequences. The lack of balance in the past practice of development cooperation has rendered the Washington Consensus outmoded.

In the past years, the Bank has decidedly steered away from the Washington Consensus, replacing it by the one mentioned before (in the introduction to Chapter 4) as the new approach to development cooperation: based on dialogue, on country ownership, on cultural sensitivity and on good governance. This is definitely what I witnessed after I joined the Bank in 1998. But it took at least five years before the Bank openly, in statements by its President, laid the Washington Consensus to rest. Even then, the 'automatic pilot' of much of the staff in giving policy advice is often Washington Consensus based.

Moreover, the line for the Bank to walk on in its policy advice on the economic organization of the country and the financial support for 'structural adjustment' is decidedly thin. The basic principles of the Washington

Box 6.1: Privatization of Railways

In 1998 one of the Presidential Awards for top team-work in the Bank goes to the team which prepared the privatization of the railroads in Latin America. At the ceremony the proud task-team leader thanks the President for the honour and narrates the main outlines of their work. Privatization was necessary because public budgets were haemorrhaging the subsidies needed to keep the system going.

No mention of consumer safety, of lower prices or of greater comfort for travellers or better connections and better mobility.

What struck some of those who attended (and who were aware of the acrimonious discussion on the sometimes disastrous effects of privatization of railroads in Europe) was that the solution (privatization) rather than the problem (huge losses for public railways) was put up front. The problem might also have been dealt with by a better organization and financial control, under public ownership (as in many West European countries).

Consensus, as coined in 1989 by John Williamson, have helped most of the rich countries to become and remain rich.[2] And they are not just there for 'naked capitalism': they are also used in an 'organized' or a 'social' market economy (as the European countries see themselves). Indeed, these basic premises of the Washington Consensus (avoid high Government deficits, avoid high levels of inflation) are sound. They apply equally, whether the country is highly developed or very poor. Yet, advice ranked under the 'Washington Consensus' is harmful if applied without context or without nuance.

Most economists, including one of the most well known critics of the Washington Consensus, Nobel Prize Winner Joe Stiglitz would also presumably agree on the rules implied in the Consensus.[3] But look at the consequences of the application of the Washington Consensus, for example when budget deficits are high and rising, as was the case in the end of the 1970s and the 1980s in many developing countries. The first question that is then asked is: Is there a way to raise taxes, without harming the economy? But when the maximum capacity for taxation has been used (and it may be limited), then it is a story of budget cutting or of reducing expenditures. Not just by small percentages, but in such a way that the budget for health or for education is reduced by as much as one third.

Having been a minister in cabinets which slashed the budget deficit (from 8 per cent in 1989 to 2 per cent in 1998), believe me, I know the pain, the agony, the intensity and sometimes ugliness of the political debate. The Labour Party I belong to lost virtually all of its support when, as a means to reduce public expenditures, we attempted to reform the Dutch disability law when it started to cater for 10 per cent of the Dutch working population. The Labour Party was almost wiped out in the opinion polls and party members cancelled their membership by the thousands. And still, the budget reductions involved were mere small percentages of the total budget.

All the greater must have been the pain and agony in poorer countries when Governments were forced to bring budget expenditures in line with revenues, as happened on a large scale in the 1980s and with sizeable reductions in budgets. Take Ecuador. It boomed when oil was discovered and explored. Its economy skyrocketed when the oil prices shot up. The government found it impossible to 'hoard' the revenues, but rather expanded its food subsidies, agricultural subsidies and social programs. However, as a result these public services came to wreck the economy because hard work and risk-taking in production became less rewarding than just 'living on oil'. When, during the 1980s, the oil income dwindled, it left a wrecked economy behind and no public money available to continue the services. The violent demonstrations in Quito in 1973, when I was briefly working in Ecuador, are still on my mind when I think about the 'adjustment' process directed at the reduction of subsidies. The anger of the mobs led to a virtual standstill of the country.

Much of the anger was directed at the World Bank, which made its loans available only on condition of structural adjustment (the structural adjustment programs, SAPs, see Section 3.3). But was this correct and reasonable criticism?

In retrospect the Bank should have left more of the initiative to the Government (Government ownership), it should have better supported the analysis capacity of that Government rather than supplying 'foreign made' advice. And it should in its advice have been more focused on the social consequences and the implied room for manoeuvre for the Government in implementing the structural reforms.

But it remains self-evident that reforms were necessary when SAPs were given to countries. The reality is that the countries were headed for a breakdown, because there was no one who wanted to finance the budget deficits. Local citizens would balk at buying bonds to finance their government even at very high interest rates and preferred to send their money abroad. To exemplify how citizens see their private interests: 40 per cent of Africa's private wealth is stashed outside the continent.[4] When the local population does not see a private interest in buying bonds, foreign banks or foreign citizens will have no gusto either to invest in a sinking ship.

Let us continue the Ecuador story above. The naïve IMF and World Bank rushed in to rescue Ecuador, putting out the fire and helping to fix the dangerous causes for fire, only to be loathed for the conditions under which they could be involved.

Let me repeat again, then: the past practices of conditional loans were not beyond criticism. First, because the speed of adjustment implied was simply both economically and politically unsound and unfeasible. Second, because of the naïvety of the use of conditionalities, putting the burden on the 'fire brigade' rather than on those who caused the fire.

The Bretton Woods institutions have learned the lesson, and the approach of 'country ownership' has replaced that of conditionalities. The World Bank no longer goes by 'condition for loans', but rather looks at the credibility of government plans. But there was also learning about the political feasibility of adjustment. The Bank learned, for example, that it is not enough to have support from the political elite for reform, but that a broad political spectrum should be involved, as is documented in an internal Bank document (PREM note 27, August 1999), citing Argentina (sic!) and South Korea as positive examples of the effects of large adjustment loans, because the reforms were widely supported.

The notion of government ownership as decisive for the success of substantial government reforms had, then, been around in the circles of development economists for at least 10 years. In 1990, Publication no. 14 of the Policy and Research Studies Series of the World Bank ('Adjustment Lending Policies for Sustainable Growth') and in 1992, Publication no. 22 ('Adjustment

Lending and the Mobilization of Private and Public Resources for Growth') said the same. In 1992, Corbo, Fisher and Webb (editors) published, 'Adjustment Lending Revisited; Policies to Restore Growth', pointing to the importance of country ownership and good governance.

But it took a while before the Bank learned that change is not a matter of 'simple economics', but of 'politics' (a word loathed at the Bank in the late 1990s) or 'institutions'. The proper environment has to be developed, step by step, to make adjustment work. The direction of the recipes might have been the right one. Yet a lack of understanding of the social and political dynamics of the country may have led to immature policy advice, to immature programs of projects that were bound to fail.

In many respects, the adjustment period is behind us. Government deficits and inflation rates were at an all-time high in the 1980s. Nowadays the outlook in developing countries for government discipline over the 'macro-framework' (budget discipline and limited inflation) is better than it has been for decades. Budget deficits are down and under control, as is inflation. Hence the need for large-scale adjustment processes, as was common in the 1980s and early 1990s of the previous century is now the exception, rather than the rule.

The privatization issue remains. And here the Bank is still trying to find its way. Privatization was the first and most prominent response to the need to increase efficiency. Inefficiency was exposed, for example, by the fact that local public factories were not in a position in which they could compete with foreign (mostly private) firms. Local citizens would be robbed of lower prices or better quality if foreign products were banned. And if foreign products were allowed, the firms would either be losing money (making a claim on public budgets) or would fold. Quickly, the US experience led the Bank to equate efficiency with transferring ownership from the public to private hands, rather than creating better conditions for firms (whether publicly or privately owned) to be more efficient.

Privatization sometimes meant that the assets were sold for too low a price, or that existing practices continued with the risks put on the government's plate and the benefits going to the private capital owner. The Chinese and Vietnamese practices of a gradual privatization in a joint process with the building up of the institutions which can guarantee transparency, good governance and the maximum competition, have now become accepted, albeit in silence and with reluctance.

There is not only not much of an eye for other models, there is also simply a lack of knowledge of the wide range of experiences of OECD countries with ownership relations (private versus public) and with organizational relations (government model or private sector model). For example, there are still European banks which are government owned and subsidized. Yet the World Bank will advance privatization of banks as the road ahead for a sound financial system in a country anyplace, anytime.

Let us not forget, however, that the Bank is also a leader in the renewal of thinking on privatization. In 2004 it published a report on reforming infrastructure [5] in which a refreshing vision of privatization is included.

Washington Consensus thinking is not only present in the preference of the World Bank for privatization of assets (whether they are part of what economists call 'natural monopolies' or are linked to private capital). It also permeates the policy advice on the openness of capital markets. Many Asian countries used to be (and still are by and large) big savers (up to 35 per cent of GDP). They are not in desperate need of the influx of foreign capital. And yet the Bank works with the IMF to help the liberalization of capital accounts. The US [6] even seems to want to drive towards a revision of the IMF contribution so that countries would be required to commit themselves to capital account liberalization as a condition for fund membership.

There is little chance for the World Bank to contribute to development if it is unable to shed fully the automatic pilot of Washington Consensus thinking. The World Bank says that the Washington Consensus period is over. However, evaluations by the Quality Assurance Group and the Operations Evaluation Department (see Section 6.4) show that naïve market thinking has not yet convincingly disappeared.

6.3 THE EXTERNAL RELATIONS BANK

All over the world, concerned and involved citizens have a quite negative image of the World Bank. Box 6.2 gives three, quite arbitrary examples. They could easily be expanded with a thousand other examples from other spheres of life.

One cannot but conclude that the World Bank has a distinctly negative image in many quarters. Part of this may be due to the anti-capitalism movement, often disguised under the cloak of anti-globalization. But another reason is poor communication, with insufficient attention to building up a constituency among the committed young in the rich world as well as in the poorer countries. And there is the part played by mistakes in the past.

The ideological framework of the Bank is that of most OECD countries, namely: markets – if well regulated – are a good instrument for generating economic growth and contributing to poverty reduction. The Bank can be criticized for having put too much emphasis in the past on the market and not enough on its own reputation. But this critique does not warrant such a negative image as many people have of the Bank.

There is a need for better external relations, using the same channels as the Bank knows and uses to advocate policy ownership in developing countries. The Bank is a public institution. It is to the Bank's credit that it opened itself

Box 6.2: Negative Images

> The Washington DC taxi driver is from Nigeria. While driving
> through Rock Creek Park, in 2002, on the fast through-road from
> the centre to the north of Washington, he learns about my work for
> the World Bank. And in response, he knows for sure: the Bank is to
> blame for most of the trouble in his country. Giving loans to corrupt
> politicians who stash the money away in Swiss bank accounts, while
> the poor people have to pay back.
>
> Or make an occasional walk through the bookstalls of Mexican
> university publishers on economics and you'll find that Bank-bashing
> is the rule in the books and journals published (2003).
>
> The 23-year-old demonstrator from Pennsylvania at the Annual
> Meetings of 2000 is equally sure: The Bank is the problem.

up for public scrutiny, ending the quasi-secrecy of the so-called technical operations and introducing much-needed transparency about its decision-making. But the external relations anchor has not been developed on a par with this. This is not because of a lack of professionalism. The department and the spokesperson until 2003, Caroline Anstey, are the best one can think of. They have very fine feelers in the outside world and excellent judgement of the impact of messages and responses. Yet, there is no systematic process to bring in the idealism of committed people in rich countries. In particular there seems to be a kingdom to be won by engaging 'young idealism' in the Bank in a constructive and consistent way. Almost every discussion meeting of World Bankers with student audiences starts off by putting the Banker on the defensive. There is no systematic constituency of stakeholders for the Bank. There exists a World Youth Bank Network (with offices in Zagreb (Croatia), Paris and Rio de Janeiro), but this network has no systematic connection with the World Bank.

Public information centres (PICs), where individuals and organizations can find the Bank's documents and publications, were set up by the Bank in the 1990s in order to enhance outreach and dissemination. At the moment, 65 of the Bank's 89 country offices have PICs. Their role, however, is limited to 'acting on demand', rather than to be proactive in generating support from, in particular, the younger age group, for the goals and approaches of development cooperation and the way the Bank practises them. By reaching out to the public more actively with information about its development policies, the World Bank could change its closed and static image by playing a more active role in creating awareness about development issues and motivating its constituencies, including the committed young.

In September 2000, Kurt Landgraf, the CEO of the Educational Testing Service, neatly summarized the challenges for the Bank for me. The Bank suffers from an 'image crisis', being a large bureaucracy which is too much intellectualizing and not enough in a strategically driving role. Improving the image should be a top priority. Contributing to awareness about development cooperation (see Section 2.3) is part of that action.

This is not to say that the Bank is completely unaware of its public relations crisis. On the contrary: it is making moves (with meetings with youth, started in 2003) to improve its image. However, I would consider this too little too late. A more concerned and substantial effort is needed.

6.4 THE MATRIX BANK

The World Bank is organized as a matrix. On the horizontal lines are the regions: Latin America and the Caribbean, Sub-Saharan Africa, the Middle East and North Africa, Eastern Europe and Central Asia (ECA), South Asia, and East Asia and the Pacific. The regions hold the money, are the demand side for Bank work. On the vertical lines are the Networks. The professionals who are involved in the Bank's work 'reside in' the Networks. The Networks form the basis for the professional support for its staff. The Bank's web site gives the following description of the Networks, where the Networks cluster around five basic areas of the Bank's work:

- The Human Development Network strengthens the Bank's work in Education, Health, Nutrition, Population and Social Protection in order to improve the lives of people in developing countries, especially the poor.
- The Environmentally and Socially Sustainable Development Network focuses the Bank on issues of the Environment and Rural and Social Development, including areas of concern such as irrigation and water resources, indigenous peoples and cultural heritage and involuntary resettlements.
- The Finance, Private Sector, and Infrastructure Network focuses on issues of capital and securities market development private sector strategies, energy, mining, telecommunications, transportation, and water and urban development.
- The Poverty Reduction and Economic Management Network focuses on countrywide economic policy and cross-sectoral issues centered on four major thematic groups – Economic Policy, Gender and Development, Poverty and Governance, and Public Sector Reform.
- The Operational Core Services Network focuses on building and disseminating knowledge, enhancing staff skills, improving team and product quality, leveraging external partnerships and developing business strategies. The Strategic Compact provides resources to

strengthen technical expertise in the areas of procurement and financial management and to support resource management reforms.

The Networks are responsible for creating professional excellence in the staff involved in the Networks' activities, by means of ensuring the dissemination and sharing of new knowledge acquired in each area, by means of hiring and training, through quality control of the products of the staff of Networks and by means of a well devised strategy in the area of concern.

In any specific activity of the Bank, the region brings in staff from one or more of the Networks, as is exemplified in Box 6.3.

In the regions, the Country Director (CD) leads: s/he is the central person in the World Bank and is in charge of one or more countries. S/he embodies the relative success and failure of the contribution of the World Bank to development. Relative, because it is country circumstances which ultimately are the main driver.

The CD is powerful as the carrier of the country dialogue between the country's Government and the World Bank. S/he is also the leader of the local World Bank office, with families depending on his or her leadership, wisdom, compassion and humanity. Take Nigeria in the past years, where World Bank staff suffered a number of armed robberies in their homes, with a car-jacking every month and the 'bad boys' as they are known everywhere wreaking havoc. Staff depend on an active and involved CD.

The CD is in charge of the budget for the work by Bank staff. This is work to prepare loans or to prepare so-called Economic and Sector Work (ESW), and to analyse and prepare proposals for Government action. S/he also knows approximately the amount of loans s/he can commit to the country within the context of the zero interest loans of IDA, and in middle-income countries the target for the lending of low-interest loans by the IBRD. The CD operates within the framework of the so-called 'Country Assistance Strategy' (CAS) which is a World Bank Document agreed upon by the senior management and the Board. These Country Strategies are translations of the combination of the priorities of the Country and the so-called World Bank 'sector strategies'. The CDs 'hire' staff from the Networks within the context of the implementation of the CAS. This is how the involvement with education in Macedonia of Box 6.3 came about.

A major constraint for the effectiveness of the Bank is that essentially the business model for the CD is cast in the stone of lending. Networks and regions are driven by the preparation of new loans and even more by the supervision budgets attached to existing loans. For every network manager, the supervision budget represents continuity. For every region manager, the lending volume represents performance. It is not just any lending, of course. The Bank has been able to develop over the years the highest standards of quality control in lending. A loan will be evaluated on its degree of satisfaction, following the completion of the loan period, by the independent Operations Evaluation Department (OED). But already at the inception of the loan and during the loan period, evaluations take place of its effectiveness. These evaluation systems truly represent 'best practice'. Let us look, for example, at the evaluation of the secondary education project for girls in Bangladesh (see Box 6.4).

The Quality Assurance Group (QAG) of the World Bank, set up in 1996, promotes excellence in Bank performance with a diverse timing of interventions. The World Bank staff responsible for the Bangladesh girls' program mentioned in Box 6.4 might have asked for a review while in the stage of preparation (a 'quality of entry review'). It might also have been reviewed in terms of the quality of supervision.

A panel of experienced Bank staff plus outside experts will assess in-depth the 'quality of entry', shortly after approval by the Board with respect to three questions:

- Are the project objectives worthwhile and the risks commensurate with potential rewards?
- Is the project likely to achieve its objectives?
- Is the underlying topic clearly articulated?

These reviews often lead to improvements of the project, as was the case with the Bangladesh girls' education program. The external Operations Evaluation Department (OED) acts under the Board and reviews the projects after completion (when the project is fully implemented). As one might expect, the quality of entry assessment is often a good predictor of the performance of the program or project.

As was mentioned above, the business model of the Bank allows for knowledge transfer and capacity building through so-called Economic and Sector Work (ESW). ESW supports the country in its analysis of the policy challenges for development. It is again the CD who decides on the purchase of ESW. The quality of ESW is controlled in the same way as that of loans through the Quality Assurance Group. Capacity creation takes place in ESW through the involvement of local analysts in the preparation of ESW. Yet in practice there are in fact many thresholds to realizing this involvement. Involving local staff is generally time-consuming, while the World Banker is in a hurry. Often the Bank staffer in charge of an ESW program has to secure the money for the involvement of local analysts through trust funds (money specifically allocated to the Bank for a specific purpose). This requires lots of paperwork, with the costs of the paperwork sometimes being close to the money being brought(!). In other words: the incentives to involve local staff in ESW are quite limited.

Box 6.3: The Matrix at Work

Azben Xhaferi, the leader of the Albanian National Party, PDSH, in Macedonia is a thoughtful, soft-spoken man. We meet in Tetovo on October 3, 1998, two years before the eruption of a serious armed conflict in this western part of Macedonia. The Bank's mission (in which I am involved as part of the Human Development Network at the request of the ECA Region) has but one goal: how to prevent the falling apart of Macedonia and how to prevent an armed conflict. Afterwards the world saw that these efforts had been in vain. Would a different course of action have been more effective? Or were the armed hostilities inevitable?

Xhaferi is difficult to gauge. Some Macedonians tell me that he is very dangerous, by appearing moderate and pro-Western, while at the same time making the preparations for an uprising and a separation of the western part of Macedonia, which is mostly populated by people from Albanian origin, in order to merge that part with Albania.

The issue at stake is a separate Albanian language university in Tetovo (with the initial costs to be financed by the Dutch Government). Max van der Stoel, the UN High Commissioner on National Minorities has already endorsed this concept. The Dutch Government has asked the World Bank for its advice in general, and specifically about the possible place such a university would have in a wider support network from the international community for the education system of Macedonia (which the Dutch are also willing to support with relatively 'big' money).

Driving from Skopje, Macedonia's capital, to Tetovo, is sheer pleasure. Green rolling hills interspersed with Austrian-type villages. More arid than the lower Alps, but lusher green than Greece. The borderline between the parts of Macedonia inhabited by the Macedonian-speaking population and those containing the population of Albanian origin is not marked, but highly present, in language, in customs and religion, and in all other traits of life. For example, Albanian Macedonians do not bank with the Macedonian banks, but among themselves. Macedonians complain about another feature: the Albanian Macedonian population grows fast, while the rest has a zero to negative population growth. The borderline is also very visible when belltowers of churches transform into minarets of mosques.

For Xhaferi, the Tetovo Albanian language university is a must in order to do away with the discrimination of the Albanian Macedonians in getting access to secondary and higher education. Only 2 per cent of the university students are Albanian Macedonian while they form 20 per cent of the population. While 97 per cent of the Macedonian children go to secondary school the figure is only 50 per cent for Albanian children. The 'other side' alleges that this is due in part to the fact that Albanian Macedonian parents (Muslims) do not always want to send their daughters to school.

A country with a strong antagonism between the two populations: so much is clear. It does not help if Xhaferi refers to the Kosovo Liberation Army and the Chechnenia rebels as a possible next stage in the development in Macedonia. Conciliation is what is needed, not divergence.

Box 6.4: Secondary Education for Girls in Bangladesh

The educational attainment of women in Bangladesh is among the lowest in the world. According to the 1991 census, only 20 per cent of women in Bangladesh could read and write. During the early 1990s, the disparity of access between girls and boys was most significant in secondary schools. In 1990, only one-third of students enrolled in secondary school were girls. The number of girls completing secondary school was less than half the number of boys.

Although the World Bank is better known for financing large infrastructure projects in Bangladesh, it has had a long involvement in supporting social sector projects, which improve and expand access to health services and education. In 1994, the Bank began supporting the government's stipend program under the Female Secondary School Assistance Project in 118 thanas (sub-districts) of the country. Total project costs are US $88.4 million to which the Bank is contributing a US $68 million in interest-free credit through its concessionary lending affiliate, the International Development Association. The Government of Bangladesh is contributing the remainder.

Initially, the project was designed to be implemented in two overlapping phases in the 118 thanas. These were identified on the combined basis of low income, low female literacy levels, and low female attendance levels. Out of the 118 thanas, 59 were covered in 1994 and another 59 in 1997. Because there were more applicants than anticipated, the government decided to implement the stipend program in all 118 thanas simultaneously in 1994 and to expand the concept to a national female secondary stipend program in all of the 460 rural thanas. The Asian Development Bank and the Government of Norway were also assisting the government with the national program. The government's actions were part of a program launched in 1994 to support female secondary education, an area in which Bangladesh has become a South Asia pioneer.

The stipend program has generated tremendous enthusiasm for female education and has boosted the enrolment of girls in secondary schools. Khodeza Akther – a school headmistress in one of the selected thanas – says, 'More girls are coming to the school because of the stipend. The scene was quite different three years ago when I joined the school. Now it seems as if the school is turning into a girls' school.' Out of a total of 738 students in her school, more than 60 per cent are girls.

The need for 'home-grown analysis' is widely recognized in the Bank (for an example, see Box 9.2: 'Problem-solving by think-and-do tanks', p.189 and 190 of the World Development Report 2003). My critique is that it takes too long to translate the excellent new insights into practice and into a business model that creates incentives for good practice.

The Bank does recognize that there is an urgent need for a change in the business model to incorporate donor harmonization and coordination, as well as capacity creation. The present matrix structure has not embodied these elements sufficiently.

6.5 THE SCALING-UP BANK

The amount of the annual transfer of funds from rich to poor countries of around (in the beginning of the new century) US $50 billion may sound huge, but it is little compared to the GDP of poor and middle-income countries (about 1 per cent). The annual transfer for health and education is equally minor. OECD estimates are that these transfers amount to US $4–6 billion per year each for health and for education, also just over 1 per cent of the total budgets for these sectors in middle-income and poor countries.

Clearly these transfers are only going to help if they are 'leveraged'; if they help a process by which the effects – for example, in health, reducing child mortality, or in education, getting children into quality schools – are larger than the amount would buy if it were not leveraged but spent by itself. However, leverage is often not really gauged in the practices of the agencies of development cooperation. Many of the transfers, particularly those for infrastructure, 'buy' buildings, roads and little else: what you see is what you get. Sometimes they buy less if the aid is tied, as explained in Section 2.2.

Sometimes even simple investment projects can buy more (and thus are leveraged) if they lead to better capacity in the country, to increased domestic financing or if the investment project has 'show window 'effects. Yet the past decades have shown that the degree of leverage should not be overestimated, implying that development cooperation has by and large played a marginal role, limited to the transfer of funds.

The more substantial role of development cooperation is played in the policy domain. Huge developmental effects can be derived from improved policies. For example, from policies which ensure that domestic funds reach the schools for which they are intended, or policies that ensure that teachers appear and teach in the schools they are appointed to.

Scaling-up has been used at least in two different forms. One form of the scale-up of the Bank is to be more efficient with 'repeat' loans in cases where the project or program has proved successful. This is working more cheaply and in that way having more impact. It saves administrative costs for the Bank.

But the constraint of the $50 billion remains dominant in the overall effect of development cooperation: there is only so much you can do with it through projects, even if the projects are handled more efficiently in their preparation and execution.

Another form would be scaling-up by focusing on the policy domain. This form of scaling-up is implied in the concept of the MDGs. Scaling-up starts by asking the question of what should be done in an individual country to reach the MDGs in that country. We noticed in Section 2.5 that there is a serious challenge in reaching the MDGs.

In the 'MDG-style' scale-up two parameters emerge: the policy change in the country as well as additional finance by the donors. The Monterrey Conference in 2002 (see Section 4.6) very much confirmed the interest of developing countries and the developed world in entering into a 'compact' in which developing countries will do their utmost in policy changes, while the donor countries will increase their financing, both in terms of the amounts (promising US $12 billion per year more) and in terms of untying and coordinating aid. This might not be enough. According to Devarajan, the additional foreign aid required to achieve the Millennium Development goals by 2015 is between US $40 and US $60 billion a year, even if countries improve their policies and institutions.[7]

The 'even if' is an important prerequisite: financial aid is only effective in development under conditions of 'good governance'. There are still many countries that need to adjust their policies and their service delivery in order to use this financial aid in an effective manner.[8]

A first, serious attempt at a scale-up was the so-called Fast Track Initiative for Education for All: all countries which had shown themselves willing to engage in the necessary policy reforms could be sure that they would not lack the finance for having all children in schools. Although a World Bank Meeting with donors in Brussels on November 27, 2002 on this topic originally showed considerable reluctance in the donor community to be engaged in this form of scale-up, the commitment to effective development cooperation ultimately prevailed (see Boxes 6.5 and 6.6), although we still have to see the implementation. The occasion demonstrated the joint work of the World Bank with that of United Nations organizations and with bilaterals in realizing effective cooperation between the different partners in development.

The original reluctance of the donor community to engage in scale-up could be considered to be cause for pessimism in development cooperation. It should be a cause for concern as well as a warning sign for those involved in development cooperation. However, the increased awareness of good and bad practices, the strategy of country ownership, as well as the increased evaluation of development aid, is a sign of improvement in development cooperation and a good stepping-stone for an increase in effectiveness.

For the World Bank, there is no choice. If it wants to fulfil its mission, it has to do the utmost to 'scale-up' its own efforts and help to create the authorizing environment to bring its partners along. Donor harmonization and coordination is an essential part thereof.

In conclusion to this chapter, the World Bank organization has been changed tremendously for the better in the past decade. Yet it may not be fully ready to accept the challenge of effective development cooperation in the first decades of the twenty-first century:

- Its management could be more decisive.
- Its university culture is an asset, provided the agenda for research is

Box 6.5: Partners in the Fast Track

Len Good, the director of the Canadian International Development Agency, Joan Boer of the Dutch ministry for Foreign Affairs, and Koos Richelle, the director general for development cooperation of the European Union set the tone when they open the meeting. 'This is a moment of truth. A number of developing countries have engaged in the contract that they will do the utmost to bring all children into quality schools, expecting that the donor countries will do their bit by bridging the remaining finance gap.' The director generals of donor countries, who are present, feel clearly ill at ease. Indeed, this was the contract, but now that the donor countries have to deliver, they see all the complications. First, this commitment will cost a lot of money from the donors, maybe as much as 5 billion US dollars a year. This amount will be used to get all the 120 million children who are out of school into school and to substantially improve the chances that children will complete their primary education and effectively learn how to read, write and do numbers. (Still, that is only about $40 per child!). Second, they now realize that they will 'lock' this 5 billion 'in' for a long period of 5, maybe 10 years. They may be happy that finally they are dealing with the real problem, that is, that the poorest countries simply lack the funds to pay out of domestic resources the teachers they need for universal primary education and will continue to lack these funds for a number of years. Third, they will have to change some of their bad habits; for example, tying aid to foreign consultants where the need is for domestic teachers, or financing one-time construction of schools rather than the recurrent costs of the teachers, or asking accountability for every cent spent according to the standards of the huge variety of donor rules rather than to the standard of internationally accepted accountancy rules.

Developing countries do not present themselves, but their presence is felt through the reports of seven countries (Mauritania, Guinea, Niger, Burkina Faso, Nicaragua, Honduras and Guyana).

Box 6.6: Hope

> Finally the meeting in Brussels showed considerable engagement to the contract for the seven countries that have delivered on their part of the deal, until it comes to discussing the press release. Only after considerable discussion do the donors accept that they now do feel responsible for paying up the (roughly) US $130 million needed to bridge the financing gap for the seven countries.

focused on the main unresolved issues of development cooperation such as governance, a level playing field in trade and the harmonization/transaction costs of development cooperation.

- Washington-Consensus thinking in its crude, naïve form needs to be cast aside, not only in official statements, but in the culture of the Bank as well.
- The potential constituency of committed youth needs to be realized.
- The matrix organization should strive for donor harmonization as well as capacity creation, rather than for individual loans.
- Scaling-up is a necessity for realizing the mission of the Bank.

Overall the success of the World Bank will heavily depend on better rules of the game of globalization.

PART III

SPINNING THE GLOBAL ECONOMY

7

Partners in Development Assistance

You never walk alone. That might be the motto of a politician, a civil servant or a teacher or doctor in a developing country. It could also be the motto of the person involved in development cooperation (like, for example a World Banker). You will be surrounded by many different 'partners' and colleagues, engaged in similar work.

For example, imagine yourself to be the minister for health in a poor country, with major challenges in health, because one in every ten children dies before the age of five (as is the average in poor countries), while the budget for health is only 1.7 per cent of GDP (as is the average in Africa) in contrast to a level of around 7–8 per cent in OECD countries. Or let us make that 3 per cent, which is slightly higher than the average in Latin America and Asia, but with major problems because doctors who are paid to serve village clinics will often not show up, or ask poor people (illegally) for contributions for services rendered, and where the trained doctors leave the country in droves (as is the case in many developing countries).

A minister in a developed country (as I also was for almost a decade) will find the problems he/she faces quite simple compared to the minister in a developing country. It may help the minister in the developing country, however, that there is substantial assistance, both in terms of expertise and in terms of financial resources.

As a minister of health (to continue the example) in the developing country, you would seek all the support you can get. But this means that you would find yourself surrounded by scores of partners who, by the way, all like to talk to you. The WHO (World Health Organization) will have an office in your country, with a number of foreign specialists who are knowledgeable about malaria, if that is prevalent in your country, and who know about other major, prevalent diseases. UNAIDS will have a specialist, either in your country or near by. UNDP has a specialist who is interested in monitoring your progress in reducing child mortality (but who may have little money for projects in health). There may be a UNICEF group in the country, involved in inoculations or in other activities. These are but a small number of the members of the UN Family (Section 7.1) who are your partners. The UN family has lots of expertise to offer, but little money.

There is of course, the World Bank, with a country director, who comes to visit you and offers help, in the form of staff members who may work with you on loans, or on analytical work. But the World Bank can only be involved if the IMF considers the macro-framework 'acceptable', which means that inflation is in check and that the government deficit is not too high (Section 7.2). The IMF may have their own thoughts on the potential for new grants or loans, because these might raise the price of local currency (the foreign money will have to buy local money), and in that way contribute to an appreciation of the local currency. But the IMF is mostly known for its role as fire-fighter, providing loans when the country is on the brink of a major economic catastrophe. Also the IMF has the responsibility for the oversight of the banking systems in the world. And, lastly, the IMF can provide loans for the improvement of the macroeconomic policy environment.

Other partners of the 'banking' type are the Asian Development Bank, the African Development Bank, the Inter-American Development Bank and the European Bank for Reconstruction and Development. Like the World Bank, these Banks provide loans for projects or programs with interest rates far below the market rate for that country. The World Bank will work closely together with the regional development banks. Sometimes there is even a division of labour (for example, there may be the agreement that the World Bank focuses on health, while a regional development bank is engaged in education). We will not pay separate attention to these development banks in this book.

But there are also the so-called bilaterals as partners for the minister (Section 7.3). All of the donor countries have their own agencies for development cooperation, many of them with offices in a large number of developing countries. Some donor governments may even have several agencies that are involved in development cooperation in the same developing country. The bilaterals annually spend some 30 billion dollars in the form of grants. From a financial perspective, they are very attractive partners to the minister, especially when compared to the UN (little money) or compared to the World Bank (loans). Yet they can also be cumbersome, because they may bring their own agenda and because they may require a lot of red tape.

The above constitutes an already considerable network. In reality, however, the partner network of the minister is even wider. There are literally thousands of small initiatives for the cooperation between hospitals or doctors of his/her country and those of developed countries. Private foreign NGOs may be involved, as well as major private organizations, like the Ford Foundation.

The evolving partnerships between the official organizations of development cooperation and the NGOs are covered in the next chapter (8).

Note that we are limiting ourselves here to the network of foreign partners. This comes on top of the normal national network of a minister, who will have to be actively engaged in the country and in the sector.

Maintaining the foreign partner network is more than a full day's work. It would be so much more effective if these partners, on their side, coordinated and cooperated more. Some examples of such cooperation are emerging, albeit on a very small scale. The Dutch government has operated, for example, through the UK aid agency in a couple of cases. Some of the bilaterals have 'bought down' IBRD loans of the Bank, which means that they have used their money to lower the interest rate (they effectively pay the interest, rather than having a project on their own) for the developing country which has taken out an IBRD loan. However, in general, the minister will feel terribly frustrated by the fact that every organization has a similar story (in most cases), but tends to come up with different advice and always with different rules for managing projects.

Despite his/her frustration, the minister in the developing country will accept all the help he or she can get. At the same time, s/he is aware of the magnitude of the flows of resources in official development assistance (ODA), looking for opportunities both in terms of the quality of the expertise offered as well as the financial resources available. Every country has a 'menu' of partners for the minister in terms of financial resources. Some bilaterals may have chosen the country as one of their priority countries and are preferred partners for the minister if they provide untied grants with little paperwork. Others may be less preferred if aid is tied, or is subject to considerable paperwork, or comes in the form of a loan. The menu may be constantly changing, depending on the politics and strategies of the partners. This is another frustrating element for the Government of the developing country: not all of the partners are in the country for a long-term commitment. Here, the Bretton Woods institutions may have a preferred status, as they are there to stay (under normal circumstances; there are exceptions, such as when the Bank stopped work in Kenya, because of the high degree of corruption in the last years of the Moi Government in the late 1990s).

7.1 THE UNITED NATIONS FAMILY

The World Bank is part of the group of international organizations, the so-called United Nations Family (see also Section 5.1). The UN and its daughter organizations stand out in this group. They are more or less part of 'world government', ruled by the 188 heads of state, which constitute the UN on the basis of 'one country, one vote'. Formally, the Secretary General (SG) is the civil servant who prepares and implements the decisions of the Council. Informally, the SG has a lot of power. The daughters of the United Nations, like the WHO or UNESCO, are also 'ruled' by representatives of countries on the basis of one country, one vote. Here, it is the Director General who assumes the role of civil servant.

Ideally, all international organizations should operate as one and negotiate joint approaches both internationally and in individual countries. In practice, there is too much the feeling of competition between the different organizations and too much energy is spent on individual rather than collective actions.

Fortunately, the international organizations have all signed up to the same major challenges for joint action, namely the Millennium Development Goals (MDGs) (see Section 2.5). There is only a chance of reaching the MDGs if it is done by joint action (see Section 4.6).

In March 2002 in Stockholm, the World Bank discussed with WHO and UNICEF ways and means to bypass business as usual and gear up the reduction of child mortality. The WHO and UNICEF, for example, can add value for the clients of the World Bank. They often have the special technical knowledge that complements the countries' and the Bank's knowledge on policy analysis and policy change where the Bank can be the supplier of the financing.

The benefits for the country of a close alliance between the WHO, UNICEF and the World Bank (if it occurs) are substantial: reinforced messages, rather than working at cross-purposes, and joint analytical work. But for the minister, one of the major advantages would be the reduction of the transaction costs of development assistance: less need for debate on projects and less burden on the scarce capacity of the civil service for working along different rules and regulations.

These benefits are visible in the areas of leprosy, polio and tuberculosis, where the World Bank and WHO have closely worked together for some time. Onchocerciasis or river blindness is perhaps the best example. On a roundabout in the middle of Ouagadougou (Burkina Faso) stands the statue of an aged man (who may be no more than 45 years of age) holding a stick, who is guided by a small boy walking ahead of him. The same statue can be found in the centre of the main building of the World Bank, close to the White House in Washington DC, and in Amsterdam. It is a forceful image of what until recently was a stark and frightening reality: insects literally eating away the eyesight. Young boys were kept from school because they had to guide their blind elders. It is gone, or mostly gone, through the cooperation among many partners, but first and foremost, the World Bank and the WHO.

While the benefits of cooperation are easy to see and comprehend, cooperation is not the rule. One observes that staff of the UN organizations sometimes find it easier to reap the internal benefits of being critical of the

Bank, to take the moral high ground and to bash the Bank for all its dirty work it has to do with both feet in the mud of actual policy-making. Some jealousy about the financial resources of the Bank might play a role as well in the attitude of some UN staff. World Bank staff tends to look down on the UN staffers as irrelevant and ineffective. UN staffers are not always willing to realize that the World Bank does indeed engage in difficult circumstances, that it works with politicians who are not always too clean, and that it does take responsibility for financing policy reform, which will not always be popular. But one also observes that sometimes the Bank is to blame for the lack of partnering, with a business model in which partnering has to be done free of costs, and sometimes with an arrogance of being smarter than the rest, even though the Bank has much less field presence and knowledge on the ground than the UN organizations.

The limitations to partnering also arise from the focus and organization of the donor agencies. In its issue of December 7, 2002, the Medical Journal *The Lancet* complains about the limited value of the WHO in the development process of countries. The complaint of *The Lancet* is that WHO staff often concentrate on the technical aspects of specific diseases, because this is generally their area of expertise, rather than on health systems (which are the integral backbone for health services). This is another example where the cooperation between WHO and the Bank might generate more than just the addition of two major organizations. The Bank is good at the broader policy framework and could do very well with the additional WHO expertise in specific diseases.

In my view, there is still a long way to go to nail down agreement on a global scale that cooperation is of benefit to all, in particular to the developing countries in which the organizations work, acknowledging the right of existence of all partners, while at the same time ensuring that all partners work according to the same strategies (that is: the strategies of the developing country itself) and work with shared priorities. The partners of the United Nations Family are then, of course, prime partners in this joint effort.

Partnering does require a good communication between the different international agencies. This should mean communication between, but also within organizations as Box 7.1 shows.

7.2 THE IMF

For the World Bank the IMF is the prime partner. The World Bank and the IMF are sister organizations, both originating in Bretton Woods in 1944. The IMF oversees the macroeconomic, while the World Bank helps countries on the structural side and on the development of institutions. The IMF also provides policy advice and loans related to the macroeconomic position of the country. Loans are in particular meant to address external balances when the

Box 7.1: Communication

Queen Silvia of Sweden asks me: 'What are MDGs?' She is the lead speaker at a joint meeting in Stockholm on March 11, 2002 of two partners of the United Nations Family, the World Health Organization (WHO) and UNICEF (United Nations Children and Education Fund) with the World Bank on how to reduce child mortality. She is also Abba's dancing queen: cheerful, engaged, but absolutely not frivolous, if the word dancing might evoke that connotation. While she speaks – very seriously, and with the right emphasis and conclusions – I hear the tune playing in my mind. Abba be praised.

I am shocked by her question, as I realize that I have failed. In public speaking one should always imagine the knowledge level of the audience, and never assume too much. I had assumed that everyone knows about MDGs – sorry, Millennium Development Goals – as they have been endorsed by the international community and so widely discussed among the leadership and the operational staff of the different organizations. But obviously the communication has had its limitations.

Not explaining the MDGs was a mistake that I had already had warning of. When I was in Geneva in December 2001, to address the ambassadors to the UN, I tried to test the waters on the knowledge of the ambassadors about the MDGs. Most ambassadors seemed only to be familiar with the first goal (halve poverty between 2000 and 2015). I sensed that the staff were better informed on the other MDGs than the ambassadors were.

country has a program in place to arrive at an equilibrium in due time. The IMF makes it possible for poor countries facing temporary shocks or capital account crises to survive without instant adjustment. The World Bank cannot work in a country if that country is not an IMF member or lacks an IMF program (is subject to the so-called Article 4 supervision, which means that there is an annual report by the IMF on that country's economic bill of health). The IMF is responsible for dealing with imbalances as they arise in the world. Many argue that the IMF is not handling the present (2004) situation of huge current account deficits in the US and vast foreign exchange reserves in Asia sufficiently aggressively: it should more strongly emphasize currency revaluations of the Asian countries concerned.

The IMF and the World Bank work closely together on standards and rules for the banking sector, financial sector assessment (on how healthy this sector is) and on guidelines for sound management of the banking sector or the management of public sector debt. In some respects the IMF is more open than the Bank: the IMF does disclose the main lines of the discussions in the Board of the IMF. On the external relations side, however, the Fund may have much to learn from the Bank (this puts the IMF at an almost rock bottom level of external relations, as you would deduce from my conclusion on the Bank's external relations in Section 6.3, which is not very positive to say the least).

IMF and World Bank now both have an independent evaluation office, located within their organization and reporting to the boards, rather than to management. The success of the Operations Evaluation Department of the World Bank has definitely contributed to the foundation in 2002 of an Independent Evaluation Office at the IMF.

In daily operations the staff of the Fund and of the Bank also find themselves working together increasingly. Still, it took more than four years of insistence on the Bank's part before the Fund changed its position on the way grants were counted in calculating the budget deficit of the country. The 'old' rule was that any money coming from the outside and contributing to government income, was counted as debt. Is this good bean counting? Economists like to compare countries to households. So, if a household receives a gift, then should it count this as a debt? The IMF used to reason: yes, you might get used to it, and not be able to do without it next year when the gift may no longer come. As early as November 1998, Shanta Devarajan tried to work with the IMF to change that view, but this turned out to be in vain. Only recently in 2003, with substantial efforts, the then Chief Economist of the Bank, Nick Stern was successful as far as sustained grants are concerned, opening up much needed room for higher aid levels. Of course, both grants (like loans) have macro consequences, like a potential appreciation of the currency (as more local money has to be bought with the foreign exchange brought in through the loans and grants). These consequences should not be ignored. But to put a grant on an equal footing with a loan simply makes no sense. The conclusion was in the end that the impact of grants on the economy of a country needs to be considered on a case-by-case approach.

To demonstrate the oddness of the generic IMF approach, consider Ireland. Ireland received between 5 and 9 per cent of GDP as grants over a long period (almost 20 years) through the CAP and through the combination of the physical and social infrastructure as well as the cohesion fund.[1] Under IMF rules, this would not have been allowed, while Ireland's development brought per capita incomes in Ireland above those of the UK and is now a shining example for many other countries.

The IMF and the World Bank always used to exchange views on the analysis of a developing country in which they worked. The Country Assistance Strategies (CAS) of the World Bank, which led to its involvement in a country, would be well discussed with IMF staff. And yet, it was a major step when the IMF and the World Bank agreed in 2000 to work with the same document, the Poverty Reduction Strategy Paper (PRSP). It was not only a major step that the two sisters worked on the same basis. It is even better that this basis is constructed by the country *itself*, thus contributing to the ownership of the policies involved. UN agencies have followed the World Bank and the IMF in their course and depart from the PRSP with their actions in a country. Also, bilaterals have nowadays 'signed up' to the PRSP as a means of organizing development assistance.

If the Bank is under attack for its application of the Washington Consensus, then this is only minor criticism compared to that of the IMF. Much of the criticism on the IMF (as on the World Bank and the WTO) is derived from the market approach that is followed by these institutions. The criticism of this approach (forcefully brought to the table by the campaign '50 Years Is Enough') is that the IMF, as well as the other Bretton Woods institutions, ignore, through their market approach, social factors and the environment (see Section 6.2 on the Washington Consensus). At the same time, the criticism also holds that decision-making is not transparent, that root causes of poverty are not addressed, and that as a result, the approach of the IMF (and others) has perpetuated the debt crisis and has led to destructive agricultural practices.

These are serious allegations, which are not always easily rebutted. One allegation is, for example, that the IMF's lack of country-specific policies has hindered the stabilization of economies, and has rendered the IMF at times ineffective at realizing its own goals. By aiming to focus only on correcting short-term balance-of-payment problems, the IMF has harmed the social fabric of the countries it claims to have helped.

Critics will give examples in Eastern Europe, like that of the devaluation of the dinar in Yugoslavia in 1986. This devaluation was imposed by the IMF in a Structural Adjustment Program (SAP):

> The resultant inflation is considered a contributing factor to the already tense environment of ethnic tension and nationalism, which has led to the current conflict throughout the region. In Russia and other former Soviet-bloc countries, the IMF imposed 'economic shock therapy' measures, which involved the sudden introduction of capitalism into what were previously command economies. The result has been widespread unemployment, in the case of Poland going from 0 per cent in 1990 to 15 per cent in 1993. This has also led to the devaluation of pensions and large cuts in social services. In Russia, similar conditions are commonly attributed to the rise in popularity of ultra-nationalism, and the rise of Vladimir Zhirinovsky.[2]

Is this not too easy? What would have happened without the IMF's involvement? What were the alternatives to the way in which the IMF was involved? There is much in this criticism that is blaming the fire brigade for the fire. This is not to say that all the criticism is unwarranted. In fact, both the IMF and the World Bank have acknowledged some of their mistakes in the past and have changed their policies quite drastically, based on some of the criticism. But the following is also true: 'The Fund gets often cast in the role of the villain when in fact the problem lies with the country itself. Corrupt and autocratic regimes, some of them propped up by the vested interests abroad are often the first to plead ownership and then bemoan the lack of it when they feel the pressure of donors and the multilateral system to rectify things' (ESAF Report: External Evaluation, IMF, 1998).

The IMF is particularly known for its role in financial crises: the fire-fighting role. However, it is also heavily involved in development on a day-to-day basis, monitoring, advising and also financing in a country. The IMF comes to the rescue with 'packages' (large sums of money) when a country collapses because it is cash-strapped and has nowhere to go to (a financial crisis). The country and the IMF hope and pray that the package will help to fill the financial gaps, but will also address the causes of the crisis. But the latter is not certain: economics is not rocket science as is nicely demonstrated in Paul Blustein's book, *The Chastening of the IMF*, (Public Affairs, 2001) about the East Asia crisis.

Yet some of the criticisms of the IMF are warranted (see Joseph Stiglitz: *Globalization and its Discontents*, Norton, 2002). Sometimes the fire department causes quite a bit of collateral damage in its engagement to put out the fire. None of this has to do with the direction of the advice: get growth going, make sure that inflation is in check and make sure that government expenditures are in line with tax receipts. It has to do with the modalities and the speed of the measures and their effect on the fabric of society. Reducing government budgets might affect safety nets, and might imply that schools or village clinics start to raise fees, because their income from the government is cut, thus leading to dropping out or an increase in morbidity and mortality.

The main target of criticism of the IMF is that it tends to see social policy as an embellishment, as a luxury, which you buy if you have the money, and lay off when times are slow, ignoring that social policy is an integral part of the economic and social dynamism of a society.

In a crisis, government policies need to be countercyclical (as they are in rich countries) and help people through the bad times when there is a drop in income. In the past, the IMF was not always quick on the uptake on these lessons. Yet in the East Asia crisis, it did allow the Korean government to more than double its spending on safety nets and it did go along with substantial World Bank financed programs to help Indonesian kids go to school by giving money to the parents on the condition that the children remained enrolled.

Criticism of the IMF does not only come from the political left. There is also criticism from the opposite side, from the advocates of market forces.

'The belief is that much foreign aid is transferred from government to government, leaving people short-changed and bureaucrats and politicians, some corrupt, the beneficiaries. This promotes a disastrous politicization of life in developing countries, as well as Western-type heavy industries rather than small firms using indigenous technology. This over-stressing of the role of government discourages private market development and curtails the flow of private capital. This process prolongs a country's dependence on official assistance, while only contributing at best a small fraction of investment. Examples of the commercial export development in West Africa and Malaysia in the early 1980s are held up as models of private enterprise performing what foreign aid could not.'[3]

The IMF is in many respects in trouble with its lending role. The main problem at the moment (2005) is that so much of its money (in total US $64 billion) is tied up with only three clients: Argentina, Brazil and Turkey. The involvement of the IMF in these countries is so large that the IMF can easily become hostage to the course of the country. The worst-case scenario of a new crisis in two or more of these countries would seriously threaten the very existence of the IMF.

Earlier (Section 4.6) we mentioned how the US Congress Commission, led by Chairperson Allan Meltzer, proposed to change the mode of operation of the Bank by abolishing loans. The same commission also feels that the IMF should abolish loans and replace them by grants.

The rationale for abolishing loans to middle-income countries is that the private sector could equally well provide such loans. This topic will be discussed in Chapter 10 with the conclusion that a better rationale for the loans of the IMF (as of those for the IBRD-wing of the Bank) is needed, but that – in itself – the possibility of low-interest loans for specific purposes in middle-income countries (still under the level of US $5185 per capita in 2004) creates added value for the world at large.

More relevant is the proposal that the Bretton Woods Commission of 1994 led by Paul Volcker seriously considered, namely the merging of IMF and World Bank. This proposal was rejected, because it was said that the emphasis of the IMF (namely the macroeconomic side) was distinctly different from that of the World Bank (namely: microeconomic). However, this distinction has become increasingly blurred, as the microeconomic foundations of the macroeconomy have become the focus of analysis and policy. A merger of the IMF and World Bank would decrease overlap, would decrease transaction costs for developing countries, would improve policy advice and last, but not least, might faster phase out the Washington Consensus from development cooperation.

7.3 BILATERALS

A substantial part of the money involved in development assistance comes
from the 'bilaterals': the rich countries that support poor countries bilaterally.
One of the major thresholds to effective development assistance is the limited
effectiveness of these bilaterals. Many rich countries find it hard to choose
between effective development assistance and their own interests. They end
up (at least in part) with 'flag planting' exercises, showing their presence without
much concern about effectiveness and sustainability. They often provide aid
that is tied to products or advisers from their own country, while at the same
time claiming substantial time from ministers, civil servants and others in the
developing country, and demanding accountability with extremely high
overhead costs.

It is only recently that bilaterals have begun to team up among themselves
so that transaction costs for the developing country are lowered. For example,
Dutch bilateral development assistance is provided through, and in
combination with, British bilateral assistance. The outcry to untie aid from
the rich country's products or advisers has been around for quite a while with
some success, but unfortunately only in a limited number of countries. The
mentality of flag planting is still around. Few cabinets have had the guts or the
conviction to see that the road away from flag planting can be well defended
in parliaments, (as has happened successfully in the Netherlands), as flag planting
is contrary to effective aid.

One of the best examples of coordination between bilaterals among
themselves and with international agencies has been taking place in Uganda
since 2000. In Uganda, all agencies are supposed to contribute to the national
budget (or parts thereof, like the education budget), which is in line with the
plans of the government (outlined in a Poverty Reduction Strategy Paper).
The difficulties involved in such a coordination are sketched in Box 7.2.

Donor coordination is advanced in Uganda, but on a scale of 0 to 100 it
may be no more than say 50 (with a worldwide average, however of no more
than say 5 to 10). In other words, there is still a world to be gained in donor
coordination in Uganda. At the same time, Uganda compares very favourably
to the overall picture of donor coordination: it is in fact exemplary.

Uganda is still not ideal in two respects:
- The accountability for the contribution of each donor has to be
  done along the lines of the donor's frameworks. The absurdity of
  this approach has been highlighted in Tanzania. Every three months
  the Tanzanian Government has to produce 2,400 separate reports
  to satisfy the accountability requirements of the donors. The
  tremendous imposition of these requirements on the already very
  limited capacity of the country should shake donors sufficiently to

Box 7.2: Donor Coordination

Paud Murphy, the Bank manager for education in Uganda asks me to join a donor's meeting, which is called at a crucial juncture of donor coordination.

Uganda is the success story in development in Africa in the last decade of the second millennium. The Idi Amin years (1971–1986) virtually destroyed the country's physical infrastructure and economy. Idi Amin was a dictator who is said to be responsible for the deaths of up to half a million Ugandans. Even more were imprisoned and tortured.

After Amin's overthrow, the country emerged, slowly at first, but subsequently realizing growth rates of an average 7 per cent by the latter half of the 1990s, while keeping inflation down. In this process, the percentage of the population in poverty dropped from 55.6 in 1992 to 44.0 in 1997 (World Development Report 2000/ 2001, Table 1.3). Yet this percentage went up again to 55.0 in 2002 (Little Data Book).

Education may not have suffered under Amin as much as other sectors. Still, by 1980 enrolments in primary schools was under 50 per cent of the age group with an average of sub-Saharan Africa of 85 per cent. In successive years, the government moved towards its goal to bring all children in quality schools with a bold move in 1997 to abolish school tuition fees, which were a major barrier against poor Ugandan parents sending their children to school. Moreover it set everything in motion to have net enrolments approaching 100 per cent in 2003 and reducing the pupil-teacher ratio from 68:1 (!) in 1990 to 45:1 (still very high) in 2003.

The government of Uganda has well thought through the steps it has to take and the donors are committed to support this by putting their money into the government budget as long as the government delivers on its course. And then all hell breaks loose. 'The government has not delivered', says the staff member of the UK Aid Agency, DFID in February 2000, 'and we should stop the donor money flow to show that we are serious'. The EU staff member and Dutch staff member are equally strong-minded in their positions. Someone asks for more precision. 'Stopping the donors' money puts the program to bring more children into school into the category of red alert. Teachers will no longer be paid and will have to be fired.' So what was it the Government did not deliver upon? It turns out that the government had committed to take seven steps in the preceding year. It delivered on all except one: the full implementation of a management information system. The evening before, when I met the minister, he was profusely apologetic, but also quite clear that he had given earlier information about the possibility of a delay, as the ministry of finance had raised a number of serious objections, which had not been foreseen.

I was watching the scene with some apprehension. Dedicated, but also young and inexperienced staffers from donor countries were

> judging the commitment of a government to bring about change, with major implications. This was the first experiment with donor coordination, based on a government commitment to change and expansion. In my experience, educational change always runs into unexpected problems and I was more surprised to see that the government had delivered on no fewer than six of the seven steps than I was disturbed by the lack of full delivery.

change their ways and rely on the country's reporting along internationally accepted lines.

- There is no integration of the policy-making of donors. This is best illustrated with the 'travel habits' of donors. Successive groups of foreign dignitaries who visit the country all make claims on the calendars of government ministers and civil servants. The minister of finance can spend full days talking to and entertaining the Danish minister for telecommunication, the Belgian deputy minister for trade, a top-level Japanese delegation, or the annual consultations of Austria (to just mention the foreign dignitaries which passed through Kampala at the time of the meeting of Box 7.2). There are at least nine bilateral donors present in Uganda with their own office. The minister of finance of Namibia said at the press conference at the Spring Meetings in 2002 in Washington: 'Do not call me minister of finance; I am the travel agent, bringing high-level delegations to the president.' It would be quite like a Monty Python video, putting successive visits in a country together and making a collage of the advice the visiting dignitaries give. Poor country to be overloaded with so many good intentions!

Donors in Uganda have not stopped their 'bad' travel habits. Nor have they stopped to ask for reporting on the use of 'their' money in 'their' national frameworks.

In principle donors agree. Every meeting of the Development Committee of the World Bank or the International Monetary Fund Committee of the IMF is a moment for a solemn pledge to coordinate. Yet there is not too much progress in the implementation. To many observers there is even a relapse into old, bad habits, as the World Development Report 2004 suggests. This fear is confirmed in the Global Monitoring Report 2004 (Chapter 11, p. 10). This report introduces a donor fragmentation index. This index only deals with the shares of individual donors (if the index is zero, then one donor accounts for all of a recipient's aid). This index – as a result – does not say anything about the degree of harmonization. The overall donor index is shown to rise from 55 in 1975 to 65 in 2002.

The best sign of the world's readiness for donor coordination is the EFA/FTI (Education For All, Fast Track Initiative), mentioned in Section 6.5 under scaling-up. EFA is an initiative of UNESCO. In 1990, delegates from 155 countries, as well as representatives from some 150 organizations agreed at the World Conference on Education for All in Jomtien, Thailand (March 5–9, 1990) to universalize primary education and massively reduce illiteracy before the end of the decade. Some 10 years later, in 2000, an EFA assessment showed some successes, but overall the goals had not been achieved. Still, the successes are substantial:

- Some 10 million more children went to school every year during the last decade.
- The overall adult literacy rate rose to 85 per cent for men and 74 per cent for women.
- Enrolment in primary school rose from 599 million in 1990 to 681 million in 1998.
- The number of out-of-school children fell from an estimated 127 million children to 113 million children.
- Globally, there was a 5 per cent increase in enrolment in pre-primary establishments.

The need was felt to renew the pledge with new vigor, which happened in Dakar in 2000, as shown in Table 7.1.

By adopting the Dakar Framework for Action, the 1,100 participants of the Forum reaffirmed their commitment to achieving Education for All by the year 2015. The Fast Track Initiative (EFA/FTI) was developed by a number of

Table 7.1 The goals of EFA set in Dakar

- Expanding and improving comprehensive early childhood care and education, especially for the most vulnerable and disadvantaged children;
- Ensuring that by 2015 all children, particularly girls, children in difficult circumstances and those belonging to ethnic minorities, have access to free and compulsory primary education of good quality;
- Ensuring that the learning needs of all young people and adults are met through equitable access to appropriate learning and life skills programs;
- Achieving a 50 per cent improvement in levels of adult literacy by 2015, especially for women, and equitable access to basic and continuing education for all adults;
- Eliminating gender disparities in primary and secondary education by 2005, and achieving gender equality in education by 2015, with a focus on ensuring girls' full and equal access to and achievement in basic education of good quality;
- Improving all aspects of the quality of education and ensuring excellence of all so that recognized and measurable learning outcomes are achieved by all, especially in literacy, numeracy and essential life skills.

Source: http://www.unesco.org/education/efa/ed_for_all/faq.shtml

partners together: the World Bank, UNESCO and bilaterals. The notion is essentially that no country will be cash-strapped if it seriously wants to reach universal primary education. The term 'seriously' means that the country should follow international good practice in, for example, teacher salaries and in recurrent costs, as well as in its own financial efforts for education. Donors will help the 'serious' countries with cash, if needed. This form of development cooperation can be considered an example of combining the efforts of the different development organizations in a focused and effective way.

Of course, EFA/FTI still needs to show its successes. While initially all partners were enthusiastic about the program, the subsequent steps will be cumbersome when donors have to commit themselves.

8

Civil Society and Development

Since the 1990s, civil society has become an important partner of the World Bank and other development agencies in fighting world poverty. Stronger democratic support by citizens is necessary to bring about the changes that world poverty alleviation entails. Such support is part of a virtuous circle.

The World Bank uses the term 'civil society organizations' (CSOs) to refer to the wide array of non-governmental and not-for-profit organizations that have a presence in public life, expressing the interests and values of their members or others, based on ethical, cultural, political, scientific, religious or philanthropic considerations. CSOs include NGOs, the organizations involved in specific development activities in the country, but also trade unions, community-based organizations, social movements, faith-based institutions, charitable organizations, research centres, foundations, student organizations, professional associations and many others. The Bank has traditionally interacted with NGOs in its operations and dialogue, giving them a prominent role in policy analysis and advocacy activities. Today, however, the Bank has begun to reach out more broadly to CSOs. Box 8.1 depicts an experience with CSOs.

The recognition by donors of the importance of civil society in a country for its development was a logical reflection of civil society's role in the development of the donor countries themselves. Private advocacy and private initiatives in areas of public concern are part and parcel of the development experience in rich countries. But also, several forms of effective development cooperation have been taking place for decades, involving private partners in developing countries as implementing agencies. This is the topic of Section 8.1.

Civil society also has other faces, like those of some NGOs from the North, with loose ties to similar-thinking groups in the South, who drive the anti-capitalist, anti-globalist movement. The major demonstrations against the IMF and the World Bank in Washington (1999) and Prague (2000) came from diverse groups. Most of the demonstrators were youngsters from the North and South advocating more development aid and more debt relief. But trade

Box 8.1: Defining Civil Society

Grace Yabrudy, the World Bank's resident representative in Mali, gave me an excellent opportunity to learn about civil society in the development process of Mali in November 2000, through a series of meetings with representatives of different civil service organizations (including non-governmental organizations, NGOs). These meetings demonstrated how difficult it is to define civil society. One knows what to exclude: government agencies and private industries (and even here there is a question mark), but it is not easy to define what is included, definitely not 'everything else'. What is included can vary from individual lobbyists, individual advocates or groups of advocates, to trade unions, women's self-help groups, or agricultural cooperatives. All of these groups have been brought together in Mali through the World Bank with the full support of the government, with the purpose of involving them in the elaboration of Poverty Reduction Strategy Papers. These PRSPs are the main vehicle for the engagement between donors and the country. They contain the drive of the government for the policies directed at economic growth and poverty reduction. By involving stakeholders and civil society in general, the likelihood that these strategies can be implemented increases. Here we see one of the faces of civil society: partner and participant in the domestic development process.

union members from the North who wanted to block imports from the South because they feared for their jobs were also present. Others turned out to be virulent anti-market thinkers. There were also the anarchists. For the latter group, the goal was clear: inciting violence and chaos.

It would be incorrect to depict the civil society movement as a group of mainly disruptive organizations, which harm development rather than helping it. As Kofi Annan said in his address to the Millennium Forum in New York on May 22, 2000: 'Barely had the pepper fog settled over the Seattle protests, before NGOs were branded as confrontational or even contrarian, disruptive or even destructive, anti-technology or even anti-progress. Those labels overlook the pioneering role of NGOs on a range of vital issues from human rights to the environment, from development to disarmament. We in the United Nations know that it was [they] who set the pace on many issues.'

For the World Bank, some of these groups (like the one consisting of youngsters who advocate a greater commitment of the rich world to development cooperation) should be outright companions and friends. However, with others a dialogue would be one between the deaf, with no sign language present (Section 8.2).

The trade unions are a special group in civil society. From my experience in the Netherlands, I cannot but consider them to be part of the development solution, both for rich as for poor countries. Yet it requires an intensive dialogue to make sure that these trade unions feel at ease with an active development policy, so that they can opt for the relative uncertainty of policy reform, rather than the relative comfort of the status quo, regardless of how 'uncomfortable' this may be for a poorly developed country (Section 8.3). The private sector is normally not included in 'civil society' even though it may be the most important factor of development (Section 8.4). A very special group in civil society in developing countries is the returning diaspora, people who have left the country to work abroad for a long time, who have the great promise of bringing international experience to the country, while at the same time being in closer touch with the country than any foreign expertise. It is also a force which is by and large untapped as a human resource (while its financial resources – remittances – do already play a substantial role in development).

8.1 CIVIL SOCIETY AS A PARTNER

The World Bank pays attention to civil society in the form of the integration between the formal and the informal institutions. It recognizes that civil society may reflect the voices of the poorest people, and may contribute to development effectiveness and sustainability. Nevertheless, this role should be in balance with the government's responsibilities.

Civil society also acts as a financial supporter of projects and programs in countries. Development assistance has not only become a matter for the multilaterals and the governments, but also for individuals and the private market. In every developing country, there are literally thousands of small projects or programs, backstopped by NGOs in rich countries. Sometimes these NGOs have a religious background, but often they are 'just' the result of private concern and private actions. In general, these small projects can be highly effective. Their total impact on development remains small, simply because of the limited scale of the projects. Yet, private grants by NGOs are the fastest expanding type of development assistance, rising by 70 per cent over the period 1997–2002 and reaching a value of US $9 billion in 2002 (World Bank, Global Monitoring Report, Chapter 11, p. 3).

The position of the World Bank is still stronger than any other partner in development cooperation, but NGOs, companies, and the role of remittances are becoming more significant. The World Bank and other multi-laterals should expect the importance of their institute to grow in the future as a convener, a catalyst and an organizer of integrated support to countries.

The anti-globalization movement has changed public opinion about the Bretton Woods institutions and their public accountability. In response, the institutes have been working to become more accessible for the public, to evaluate their policies, as does for example the OED of the World Bank and the newly created Independent Evaluation Office of the IMF, and to make their policies and organization more transparent and democratic. However, theory and practice still show wide gaps, both on the side of the multilateral institutions and on the side of the targeted and involved developing countries. According to the organization called Charter 99, 'the charter for global democracy', there are the following three immediate challenges that the multilateral institutions such as the World Bank need to face in order to become truly effective:

- Democratic reform of voting and decision-making.
- Changing the three economic organizations of the World Bank, the IMF and the WTO from being maverick agents of the industrialized countries to a coherent and democratic family of global institutions for tackling global problems and clearing up the confused hierarchy between the UN and these three organizations.
- Growing a new constitutional settlement for the world economy from the roots up, with citizens, not civil servants, setting the pace: a declaration of democracy for the brave new economy.

There are serious doubts whether these suggestions by Charter 99 will indeed lead to improvements (see also Section 5.4). The formal democracy of voting and decision-making at the UN agencies is definitely not a shining example of effectiveness. The call for more 'citizen involvement' seems to ignore the democratic process within countries (which fortunately has taken a firm hold in an increasing number of countries). Bypassing governments in development cooperation (as Charter 99 seems to call for) is not a solution, but rather weakens the position of governments in their efforts to improve governance.

The tension between civil society and the official organizations of development cooperation will, no doubt, remain. This is also a healthy tension, however, as it constantly leads to challenges between the two and to countervailing powers. This is also a way of saying that I do indeed see civil society playing the role of an important partner in development cooperation.

8.2 Engaging Public Opinion

The involvement of civil society in development cooperation is a necessity because of its stakeholder position in achieving legitimized and effective public policies. However, the World Bank, like most development agencies, has a hard time involving NGOs because of the complex relationships between the state and the NGOs. Who are these NGOs, what is their legitimacy, and to whom are they accountable? Are they mere advocates for special interests, or worse, forms of self-employment for the sake of self-employment? These questions are particularly relevant in democracies. On this point, the world has changed drastically in the past decade. Between 1987 and 2001, the number of democracies grew from 66 of a total of 164 countries, to 121 00 of a total of 192 countries.

These questions are easily answered in robust states, states that have had strong democratic institutions over decades, where an active civil society is part of the internal dialogue feeding the democratic process. Robust states themselves will encourage and facilitate a thriving civil society. Development agencies will not have to worry about the promotion of civil society in such states.

In weak states, however, a strong civil society might elbow out the democratic process. Undue support for civil society might put parliament and the cabinet in a position of weakness. It is a matter of balance. Is civil society an answer to the very weak states, to LICUS (Low-income countries under Stress)? LICUS expresses the concern about the downside of the focus of development aid on the 'good performers', on places where money works, where there is ownership of the improvement of governance, of 'good policies' and of the improvement of institutions. This concentration may have helped bring such countries into their weak state. Kenya was by and large shut off from aid when it became ineffective during the Moi years. The recent change in government opens up new possibilities. It is quite impressive how much emphasis the new government initially had placed on good governance (something which is very much based on popular feelings). The transition, however, has turned out to be difficult. The fact is that many poor people live in countries where the government does not show such ownership. Zimbabwe and Angola are other examples (next to Moi's Kenya): donor flows might lengthen rather than shorten the period of lawlessness and a corrupt government.

Civil society and other partners (notably UNDP) can be an alternative in contributing to development when donor flows based on good governance are not possible. However, it is important to retain engagement of the other partners of development cooperation, like the multilaterals and the bilaterals, for the moment when the time is ripe and the country decides to rise from its ashes, so that a speedy involvement of donors can stimulate the recovery. Balance is the watchword, while realizing that the engagement of civil society in development plays a key role in promoting state and market transparency and social equity. It lends voice to the people.

For the World Bank, engagement of civil society is part of the job; a serious part, which means that memory is built up, that there is an understanding on the side of the World Bank staff of their counterparts in civil society. Involvement in civil society is not an easy or fast process, and often results in a gap between promise and performance on both sides. The results of an NGO study by the OED[1] indicate that the language of NGO and CSO involvement in Bank-supported projects outstripped the reality. 'The demand for partnership with NGOs and CSOs exceeded the supply of willing and able partners. Equally the Bank and borrowers tried to do too much, too quickly, without building up their own capacity to work with NGOs and CSOs and without clear indicators of progress'. The report of the OED is summarized by the following findings:

- NGOs/CSOs have been underutilized in Bank work.
- Consultations with NGOs/CSOs remain tentative.
- Working relationships among partners are often ineffective; clear signs of basic agreement are needed for effective collaboration, and there is a need for a supportive environment.
- Participation of NGOs and civil society organizations in some project implementations has increased.
- Government scepticism hinders engagement with NGOs.
- Monitoring and evaluation of Bank NGO/CSO activities is weak.

Strategic partnerships in an encouraging and supportive environment, together with NGO participation in projects and CAS preparation and monitoring are two of the most important recommendations of the OED to the Bank. Gradually, the development community (including the public policy analysis of the rich countries) has become aware of the importance of a society's transparency, not just as a goal in itself, but also as a means to give an effective voice to citizens. Transparency has become a key word in development. Civil society has always been a proponent of transparency, as it serves civil society in its advocacy and its other contributions to development. To give an example of the importance of transparency: in Uganda during the period 1991–5, schools received only 15 per cent of what the government contributed to the schools' non-wage expenditures. The bulk of the allocations was either used by public officials for purposes unrelated to education or (as the research report euphemistically states) 'captured for private gain (leakage)'.[2] This was the result of a widely published tracking survey. Five years later, a similar survey shows that 90 per cent of these discretionary expenditures reach the schools. This demonstrates the power of publicity and transparency. A power which is largely untapped in many developing countries and which means that the voices of the poor remain unheard or are smothered.

Another 'leakage' that occurred in Uganda (as in many other developing countries) was the money that went to 'ghost' teachers: teachers on the payroll who never or only rarely turned up in school. In 1995, it was estimated that as much as 20 per cent of the government budget went to ghost teachers and was thus lost for education. The publication of (comparative) figures of school attendance of teachers (not of students) has also played a substantial role in reducing this percentage, in a similar way as the case for non-wage expenditures.

The Ugandan example is a powerful one. With this success in the use of transparency as a means to improve the allocation of public resources in Uganda in mind, 'tracking surveys' showing where the money for education allocated by the central or regional government goes, have become a regular part of the World Bank's assistance in many countries.

The dialogue between the donors (including the World Bank) and the NGOs is not an easy one. Part of it is even a dialogue of the deaf. This is the case with the NGOs that have a specific anti-capitalist inclination. However strongly the Bank pushes for a strong state, for good governance, for the environment, for priority of the social sectors, these groups remain opposed to the central notion of the Bank's work that the system of a planned (communist style) economy has failed and that coordinated market economies (with government coordination to ensure the proper working of the market *and* to ensure acceptable solid outcomes), however imperfect, are superior for achieving better living conditions in a country's poorer parts.

8.3 How Civil are Trade Unions?

The Venezuelan or Senegalese teacher trade unions are not the progressive forces that will help to get more children into better schools. On the contrary, they are part of the problem and are far removed from being the solution that they should be. To bring them closer to their desperately needed role – to help the country help itself – they need to be *in* on the dialogue between the Bank and the country, however frustrating that may be.

Venezuela is such a beautiful country: beautiful people, beautiful countryside. It makes one weep to see how it is literally propelling itself into a downward spiral. Despite a huge oil export, GNI was in 2000 $5740 – far below what it was some 10 years ago, with education on the wrong side of the development equation and teacher unions unwilling to change the situation (see Box 8.2).

It remains amazing how, worldwide, teacher unions seem unable to capture the ground they need and deserve. But then again, the bureaucratic approach of a Bank, driven by abstract analysis and cold reasoning, does not help much either. Trade unions need to be involved in the country dialogue. They do represent an important interest in the country.

Teacher unions are not the exception in not being able to look for inclusion. Trade unions in general have the problem of selling to their constituency (the workers who are 'in', that is, those who have a job) the advantages of bringing more people in, even if it is at the cost of the wages and benefits of those already in. A few weeks before he died, Jan Tinbergen, the famous development economist and Nobel Prize winner, told me to read Jacob Marschak's 1929 article (in German) 'Die Lohndiskussion' ('The Wage Debate'). It made me realize that the discussion is a very old one: workers who have a job will try to maximize their benefits and wages, even at the cost of unwittingly excluding others from employment: what is often called the 'insiders' versus 'outsiders' conflict.

Box 8.2: Teacher Unions in Merida

In March 1998 we are sitting together in Merida, the capital city of the province of that name. 'Only' 7 of the 17 national teachers unions are present. I have the privilege of speaking with three of them. We go through the education agenda. Venezuela ranks low in educational achievement, far below that of other countries with lower per capita incomes and per student expenditures. Visits to schools like the Simon Bolivar School or the Prado Verde El Valle School in Merida, illustrate everything one knows from the impersonal statistics: teachers are devoted, but also not always too conscious of quality. The maths teacher in the 5th grade (9-year-olds) believes that 3 divided by 3 is 0; afterwards it turned out that only one of the other students (no surprise) had the right answer. Even dividing 21 by 7 turns out to be a mystery for most kids. Teachers work 5 hours a day and retire with 80 per cent of their salary after 25 years. The number of fully paid teachers (non-retired) who actually turn up is no more than 70–80 per cent of the total. Yes, the inspectors come once a month, but they either turn a blind eye, do not see, or are ignored. In many classes there are no or very few textbooks – definitely not one per student (the textbooks can be found in a warehouse, explains a civil servant, but we will get them out soon). This is all irrelevant for the teacher unions. They care about ideology, the role of the state in society and teacher salaries. Yes, teachers are politically motivated and many enter national or regional politics. But the teacher unions are not interested in educational policies, while there is so much political credit to be earned from parents and ordinary citizen, by honest, credible improvements in quality and access.

Trade unions can only be progressive if governments allow them to be progressive. There must be a willingness on the part of government to exchange promises of more inclusion for the promise on the part of the trade unions to help in the reforms that will improve the investment climate and the creation of employment. This is what makes trade unions and the World Bank partners. Employment creation is the best means of poverty reduction and links trade unions and the World Bank.

Social contracts between trade unions, employers and the government have been the basis for most of continental Northern Europe's way out of the employment crisis of the 1980s. These were ways of bringing the unions in as forces of innovation, rather than fighting them as forces of conservatism.

There need not be a contrast between such policies and 'core labour standards.' The ILO (International Labour Organization in which trade unions, employers and governments cooperate) has made – under Hansenne, Director General (from 1989 to 1999) – the promotion of 'core labour standards' the main point of its agenda. When trade unions and the World Bank met for the third time in October 2002, it was clear that the two organizations work very well together on all of these standards with the strong support of countries like the US and Germany. The core labour standards are:

- Abolish forced labour;
- Abolish child labour;
- Abolish job discrimination;
- Allow freedom of association.

On the first three, the ILO found the developing countries on their side. The countries enacted legislation in line with the standards. The fourth point was a different matter. Several countries have not ratified the international treaty on this subject (including China). It remains a point of debate between the trade unions and the World Bank to what extent the Bank should advocate the 'freedom of association,' the right to have and become a member of an active trade union. The World Bank obviously supports this, but cannot apply 'conditionalities' to enforce it (this is equally obvious now that the World Bank has generally dropped the notion of conditions and works more by way of country ownership). Yet the Bank is often chided by trade unions and some of the shareholders of the Bank (notably the USA) for not advocating strongly enough the right of association.

Trade unions in the rich North have decidedly acted ambiguously in response to the quest for convergence. Officially they support convergence and development assistance. But when it comes to the relocation of jobs they often react with a request for protectionism, as is exemplified in Box 8.3.

The combination of trade unions in the South which are hesitant in supporting desperately needed change, and trade unions in the North, which turn out to be protectionist when the South is gaining ground makes up the answer to the question: How civil are trade unions? The answer is that trade unions could be far better and stronger agents for convergence than they are now. There is a need for a proper, well-constructed debate between the trade unions of the North and the South.

Box 8.3: Protecting Jobs at Home?

In an address in the Washington Cathedral in June 2001, President Sweeney of the AFL/CIO blasts the World Bank. Is this indeed based on a desire to help poor countries? It is more likely that President Sweeney was trying to protect US jobs, even if the protection of one such job may mean the loss of scores of well-paid jobs in developing countries.

8.4 The Private Sector

Development cooperation in the form of financial transfers (official development assistance), which amounts to about US $50 billion, is dwarfed by the private capital flows to developing countries in the form of liquidity and foreign direct investment (FDI), which amounted to roughly US $300 billion a year in the latter half of the 1990s, helping to increase economic growth and to reduce poverty. Although this flow has decreased since then, FDI is holding up nicely with a level of around US $150–190 billion (see Section 2.2, Table 2.1). However, FDI is very much concentrated in a limited number of countries and is of little help to the majority of the poorer developing countries.

Development cooperation aimed at increasing the flow of private resources, in particular FDI, to developing countries is a double-edged sword. It brings in investment, the much-needed cash, but also experience and technology. Moreover, it signals to the local investors that it is wise to invest in their own country, rather than sending their money abroad. The signal is that the investment climate in the country is good. Improving the investment climate is one of the two pillars of the World Bank's development strategy (the other pillar being focused on human development). The impact of the role of the investment climate can best be illustrated with the result of a study of the Confederation of Indian Employers comparing the business costs in India and China of well-defined products (for example shoes or textiles). It turns out that these costs are higher on all counts in India than in China, whether it is the costs of taxation, utilities or finance, or money (internal costs); this is not as much through 'official' costs as through 'unofficial' ones, such as tax inspectors demanding more than the official rates (to supplement their own salaries), utility costs being high because of non-payment by substantial blocks of consumers, and high interest rates, equally due to non-payment by others. At a colloquium in January 2001 the study was discussed. The chairman of the Confederation exclaimed when he presented the findings that he, too, would rather invest in China than in India. It is not highly surprising either that on average China received a net FDI of almost US $40 billion a year in the 1990s against a meagre US $1.5 billion for India.

One needs not only to focus on the improvement of the investment climate to attract FDI. The investment climate also promotes the retention of local savings and prevents the flight of domestic savings to other countries, as is so prominent in most of sub-Saharan Africa and to a lesser extent in Latin America (see also Box 9.3).

The net FDI inflow is both an indicator of development and a factor in development. FDI is, of course, different from the short-term capital flows, which can be brought in and also pulled out of the country in nanoseconds, creating substantial risks and vulnerabilities against which countries need to guard themselves, in line with what gradually has been recognized as good practice; namely, to keep a sufficient reserve of foreign currencies.

The organized private sector is often very small in the poorer developing countries. For example, in Yemen or in Mali, there are only two companies that employ more than 1,000 persons. A substantial increase is needed to create a middle class which in itself is a 'civil society' that will advocate for the political climate for faster development. Where a substantial private sector exists – as in India or Morocco – it does more than contribute to economic development. It is often also effective in helping to deliver human development through health facilities, through support in combating HIV/AIDS infections by supplying anti-retrovirals to those infected, and in stimulating education. Sometimes the private sector will even (as in Morocco) provide schools and teachers for primary education for other children in addition to those of employees.

However, there can be downsides to FDI and the presence of multinational enterprises (MNEs) in developing countries. An important precondition is that MNEs behave in a socially responsible manner when located in developing countries. Practice has shown (e.g. with Adidas, Ikea, Nike, Shell, IHC Calland) that MNEs can increase corruption or can have a negative influence on the environmental or local social situation.

The year 2002 was an important year in furthering the role of private – public partnership in fighting poverty, corruption, inequality and environmental degradation. The World Summit on Sustainable Development, combined with the corporate governance scandals in the US, put ethics, transparency, accountability and private-public partnerships firmly on the political agenda.

In this time period of governance scandals, anti-globalists and inequality, companies invest in Corporate Social Responsibility (CSR) for four reasons. First, companies need to regain the trust of the consumers by safeguarding or rebuilding their reputation for transparency, integrity and social engagement. Second, more and more employees appreciate working for a socially responsible company, which makes CSR an important aspect for Human Resources. Philanthropy is the third reason for companies to invest in socially responsible activities. Fourth, corporate responsibility may appeal to consumers and in that way contribute to profits.

Partnerships with the different segments of society are one way for companies to show their Corporate Social Responsibility (CSR). Currently, more and more companies start a dialogue with civil society, by inviting NGOs, governments etc. to discuss their operations in terms of their contribution to society.

In Europe, Norway and Sweden have always been well known for their global commitment, which shows from their high level of development aid and by their companies' interest in CSR. 'An estimated 95 per cent of all Norwegian SMEs with between 50–249 employees are involved in social activities making Norwegian's SMEs of this size the most socially responsible in Europe' (Campaign report on European CSR excellence, 2002–2003).[3] The House of Representatives of Belgium passed a law in January 2002 aimed at promoting socially responsible production. This law enabled a multi-stakeholder committee, which reviews social audits of companies in order to determine whether their products can get a Social Label. This label guarantees that the product is not manufactured by forced or child labour, and that the workers are protected against discrimination and have the right to organize collectively. The UK passed the Pensions Act amendment in this same year. This amendment has made it mandatory for all pension funds to disclose whether they take into account ethical, environmental and social considerations when making investment decisions.

At the national levels of developed countries, CSR has started to lift off. Nevertheless, at a global level CSR is not yet integrated or even fully accepted. International laws are not yet in place to protect developing countries from the possible bad practices of MNEs, even though progress has been made with the OECD agreement to combat the corruption induced by MNEs in developing countries.

8.5 Supporting Civil Society

There are several ways in which the World Bank can (and does) support the development of civil society, in order to reach the desired balance between the multilateral institutions, government and civil society. This can be direct support, by giving civil society a concrete voice in the policy and decision-making of the World Bank, or indirect support by policies on topics such as CSR.

In June 2003, the World Bank had a meeting with the external advisory committee on the Bank's New Practices in Civic Engagement, Empowerment and Respect for Diversity (CEERD). Managing Director Mamphela Ramphele noted that the Bank has become wiser about the importance of ownership, capacity building and partnerships in development. 'We have a role to play in helping governments create an enabling environment for civic engagement, so that ordinary citizens can really feel ownership.' In order to reach this goal Mrs Ramphele refers to the need for support from the World Bank's different partners in the field of development assistance. However, another important precondition for the World Bank to realize this goal is to increase their external communication in order to create a knowledge transfer from the Bank, not only to the different governments, but also to the public, the young in particular. Applying more active external communication means to approach the young and the rest of the public actively, instead of waiting for them to ask for information.

In 2003 the World Bank took the initiative during the run-up to the G8 Summit in Evian (where the Millennium Development Goals were discussed) to collaborate with CNN International on three 30-second informational vignettes. These conveyed the message that universal primary education is critical for poverty reduction. The spots were broadcast on CNN International in Europe, Africa, South Asia and Latin America, reaching a potential audience of more than 500 million households.

In addition, the World Bank put a link on its web site for young people which explains the development topics and news in easily understandable terms. Moreover, in initiatives such as Youth Groups Speak Up, children are asked to give their opinion in forums. An example is the strategy on children and youth that is being written by the World Bank to make sure that its development projects reach and benefit young people as much as possible. With a draft of the strategy written, the Bank has invited young people from around the world to participate in on-line discussions to share their views and give comments on the draft.

When it comes to congresses and the representation of countries by young people, the World Bank only refers to youth organizations that organize youth congresses and meetings, such as the Global Youth Parliament, instead of organizing these themselves. These congresses or meetings could be organized parallel to the official World Bank agenda and should be accessible to the youth of all involved countries and for young people from different 'social levels' and backgrounds in education. Using youth ambassadors whose function is to relate to the different members of civil society and the World Bank is another possibility. These are two ways in which the youth World Bank organization could invest in public awareness and future relationships. Examples such as commercials or the publishing of the World Development Report increase the public knowledge about development issues. Initiatives such as these should be used more extensively in order to change the current inaccessible character of the World Bank, and to develop the public knowledge on development issues in order to create a stronger civil society and to formulate representative development policies.

PART IV

A PROSPECT FOR DEVELOPMENT COOPERATION.
A CHANCE FOR THE WORLD BANK?

9

Successes and Failures

Is 60 years of development assistance enough? This question is a paraphrase of a statement made in 1994 by the campaign '50 years is enough' (see www.globaljusticeecology.org). We mentioned in the introduction to chapter 5 a strong message of this campaign: we (the rich countries) need to do more, but we also need to follow out different ways of committing ourselves to development assistance, now that we have failed to achieve the substantial poverty reduction we had expected in the past 50 years.

The campaign focused on the huge levels of debt (in relation to gross domestic product), which suffocated development in many of the poorer and very poor countries. There was strong and widespread support for the campaign, engendered in particular by the organization Jubilee 2000 (www.jubilee2000.org). Its tireless leader Ann Pettifor managed to create a broad coalition for debt relief with such unlikely alliances as Puff Daddy and the Pope, Jesse Helms and Bono, the Sisters of the Sacred Heart and the Spice Girls.

July 2004 marks the 60th anniversary of the Bretton Woods meetings which led to the birth of the World Bank. It is time to take stock once again and to notice that in the past 10 years on the one hand much has changed for the good, and yet on the other hand there is an urgent need for further and more radical change in development assistance. I am not suggesting such radical changes as an experiment. Rather, they are the translation and implementation of the lessons we learned in development cooperation during the 1990s. The early years of the new century have shown too little, too late, in terms of implementation of what we know to be the right course. In particular '9/11' seems to have halted the process of the desperately needed transition of development assistance.

This chapter deals with the lessons learned in the 1990s. Debt – the rallying point of the campaign '50 years is enough' – has been relieved in many of the poorer countries, but debt relief turned out only to be effective development assistance under circumstances of government ownership of policies which are internationally known as 'good practice'. Also, debt has so far been relieved 'too little, too late'.

Section 9.1 touches on this point as the main element of effective development assistance: government ownership for poverty reduction. Ownership is not just a matter of lofty statements, but implies the demonstrated willingness to commit to the difficult political processes which are a sequel to such ownership, like keeping inflation low or fighting corruption. 'Focused aid' is the expression of the World Bank, which means: bring development assistance to the places where it works, where it is used properly and does not leak away. Craig Burnside and David Dollar[1] see in this the main reason why development assistance in the 1990s has become much more effective than in the 1970s and 1980s. Their analysis carries a lot of conviction. It also makes a lot of sense.

Yet focusing is not as easy as it sounds (Section 9.2). We need transparent criteria for focus, based on measures of good governance. At the same time, focusing raises the important question of the development interaction of rich countries with those poor countries that are 'out of focus' and would not receive development aid under the criteria of good governance. These countries cannot be helped yet financially, because they are at war, suffer from civil strife, or are peaceful but with a corrupt government. To put it more generally: these are those countries that cannot or do not want to commit to ownership for 'good practice'.

Debt relief can be a form of effective development assistance, if it is focused in the same way as regular financial assistance. The case for debt relief as the preferred alternative above project or program financing can be made with conviction by comparing the transaction costs of a one-time debt reduction with a stream of annual development financing of the same size (Section 9.3). There is ample evidence that the level of debt relief has been too low.

Among the failures of development assistance in the 1990s and early 2000s should be reckoned first of all the inability of the donor community to follow up on the notion of focus (Section 9.4). Second, the development assistance community has failed to sufficiently embody the lesson that its main goal is to 'create capacity', to increase the room for manoeuvre for governments of developing countries 'to do the right thing'. It still has to apply the lesson that development can only come from 'within'. Third, the dialogue of development assistance, which needs to be culturally sensitive towards the developing country, is in general still donor driven, without much knowledge and understanding on the donor's side of the local situation. Decentralization of development cooperation away from the rich countries and towards the developing countries is what is needed. In summary, the new development paradigm described in the introduction to Chapter 4 has only half-heartedly been implemented.

A major failure is the lack of harmonization and coordination of the development assistance community (Section 9.5). It is a glass not nearly half full. Even in 'examplary' countries like Uganda the glass is more than half empty. Also, despite the Monterrey Consensus, the rich world failed in translating its stated generosity into an actual freeing up of money for poor countries – even going against its own long-term interests.

Three other failures of the 1990s have been mentioned before and will not be repeated in this chapter:

- Government ownership and good governance have been heavily affected by 'induced' corruption. The 'inducement' came from multi-national enterprises and is – as yet – insufficiently put in check through the OECD convention or UN actions.
- The trade playing field is not level and heavily disadvantages developing countries.
- There is insufficient ownership among committed (young) people in rich countries for effective development cooperation.

These points are absolutely not new or shocking. They are widely recognized. For example, in the Annual Review of Development Effectiveness (ARDE) of the World Bank's OED of 2002 (called 'Achieving Development Outcomes, the Millennium Challenge') a similar conclusion is drawn. This report concludes that the World Bank needs to be clearer in the definition of the objectives and targets of the Country Programs, in order to reach the Millennium Development Goals. In addition: 'The Bank must move from recognizing the multisectoral determinants of development outcomes to developing and implementing cross-sectoral strategies. And the Bank must further clarify and rationalize its role in global programs. Above all, the Bank needs to more fully – and urgently – assess the implications of the MDGs at the corporate, country, sector, and global levels, and address these implications in its use of lending and administrative resources.' This evaluation reveals the low speed of transition from the old paradigm to the new.

The analysis and discussion of this chapter are the stepping-stones for the next: a platform for radical change.

9.1 OWNERSHIP AND FOCUSED AID AS A SUCCESS

Developing countries themselves will always be the major force in development. That has been a truism since the early days of development cooperation. If one only looks at the size of development assistance in relation to the GDP of developing countries (on average 1 per cent) then one realizes immediately that the tail cannot wag the dog.

Development assistance of a serious size will only 'work' if the country truly is engaged in pursuing sustainable poverty reduction, if there is country ownership for development. Country ownership means that there is a strong will in the country to overcome the difficulties involved in creating better governance, better institutions and to pursue – against the vested interests – policies which have proven to be 'good practice'. But then – as might be the reaction – are there not countries where such country ownership for sustainable poverty reduction strategies is absent or by and large lacking? Unfortunately, the answer is yes. In Chapter 3 we presented Lant Pritchett's analysis of divergence in the world as the result of an overwhelming 'first mover' effect of rich countries, which have their institutions and governance reasonably well in place, taking precedence over the 'initial income' effect (it is easier to develop when you are less well off). This analysis is an expression of the unfavourable conditions for development in the institutions and governance of the countries concerned. It is also a result of civic conflicts and failing governments in quite a few of the very poor countries (see Section 3.5).

Focusing donor aid has been the key to success of the development effectiveness in the 1990s. When aid goes to countries without good governance, the money may end up in the wrong place, or may not be used effectively in the right places, because of leakages. But then, one should realize that the 1970s and 1980s were characterized by development cooperation that did not depart first and foremost from effectiveness, but was rather under the sway of the political dimension, used to buy friends. I still remember vividly the huge amounts that went from the Dutch taxpayer to Sudan to support the balance of payments (even as late as the early 1990s). And the Dutch were not the exception; they rather conformed to a rule.

Focusing has been (and should be) very much aligned with general budget support. Only recently has the dimension of specific sector support (or specific budget support) in education and health been 'discovered'. A country like Gambia might not do very well overall on governance, but it turns out to have a remarkable absorption capacity in education. In education, additional donor aid might help Gambia to reach universal primary education much faster than when the country was left to the old ways of development cooperation.

A lack of focus is not the only problem. There is also a lack of commitment to the financing of sustained or long-term recurrent expenditures in the countries in focus. Donors will have to give up one of their pet constraints on aid if they want to be effective with focused aid. One such as pet constraint is the adherence to capital spending, while recurring spending is seen as a sin: they like to donate just once and for all (often to come back next year and do the same). In education, donors have had a tremendous preference for the one-time financing of buildings and equipment. They must have realized that this was odd: to provide education you first and foremost need teachers; that is as true in Gambia as it is in Switzerland. Developing countries do not lack schools, but they lack the money to buy the full package.

Of course, donors are wary about being drawn into a sector in a country for what may seem like a long time. At the same time, there is no alternative. Reaching the MDGs is only possible by a long-run commitment. Debt relief may come in at this point as a nice form of 'recurrent financing': debt relief offers the country the chance to free up resources for recurrent financing.

At the front of creating more leeway for recurrent financing, there is now some progress with donors being more inclined (as the Development Committee of October 2002 showed) to engage in the financing of recurring expenditures.

Financing recurrent expenditures for a specific sector does raise the general point of the fungibility of money. Extra financing from donors for education might end up being used for extra purchases of weapons, if the country reduces its own overall spending on education in the presence of donor money and uses the freed up resources for weapons. Fungibility is a reality one has to be aware of. Such an awareness can be expressed for specific sector support, by putting it in the context of an overall agreement with the country on its spending (also on other sectors). The PRSP provides such a framework.

There is still a world to be gained by an increased focusing of aid. There is also a world to be lost if the rich countries revert to past bad practices and start buying friendship in the war against Muslim fundamentalism with ODA, ignoring the criteria for focus.

The foregoing argument may seem to imply that one can easily distinguish between countries for focus and not-for-focus. This is absolutely not the case, as will be exemplified in Section 9.2.

We are starkly aware of the criticism that focusing may mean that the most needy people will be bypassed. The most needy people may be in the least well-governed countries. In the World Bank this has been debated under the 'code word' LICUS (low-income countries under stress). Is it possible to develop an alternative approach for such countries? Yes it is, and it is important. But it is an illusion to believe that development assistance would be equally effective in LICUS countries as in countries with good governance and country ownership. An alternative approach aimed at breaking the governance deadlock is needed in order to provide the stepping-stone for more and better assistance. Such an alternative approach has to start by immobilizing the factors that contribute to the governance failure.[2] Chapter 3 provided an overview of the international factors that cause wars and civil conflicts. For each separate case, a separate approach is needed to create an environment in which there is no chance for opposing groups to buy weapons through embargos, through consumer 'strikes' (like for the 'blood diamonds' harvested by Taylor in Sierra Leone and used to buy weapons for rebels) or through diplomacy (for example, Georgia needs diplomacy to reduce the pressure of the Russian-supported rebels in Abkhazia).

9.2 CLARIFYING OWNERSHIP AND GOVERNANCE

Nowadays the World Bank, as well as many bilaterals, has engaged in country 'selectivity' in order to be effective in development cooperation. Over the years, the World Bank has developed an index for governance: the CPIA (Country Policy Institutional Assessment). This index is based on the World Bank's assessment of 24 parameters of a country's governance. Interestingly enough, there turns out to be a high correlation between the many different indicators of the governance of a country and the corruption index of Transparency International.[3] The CPIA is used to distinguish between countries where budget support works because of good governance and where projects (sometimes of only a limited scale) may be the only way forward, because of limited governance or abundant corruption.

Let us be clear that the selection of countries 'with' or 'without' good governance is by no means a simple, technical step. It involves substantial further analysis, because the indicators will hardly ever be at the extremes ('good' or 'very bad'), but rather will be somewhere in between. Hence, donors have to focus on trends in the indicators over time, so that they can support the countries that are on the right track. An example of the difficulty of assessing the readiness of a country for (increased) donor aid is given in Box 9.1 for the education sector. The Netherlands is one of the bilaterals, which has engaged in country selectivity based on good governance. In his article 'Taking a close look on Herfkens' selectivity policy', Dirk-Jan Koch describes the appropriateness and effectiveness of country selectivity of Dutch development aid.[4] Koch shows that the selection process in the Netherlands has not always been free from political bias. In one quarter of the cases, the selection of the countries proved to be based on previous relationships and old colonial ties instead of good governance and a high poverty rate. In all the other cases these historical relationships or ties also proved to be of some importance. Koch proposes that the criteria should be applied in a more transparent manner and that donor governments should stimulate the leaders' ownership of development, as well as better coordination and harmonization among the different donors. According to Koch, one way to increase the ownership of the leaders is the common pool approach. This means that all developing countries can apply in a tender by handing in detailed development plans, which allows country ownership since it allows governments to plan and use the money in their own way.

The two latter suggestions cannot be anything but supported. It is of the utmost importance that the World Bank makes the CPIA ratings public and that an international agreement is reached on the criteria for focus in relation to criteria for the PRSP (Koch's detailed development plan).

Box 9.1: Nigeria's Ownership of Education Reform

If Nigeria were to be chosen in 2002 to be one of the 'fast-track countries' in the World Bank drive for Education For All (EFA), it would receive all the external financial support it needs to get all children in quality schools. Quality means that the children stay in school and do not leave before they can read and write and can do some 'numbers.' With 125 million inhabitants, Nigeria is Africa's most populous nation. It is also Africa's top oil exporter. But 90 per cent of its people still struggle to make ends meet, trying to survive on a per capita income of perhaps $200 per annum.

Nigeria certainly needs to boost its education performance. According to the Education For All 2000 assessment, education statistics for 1996 show that only 14.1 million children out of the 21 million children of school-going age are enrolled in primary schools. The completion rate was 64 per cent while the rate of transition to junior secondary school was 43.5 per cent. There is overwhelming evidence that these vital literacy indicators have not improved in the 1990s.

The President, Obasanjo, is devoted to poverty reduction in general and to better education in particular. The President is strongly supported by Clare Short, the UK minister of development, who sent a letter to Jim Wolfensohn, the President of the World Bank, more or less demanding that Nigeria should be part of the fast track.

However, there are firm and strong criteria for admission to the fast track, with the main question being whether the country does everything in its own power to ensure quality education, like ensuring attendance of and reasonable pay for teachers, or more generally spending enough national funds on education. The President's position may be a breath of fresh air, but needs to be followed up by concrete action in Nigeria.

Clare Short and Obasanjo agree that their case for better education in Nigeria would be substantially enhanced if the UNESCO 'High Level Meeting on Education for All' were to be held in Abuja, Nigeria's capital, in November 2002. This is the annual meeting of leaders of international organizations involved in education, as well as ministers of education and ministers of development of donor countries.

However, President Obasanjo turns out to be – at this time – a lone rider in the night. The international consensus on education has not yet permeated much of Nigeria's government. Government accountability falls short and the political focus on managing the economy and the budget remain too short-term and will likely become increasingly so as the national elections in the spring of 2003 are rapidly approaching.

The UNESCO meeting fizzles out. The representation of donor countries is virtually nil (with most notably Clare Short absent). Moreover, it takes place amidst the fighting between Christians and Muslims over the beauty pageant close to, and in, Abuja.

Still, President Obasanjo needs all the support the international community can give, because he is considered to be a voice for the future, for better living conditions, even if he is only 'hanging in there'. It was to be expected that his transition from jail in 1998 (he was jailed by the late military dictator General Sani Abacha in 1995 on charges of plotting a coup along with 43 other soldiers and civilians) to his presidency starting in 1999, would not be smooth. He lacks the active network which could bring together a strong team to support him. The hope is (in 2002) that the elections of 2003 (which Obasanjo won easily) provide a stronger mandate and platform for him to lead his country out of its development impasse.

This assumes that he is the right person to turn around the impasse in his country and that accusations of abuse of power and misappropriation of public funds by parliamentarians from his own party are false.

Aside from governance issues Nigeria has been plagued by communal and religious conflict across the country. It is estimated that well over 10,000 people have lost their lives since 1999, which is an increase since the military era.

Poverty in Nigeria is huge, and yet foreign aid money is not the solution; rather, it is the will of the élite to rally around a common perspective of good governance. This means that the international community can help by being involved, by helping Nigerians analyse and find ways out of the impasse.

This also becomes the deal with the 'fast-track initiative.' It is not money, but analytical support on the level of the states to develop and implement sound educational plans, or some money to build capacity to 'run' an education system, which is needed.

Here, the World Bank, like other donors, gets into trouble with a fine balance. In some countries, like Nigeria, extra money might not help, but would rather delay the development process, because it fuels an old system of bad policies. Yet, to remain involved – which indeed is essential – money may need to flow. That would be fine, if it were used for capacity creation or pilot projects. However, the case that the money indeed contributes to capacity or that the country will learn from the pilots needs to be made convincingly. All too often, pilots are just islands of excellence, accidents or incidents without any further impact, while 'capacity' creation is often not found in evaluations of projects. And often, as in Nigeria, remaining involved means that donor money flows to infrastructure.

At first sight this may seem the right approach, because we know that in poorer countries the infrastructure is indeed desperately lacking or in a desperate state.[5] Laying a road, putting up a few buildings for markets and stores and enterprises can kick-start an upward development spiral. Yet this should come from within, and not with the big bucks from outside, with big bulldozers and machines to lay tarmac. Also, there needs to be a clear indication of a strong commitment of the leadership of the country to good governance of the infrastructure and for a corruption-free approach to investing in infrastructure. To focus on the latter: infrastructure is – as also in the developed world – a sector which is easily fraught with corruption. It should be the last sector to get involved in, in a country with a shaky governance.

So while donor or World Bank support for infrastructure may seem the right approach 'to remain involved', it might on second thoughts turn out to be the least preferred option. Investing in infrastructure (the traditional ballpark of the World Bank) might be counterproductive for development.

The lesson here is to watch the soil carefully. Sowing on rocks will not be fruitful. Only when the leadership of the country is dedicated to (and effective in) improving governance and policies, can development be spurred with the support of donor money. Such a conclusion may leave the development community in disarray. It might respond by stating: 'But we should help the poorest people.' Indeed, the humanitarian line is important. Yet, one should make sure that such direct aid is not to the detriment of long-term development by keeping corrupt systems in place, corrupt politicians in office or 'bad' policies unchanged. Moreover, the applied selectivity of countries should truly be based on good governance and development needs, instead of being based on the 'buying of friendships' or on old colonial ties.

Governance and leadership go hand in hand. Box 9.2 exemplifies this for the case of HIV/AIDS in Burkina Faso.

9.3 DEBT RELIEF: A SMALL STEP

There has been a strong urge for 'debt relief' in the past decade from the passionate believers in bridging the divide between the poor and the rich, who were angered when they realized that the flows from rich to poor countries became negative, in other words that the poor were financing the rich. The debt activists were effective. Debts have been reduced and debt relief has been effective as well. It was also long overdue when in 1999 the G–7 drew up the Cologne Agreement, limiting repayments on debt to a maximum payback of 150 per cent of export earnings. Not only did Jubilee 2000, which advocated so strongly for debt relief, get its day in court, it got a concrete result. For the

Box 9.2: The Battle Against HIV/AIDS in Burkina Faso

How does one communicate about HIV/AIDS if people cannot read, if there are no phones, if there is hardly TV? Traditional meeting places might help. In a cascade approach the government became active in training the trainees to train the dolotieres about what causes HIV/AIDS and what does not. Dolotieres are the local (female) beer brewers and bar tenders: the centre of the village's social life. It is frightening to hear from them how many misconceptions exist, like: HIV/AIDS is the result of eating a certain root; it is transmitted, like malaria, through a mosquito; it is just another illness you can catch, like the flu. In the meantime, infection rates are quickly rising, not least because of the migration of so-called Burkinabé-men to Côte d'Ivoire to work as migrant labour, to come back to visit their wives once or twice a year with a good chance of bringing the killer disease along.

On November 6, 2001, the government celebrates the launch of its campaign against HIV/AIDS. It is difficult to get into the hall because of the crowd and of the limousines. All the ministers will be there. The ambassadors of most of the countries represented in the country are there. The waiting is for the President. He is a formidable man in stature and in politics, an ex-military man who runs the ship sometimes too tightly - so that a critical journalist recently disappeared - but who has also brought stability and a substantial improvement of living conditions to Burkina.

The World Bank has invested substantially in the dialogue with Burkina on HIV/AIDS with Mirjam Schneidman in the lead. As an active task-team leader, she uses every opportunity to bring in people from other countries to pound the government on its responsibility, showing what could be accomplished elsewhere (like in Senegal or Uganda) in keeping infection levels on a low level or reducing infection levels, and showing what will happen if the government does not substantially ratchet up its involvement. The World Bank itself has been learning as well, from experiences in other countries. Initially the World Bank approach to HIV/AIDS in Burkina was severely criticized, because it did not involve the health system as a whole. In a later stage, this was amended. While the fight against HIV/AIDS has to be fought on the fronts of all sectors, the health sector itself plays a crucial role.

Condom use is the point, in a society where men are not particularly fond of using condoms – to say the least. Only with good examples and leadership can these reservations be overcome.

In the meeting hall the drums have halted and the dancers are now still. The President speaks. Jokingly, he bashes the minister of health for his laxity. But he also brings out the c-word (for condom) as part of the 'mobilisation totale'. The whole hall has got the message. The government is serious about fighting AIDS. He is quite clear about the bottlenecks: information, knowledge, difficulties in getting HIV/AIDS tests done (and the costs of these test which could be $1 but often are closer to $5), the availability of the tests and the costs of anti-retrovirals.

The dialogue on AIDS was a particularly difficult one, because it took place in the general context of better governance, and the respect for human rights. In this context the line of connection is quite thin. The Bank's support for the fight against AIDS should not weaken its position on human rights and on corruption.

When the drums and the dancing resume I feel that the dialogue has had another success.

World Bank it became much easier to pursue the Highly Indebted Poor Countries initiative (see Section 3.3), which led to a substantial reduction of the government debt of poor countries, and which had engaged in clarifying how the lower level of government expenditures would benefit the poor. Such a clarification had to be laid down in a Poverty Reduction Strategy Paper (PRSP), a substantial document, demanding a time-consuming preparation process. An interim PRSP (a short-cut for a PRSP, without much consultation and thorough analysis) might suffice to be eligible for debt relief, in order to speed up the process.

Should the money for development cooperation (which – as the saying goes – can only be spent once) be further allocated for debt relief or for specific projects or programs through budget support or specific financing of these programs or projects? Focus (in terms of the country concerned and maybe the sector concerned) is important for effectiveness. Focus should be derived from Government ownership and 'good governance'. Once focus is established, then the financing of programs or projects through debt relief becomes a very interesting option. For example, good education plans could get external financing through increased debt relief, rather than recurring donor support. In other words: debt relief should be viewed as a financing form of development cooperation, not as an issue in itself.

Debt relief can be far more efficient as a form of financing-focused development assistance than as usual, annual financing through budget support or specific project or program financing. The transaction costs are much lower. A major obstacle in the way is the practice on the donors' side. The World Bank, for example, cannot 'just forgive' debt, without compensation by other donors. In their turn, donors want to see their money earmarked for 'new endeavours', often not realizing or not willing to defend in their parliaments that debt relief can also lead to such 'new endeavours', albeit without the opportunities for flag planting. In other words: there is major room for far more debt relief, even within the present confines of the total budget for development assistance.

Debt relief as an expansion of development aid is then no longer a question. An expansion of aid is long overdue and debt relief will be part – as a form of focused financing – of its allocation.

9.4 Old Fashioned 'Advisory' as a Failure

The corollary to effectiveness based on government ownership and good governance is that development assistance should aim at creating room for manoeuvre for countries, should be attuned to the culture of the country, should be in a listening mode and ought to be wary of supply-driven technical assistance. As the WDR 2000 states:[6]

> Turning more responsibility over to recipient countries for designing national development strategies and leading consultation meetings will require rapid capacity development. Recipient countries will also need strong auditing and accounting skills if donors are to relinquish monitoring and control of projects. But technical assistance, the obvious choice for building capacity, has a spotty record at best, particularly in countries where capacity is already weak. The main reason is that it has often not been demand driven – it has often been tied aid and designed to develop capacity only in donor-supported activities. Instead, technical assistance should be incorporated into a national strategy and expenditure plan, with the recipient government deciding what assistance it needs and who should provide it. This is likely to require initial support to countries on how to use the market for technical assistance.

Effective development assistance is not only determined by the policies, but also by the culture of those who bring these policies into practice. The World Bank has a strong culture, which can both stimulate as well as prevent the effective implementation of development policies. Some of the basic requirements for World Bankers are to be able to listen and observe and to judge only after careful listening and observation. They should seek open communication and in particular aim at increasing the room for manoeuvre of their counterparts. Careful listening is imperative for the World Banker as is illustrated in Box 9.3. At the same time, the Bank has to come to a judgement over whether the country deserves support, and if so, what the support should be for. In this respect the new development paradigm makes the work of professionals in development cooperation not easier, but harder. There are no simple rules (like in the Washington Consensus) to work by.

Box 9.3: *Listening and Observing in Yemen*

Minister Sofan of Yemen is an outspoken as well as a very powerful person. At lunch (in 2001) with seven cabinet ministers, there was a virtual subservience of the other six to Minister Sofan. They asked him whether they could speak, praised him for his leadership and laughed outrageously even the dullest of his jokes. Still, he has helped to manage the country well.

The World Bank has been a good listener and did not push the agenda of policy improvement beyond the room for manoeuvre of the country's leadership. For example, there is the water agenda. Water is very scarce in Yemen. Poor people at the outskirts of Sana'a may have to pay as much as US $0.40 a gallon, while the rich in the centre have free water. Gradually, the government has engaged in a discussion on water with its constituents, realizing that while water is scarce for the existing 16 million Yemenis, it will be too scarce for the 60 million Yemenis in 2050.

At our dinner, Minister Sofan tries to escape critique on the lack of economic progress and the lack of policies to vigorously promote employment, with a quip. 'You know,' he says with a wink, 'we are the best producers and exporters of people.' Gianni Brizi, the resident representative of the World Bank and a highly effective and committed staff member does not take the bait: 'That, Your Excellency, is hardly a comparative advantage of Yemen. And unskilled labour is not in great demand as an import product.'

Indeed, Yemen does 'export' people. Many Yemenis work abroad, in other Arab countries like Saudi Arabia, with often little security (most of them were sent back when Yemen supported Iraq in the 1991 Gulf War) and in dismal working conditions. Yet remittances are a major boon for the economy. Remittances, foreign aid and oil revenue amount to as much as 10 per cent each of Yemen's GDP: in itself an excellent basis for fast development.

The main topic of the evening is the need for FDI in Yemen. For that purpose, Gianni has invited the two main industrialists of Yemen, Abdussalam A. Al-Athwari, General Manager of the Association of Yemeni Industrialists, and Abdul Jalil Tabed. Among the guests, there is full agreement that at this stage of development, Yemen needs to see the emergence of a class of small and larger entrepreneurs. For me, this was vividly illustrated in Ibb, a city with more than 200,000 people without any industrial activity. Small industries are absent. There is not even a garage in sight. Everything is imported. When a house is built, the stone, wood and labour are from Yemen; the rest is all imported, including the nails in the wood, the metalwork for locks and door hinges. It is called the Dutch disease: too much money coming from 'easy' sources, like remittances, foreign aid and oil, and not enough incentives to work hard and earn a living on their own. The advantages for rapid development seem to have turned upside down.

The industrialists quickly take the opportunity to attack poor Minister Sofan. One says:'I have not invested a single penny in

Yemen, although I love the country. My investments are in Oman, where I have a reliable tax collector and reliable costs for utilities and capital.' He adds: 'and you should subsidize us.'

Gianni has organized this brilliantly. There will be no effective foreign investment if national savings flee the country, in search of better investment opportunities, if there is no good investment climate. The minister will not acknowledge this on the spot, but does ask about ways and means in which the international community can help to establish a better investment climate.

The World Bank has increasingly recognized that homegrown analysis and policy advice is most effective. That is also the reason for me to be in Yemen, as Vice President for Development Policy in the Development Economics Department of the Bank. The Bank attempts to help the Yemeni government to set up an independent

Box 9.4: Room for Manoeuvre in Poland

The country director for Poland and the Baltic States, Basil Kavalsky, puts it squarely on February 23, 1999: 'We cannot work with this minister of education [this is minister Handke]. He has no confidence whatsoever from the ministry of finance. As soon as he starts to speak, his colleague Ners, the deputy minister responsible for loans with the World Bank, who sits most of the time next to Handke in Polish World Bank discussions, will turn to the other side, away from Handke, to start a conversation with his neighbour.'

What Basil says reflects accurately what I saw happening the other day.

How could things have come this far with the brilliant minister Handke, with whom I got acquainted three years before when I was myself minister of education in the Netherlands – as a leader in thinking about the transformation of Soviet-style education to modern education? And what was the role of the World Bank, if any, in his political downfall?

A downfall it was. Already in February 1999 Handke's position was shaky at best. Rumours were that he would be replaced as early as April. Handke himself seemed to indicate that he felt that his days as a cabinet minister were over.

Minister Handke presented his ideas on the transition in education to a forum of education ministers from the EU, Central and Eastern Europe, at a meeting in Warsaw in 1997. We were all impressed. There were notions here which would indeed make a difference. Poland has a strong educational tradition, but still ranks – with other traditional education giants like Russia and Hungary – well below the top achievers like Japan, Finland, Canada or the UK (data from the Project on International Student Assessment for the performance of 15-year-olds).

As always, education reform (I use the Bank word reform) ends up in the wrangle with the finance ministers. Poland is not an exception to this rule. And here, in this wrangle, Minister Handke lost his ground.

Ministers of finance are amply supplied by their civil servants with material to enforce greater efficiency in schools. Cut the teachers' salaries, cut the benefits at work or retirement, increase the workload, whether by class size directly or, more indirectly, by closing down small schools. Ministers of education resist and resent these 'attacks' of the stern efficiency thinkers. They are aware of the unrest and turmoil which such efficiency measures bring. But they need to have the ministers of finance on their side to finance the new programs which can help modernize education, to improve quality. There is a narrow bridge then, which the two can build between efficiency and quality. It involves seeking the room for manoeuvre for efficiency. That is, efficiency increases brought about with a human face.

The Polish discussion got stuck on the efficiency side of the divide. Polish schools are on average very small and have become substantially smaller in the past decade due to the fall in the birth rate, which is a common phenomenon in European countries. Schools experienced a decrease in enrolment of more than 20 per cent in the 1990s. The number of teachers per school has remained the same, leading to a substantial decrease in the number of students per teacher. 'Inefficiency' this was called by the minister of finance, and the minister of education replied, 'All right – we'll take that route and will then move to the quality discussion.' But that turned out to be idle thinking. The minister got stuck in the implementation of the move to close smaller schools. That move was the – quite naïve – translation of the agreement by the minister of finance: closing all smaller schools. Of course, rural areas went into a frenzy when they saw that the only school in their area would be closed. People are attached to a school nearby for more than the education of their children. Yet, when the minister realized that his move was too technocratic it was already too late. He was bogged down in the only education debate in Poland in 1999: to close or not to close. No one remembered the old days of the call for education improvements. Those ideas and plans had been blown away like the morning mist.

At the same time, the dialogue in development assistance should aim at increasing the room for manoeuvre for the government to 'do the right thing', as Box 9.4 explains.

Was there room for manoeuvre in Poland? With hindsight one should conclude that indeed there was far more room for manoeuvre, if the cultural reality of Poland had been taken into account. This reality is that schools in small villages are considered close to sacred. They also stand for the presence of teachers in the village, which contribute in many more ways to social and cultural life in the village than just through the school. This is not only felt in

Poland, but in many other countries as well. And Poland might have learned from the way in which other countries dealt with the closing of small schools, where the small schools in the sparsely populated countryside were explicitly saved. There was, for example, the experience of the Netherlands where small schools were closed with the motto: 'bigger if possible, small if needed' and the sparsely populated countryside kept its very small schools. The efficiency policy in the Netherlands also included a bridge between the financial proceeds of closing small schools and the use of money for quality improvements, helping also to bridge the political gap.

In Poland it was not the fault of the World Bank that the case of the efficiency improvement in education (by means of closing many small schools) was lost. The World Bank task team leader in charge of education at that time was Tom Hoopengardner. He was conscious of the cultural dimension and the political economy of educational reform, carefully avoiding the term 'reform' in discussions. This approach was in sharp contrast to the technocratic side of the Bank. Bank staff would generally use the term 'educational reform' when speaking about educational change (in the way this is also done in academia). Politically, the term 'reform' is deadly. People like 'evolution', 'improvement', 'modernization', 'transition', but not 'reform', which implies for many people that the old habits were bad and new ones have to be learned.

Augmenting a government's room for manoeuvre is strongly intertwined with listening, and with sensitivity to cultural differences: a main element of the new development paradigm (see Chapter 4). The difficulties in applying cultural sensitivity are obvious. Cultural sensitivity does not preclude change. Culture is not identical to the existing organization of society.[7] An example is the dialogue of the World Bank with the Moroccan Government on primary education. The listening Bank hears (and reads) in the Moroccan monthly (in French) *Pedagogical Problems* that 'culture should not be reduced to merchandise' (Nov. 2002, pp. 21–3). The article alleges that, while in the past great nations would impose their culture, their technology and their values through the intermediary of their military and their missionaries, they do so now through development cooperation. The World Bank is highlighted as one of these 'cultural imperialists' (the word is not used, but very much implied). The article goes on to plead for a cultural diversity, for a true meeting of cultures.

Why this quotation? Because in the same issue, we encounter what the writers mean by culture. We read of the resistance of a number of Moroccan educational organizations against the proposals of the Royal Commission on Education, the COSEF (Commission Spéciale d'Education-Formation). Their point of resistance is formulated in the introduction: 'The insistence of the representatives of the World Bank in Morocco on privatizing education in our country, shows that proponents of free markets at the international level and the pupils of the laissez-faire economics of our governments put our public school in the limelight of the merchants and seek to transform education into merchandise.'

The circle is closed. It is the projection of culture as the figleaf for the protection of a system which has kept illiteracy at more than 50 per cent for more than 40 years, 2 to 3 times higher than that in Tunisia or Egypt. And where is privatization proposed in the COSEF proposals? There are no proposals for the privatization of existing schools. Rather, the reports express that new schools should be community driven and community owned, presumably with salary scales (far) below those of the government's official scale.

Culture is one of the most elusive concepts for the World Banker, who is often trained as a top professional at an American or English University. And, as a result, the Bank often simply fails in being a good dialogue partner. Dialogue in a multicultural environment requires more than the analytical skills of a top economist. Listening means: to be able to understand what is transmitted, both in its overt and its hidden elements. Dialogue means to help to create a climate of understanding and to build on mutual reinforcement. Knowing about the main traits of a country and the things that many people in it cherish makes a conversation so much easier and lighter. Quoting Nagib Mahfouz, the famous Egyptian Nobel Prize Winner for Literature, opens the hearts of many Egyptian counterparts. Not knowing the profuse use of poems in Yemen is a hindrance.

There are other serious questions about culture and competitiveness which the World Banker should be aware of. The simple assumption that competition works exactly the same, whether it is in the US, in Europe or in Africa, does injustice to the different ways in which people relate to each other. Some civilizations may be more geared to value loyalty and family above honesty and trust outside the smaller circle. The pressures of globalization on these civilizations are tremendous, as they find it hard to combine the old value system with the norms of worldwide competition.

Culture does play a role in the fight against HIV/AIDS. HIV/AIDS may be one of the greatest threats to development in many countries. The epidemic is still on the rise with only a few countries finding a solid answer and a great many still in the state of denial. For example, in India, in February 2002, I received an extensive briefing by the Indian Government official in charge of the fight against HIV/AIDS. Prime Minister Atal Bihari Vajpayee had made a significant speech on the threat of the epidemic on the country's Independence Day in 2000, which gave hope for an active fight against HIV/AIDS. However, since then it has remained quiet. The briefing explains why: 'It is under control'. Here speaks a very well educated, wise person with commitment and engagement, completely ignoring the fact that the epidemic is on the rise virtually everywhere in India and that the decrease in infection rates somewhere down the line in 2004 or 2005, projected in the briefing of the official, could only happen by a miracle. In June 2004 there was another major speech, this time by Ms Sonia Ghandi. She acknowledged that the past had been a time of denial, that the projections had been plainly wrong and politically influenced. But she was still not very clear on the need for a change in attitudes, for a change in culture, if the fight against HIV/AIDS is to be successful in India.

Listening also depends on being able to listen. The World Bank used to be highly centralized and sometimes – in the past decades – even prided itself on not knowing the local circumstances. 'Experts' would be flown in who 'knew' the country from the available data. Even if the staff was interested in listening, they were at that time simply not in a position to be listeners. President Wolfensohn has had the courage and vision to turn the Bank culture around and initiate a substantial decentralization, with at least 500 of the international professional staff, including the majority of the country directors (the lead persons in the dialogue between the country and the World Bank, see Section 6.4) in the field. Still, the internal (Bank) turn-around in culture from technical know-how to listening and judgement requires continued attention. I realize that the balance between on the one hand ensuring coherence with World Bank policies (which is a force for centralization) and, on the other, listening and building up a memory of a country's circumstances is a very fine one.

One of the major challenges for the development assistance community, including the World Bank, is to support the initiatives of developing countries. In that way 'cultural consistency' is ensured. One such initiative is the New Partnership for Africa's Development (NEPAD). It is set up and owned by some of the leaders in Africa (including Nigeria's Obasanjo). It had a tremendous appeal and deserves all the support one can give.

Listening and observing are – of course – in contrast to the application of the standard structural adjustment methodology as the high road for political and economic reform. Market solutions remain the turnpike for development, but as a means and not as a goal in themselves. For market solutions to work, one needs good governance and good institutions as well as a path for change that fits into the national culture.

9.5 INSUFFICIENT COORDINATION AND INSUFFICIENT GENEROSITY AS A FAILURE

The biggest problem in aid is perhaps its dividedness. For example, the total of US $814 million (The Little Data Book, World Bank, 2004), which Uganda received in 2002 does not come in through one source, but is divided between at least 40 different donors. All these donors have their own accountability system. They also all have their own rules of engagement with Uganda. Also, all want to come and visit, discuss and advise. Preferably they want to see the Prime Minister. But in any case they will take up so much of the time of the

Government and local officials that it is constantly draining the local capacity, which happens to be already spread thinly.

To make things worse, some organizations do not bring in money, but have the money tied to certain goods, like foreign advisers or specific, foreign-made goods, while the same goods and services could have been bought with a fraction of the donated money, as in Uganda (see Section 2.2).

The dividedness of aid mentioned above and noted in Section 7.3 on bilateral aid agencies also means a considerable reduction in the real value of aid. The transaction costs of divided aid are high. I am not aware of calculations on these transaction costs, but would not be surprised if they are easily between 5 per cent (for large grants and loans) and 25 per cent (if the development aid is relatively small). The size of aid counts as well. How beneficial large, sustained flows of aid can be, is demonstrated in Ireland, which received over a longer period 5–9 per cent of GDP from the EU as aid (see also Section 7.2). At the same time, this aid was absorbed in a country which 'did everything well', also when difficult decisions had to be made by politicians. In all respects, as F. Desmond McCarthy shows, Ireland was a model pupil in applying 'good practice' and maintaining a solid macroeconomic framework.[8]

All in all, the rich countries have a substantial agenda to answer to in order to be considered reliable development partners who indeed seek the long-run convergence with poorer countries and prosperity of all. An important precondition in winning this trust will be to show interest in the local problems and ownership: to let developing countries determine themselves which priorities they address and what sort of aid they expect to be most efficient, and to create a global platform for effective aid.

10

A Chance for the World Bank?

A future for the world can only be a future with convergence between poor and rich countries, a future with a substantial reduction of poverty. And yet, the past has been one of mainly divergence, despite great efforts of developing countries to improve their governance, despite their commitment to create institutions and despite the pains and suffering of putting a good macroeconomic framework in place. The latter is a point to be underlined. In the 1990s developing countries went through great struggles to ensure that government deficits were kept low and that inflation remained in check. The implied suffering should be clear for citizens in Western Europe. They witnessed the trouble which, amongst others, Germany and France had in 2003 and 2004 (and still have) to keep their government deficit under the maximum limit of 3 per cent GDP as agreed upon within the stabilization pact at the introduction of the Euro. By contrast, many developing countries have had to enact far greater budget cutting operations than these two rich countries in order to keep their government deficits under control when oil prices rose and export prices for their commodities declined.

The New Partnership for African Development (NEPAD) is another expression of the commitment of (African) developing countries to do the utmost for their own development. This partnership does potentially have 'teeth'. It includes, for example, public governance audits. Of course, much depends on the implementation of these commitments.

The developed world has also tried its best to make resources available for development assistance and by gradually improving the efficiency of the allocation of these resources. Still, what has been done is not enough: the divergence continues by and large, fortunately with some important exceptions like the mammoth countries China and India and some of the Asian Tigers. It is even worse: in terms of the focus of development cooperation, namely the Millennium Development Goals (MDGs), the first decade of the twenty-first century has also been lost for a successful achievement of the MDGs. A successful achievement of the MGDs is not (yet?) in sight.

Radical changes are urgently needed to achieve convergence and come closer to the realization of the MDGs. I call the changes 'radical' even though they imply simply 'doing the right thing': practising what we know to be 'good international cooperation or international assistance policy'. One might excuse the development cooperation practice of the 1970s and 1980s for not being effective as there was still a considerable lack of knowledge or misunderstanding of effective development cooperation. However, in the 1990s the main elements became much clearer. The development paradigm has become broadly shared. There is no way to hide. Radical changes ought to be made now, meaning that the hard-won lessons of the recent past have to be put into practice. These lessons apply equally to the practice of development cooperation and to its context.

One main lesson we have learned is that 'buying' political friendship in developing countries is not an effective form of development assistance. On the contrary: the Cold War, which regularly included this type of development assistance, often as a means to create or keep political allies, has led to a waste of money, possibly even going against development when it supported corrupt regimes, and contributed to the debt burden of countries. Examples are the development assistance going to Mobutu's Zaire or to Saddam's Iraq. The demise of the Cold War provided the perfect stage to shed old (bad) habits of 'buying friendship'. Indeed, development assistance did turn a corner and has become far more effective (by an estimated factor of 10) through an increased focus. Unfortunately, September 11, 2001 proved to be another turning point. The brutal attack on the Twin Towers marked the start of the war on terrorism, which has brought back a ghost of the past, namely that of 'buying friendship' without a development assistance focus, thereby possibly strengthening corrupt regimes and blocking or slowing down development. To exemplify: countries like Tajikistan and Uzbekistan, which resemble – in terms of governance – the worst cases of the 1980s, have now been embraced by Western development assistance.

In other words, I fear that the window of opportunity for development cooperation has been closing rapidly. All the more reason to ring the alarm bell, to raise the red flag and re-open the window, while applying the lessons learned in development assistance.

Radical change is needed because too much money and energy is lost in flag planting, in tied aid and in uncoordinated reporting requirements imposed on developing countries (Section 10.1). Radical change is also needed because the committed people in donor countries, in particular the young, are estranged from the main organizations of development cooperation, like the World Bank and the IMF (Section 10.2). Improvement of the rules of globalization aimed at creating a global level playing field in trade and in governance requires decisive steps: trade restrictions should be abolished in rich countries for agricultural imports from poor countries and the international anti-corruption laws of the OECD should be enforced and policed, while the flows of development assistance from rich to poor countries should be augmented (Section 10.3). The present situation of a 'reverse flow' (namely from poor to rich countries) should be quickly made a demon of the past. The diaspora with its potential to help countries with human capital or with remittances (Section 10.4) can strengthen the platform for convergence between the countries of the world and improve the chances for the World Bank to operate effectively and efficiently. There is some debate on the need for the World Bank and the IMF to provide loans. In Section 10.5 we concluded that there is little reason to assume that the private sector could take over the work of the Bretton Woods sisters to achieve the MDGs. The main lesson of development cooperation is summarized in Section 10.6: perseverance and boldness are essential to realize this chance for the World Bank, which has been the focus of this book as the embodiment of development cooperation.

10.1 INCREASE EFFICIENCY AND EFFECTIVENESS

The 1990s have been a time of an unparallelled increase in the efficiency of development assistance (getting results for the 'buck' in terms of lifting more people out of poverty) and in effectiveness (reaching the poverty reduction goal of halving poverty by 2015). Since the 1990s IDA loans have also become more efficient: the percentage of projects at risk of not reaching their objectives has dropped from 28 per cent in 1996, to 13 per cent in 2001.[1] The increase in efficiency during the 1990s was realized by a better targeting of resources on countries with 'proven' (i.e. based on performance) good policies. Moreover, development assistance has become more critical about its own functioning, since there is better quality control. Finally, effectiveness is now measured by the empowerment of the developing countries to improve their situation. In addition, the coherence of projects has increased through the introduction of the Country Assistance Strategy (CAS) by the World Bank for its own operations and, in the late 1990s, by the introduction of the Poverty Reduction Strategy Paper (PRSP) of a country as the basis for development cooperation, covering all operations of donors.

Radical change is needed to continue along all the routes which have been shown to be promising and inviting for convergence and for reaching the MDGs.

Focus aid according to good governance. Break the iron deadlock of the war on terrorism to spur once more the focus of development assistance on good performance. This is the radical change needed at this time, both for the World Bank as for other bilateral or multilateral agencies. In many respects, it is astonishing how long it took Westerners to discover the importance of good governance for development. They could have been aware of Ambrogio Lorenzetti's frescos, which were made in Siena in 1338. There are two sets of them: one set showing good government and its effects on city life and on the countryside (see Figures 10.1, 10.2 and 10.3), and another set showing bad government and its effects.

One may disagree with Lorenzetti on the traits of good and bad government, although many of the characteristics depicted by him still appear to be relevant. Good government is characterized by the rule of law, with proper enforcement, depicted by Lorenzetti by the central place of the giant judge/governor in the middle of his fresco. This giant divides the citizens into 'good' citizens (to his right) and 'bad' citizens (to his left). The 'virtues' of good government sit at both sides of the judge. They are: peace, perseverance, carefulness, magnanimity, temperance and justice. With a good government, the city is booming and the countryside is prosperous. Interestingly enough, there is no sign – in Lorenzetti's view of good government – of 'competence' or knowledge about international good practice, including the wisdom and ability to find the room for manoeuvre to implement good practice (which might be another way of defining leadership). Bad government, in Lorenzetti's fresco, is the rule of a devilish tyrant who appropriates the goods of the citizens. In the streets and in the countryside there is violence, while the economy has come to a standstill.

In applying the focus of good governance to development assistance, it will be essential to create transparency on the parameters of good governance. Openness over the Country Policy Institutional Assessment (CPIA) used by the World Bank to measure the quality of governance is essential for a development philosophy in which transparency in general plays a central role. There is no reason why the CPIA should be kept secret. Until recently, the Board of the World Bank prohibited publication because of an opposing coalition of board members who felt ill at ease with the resulting measure. The coalition consisted of two groups: one group which feared for some of their constituent countries (where governance was at a low level) and another group of board members representing mostly donors who would be challenged in their bilateral aid if the CPIA were to be published. They might find out that their own bilateral aid lacks the focus needed to be efficient.

The only flag to be planted is that of the developing country. Harmonize aid. The government of Tanzania has to produce 2,400 reports for its donors every three months. School benches for Tanzania, donated by Japan, have to be purchased in Japan. There is overwhelming evidence of 'bad' donor behaviour here. 'Bad' because donors know that their dollar, euro or yen is only partly efficient, because of flag planting behaviour, of tied aid or of unnecessary transaction costs imposed on the developing country.

Transaction costs need to be minimized by reducing the paperwork for the developing country. The simplest way to do this is by adding donor money to

Source: http://www.kfki.hu/~arthp/index1.html

Figure 10.1 Good government

the country's budget within the PRSP and with accountability through the same procedures that apply for the rest of the government budget – provided international standards are accepted. This procedure would eliminate tied aid, where developing countries are forced to work with consultants and materials which represent – in value – just a fraction of the costs the donor has

Source: http://www.kfki.hu/~arthp/index1.html

Figure 10.2 Effects of good government on city life

Figure 10.3 Effects of good government on the countryside

laid out for them. Donor flag planting would be avoided as well, avoiding in this way prestige projects with a heavy emphasis on the physical infrastructure – while the real problem for the developing country is the lack of resources for recurring costs. It is not the school building or the hospital, which is the bottleneck for development. The bottleneck is the teacher, the nurse and the physician. Budget support is the road ahead for development aid.

Harmonization of aid goes hand in hand with a focused approach. It should cover all of the aid that goes to focus countries. Yet the 2004 reality is that only some 5 or 10 per cent (!) of all aid in focus countries is harmonized, while the World Development Report 2004 notes that there is a *decrease* in harmonization. It should be based on one, and only one, (joint) analysis of all donors with one conclusion (i.e. to support the PRSP), rather than the sometimes literally thousands of analyses by different donors and their widely varying conclusions. It could increase the quality of the analyses by involving what would be internationally regarded (including in the developed world) as top advice. Top advice is only possible with a thorough sensitivity to the local culture and an awareness that advice should create or widen the room for manoeuvre of those who have the responsibility for local policy. The other aspect of it is technical competency in socio-economic analysis and policymaking. Harmonization would lead to a serious reduction of the claims donors make on the time of the governments of developing countries.

The World Bank is in a natural position to work together with bilaterals and multilaterals as the convener for country analysis and for the harmonized donor approach to the country. The World Bank and the IMF have built up a strong tradition of thorough analysis, more than any other bilateral or multilateral. As a major donor agency, it could be the *intermediary* in countries with good governance between all donors and the government. A chance for the World Bank?

Harmonization through budget support is not a solution in countries which fail to meet the standards of (sufficiently) good governance, like Nigeria or Venezuela. But it might at least triple the efficiency of development assistance for the thirty or forty developing countries which at present fully, or partly (for certain sectors) satisfy the criteria of (reasonable) good governance. In other words: as a rough estimate, at least three times as many people could be lifted out of poverty, if only donors would be willing to apply the lessons they have learned.

The effect would be made even greater by a further focus: pulling inefficient assistance out of the countries with low levels of governance (so-called LICUS countries) and putting it into 'high' governance countries. The LICUS countries need attention, but this will be less in the form of money and more in the form of diplomacy, weapons embargos, policing, etc.

10.2 INCREASE PUBLIC SUPPORT

There is no doubt about the commitment of the rich world with regard to poverty reduction or the MDGs: daily we can witness that new radio and television campaigns which appeal, for example, for the causes of war children and HIV/AIDS orphans or to other specific groups, are highly successful in raising money. For micro-initiatives, like building a school in a village, it is even easier to find money. Young and old support the notion of worldwide poverty reduction when it comes to concrete small-scale initiatives. These initiatives, however, are not going to win the day. They are too small to a make a significant dent in the poverty of so many. Poverty reduction can only be achieved on a substantial scale through large-scale efforts, through the official channels.

On the larger scale, in the commitment to reach the Monterrey Consensus of 0.7 per cent of GDP, there is some progress. Some progress, but not enough, and not sufficiently supported by the citizens and leaders of today and tomorrow; because there is distrust in the effectiveness and efficiency of the official organizations.

The World Bank (and even more so the IMF) is distrusted and is the target of criticism by many who are committed to development cooperation. In particular committed youth, the backbone for the future support of development cooperation, shows great reservations about the World Bank (and the IMF). The two organizations embody the main thrust of development assistance while bilaterals and other multilaterals work mostly according to the same philosophy as the IMF and the World Bank (albeit insufficiently coordinated). In other words: there is a huge void between youth and the practice of ODA. In part, the distrust is linked to insufficient progress in increasing the efficiency of development cooperation (the preceding Section, 10.1) or in improving the rules of globalization (the next Section, 10.3). It is also partly due to a simple lack of communication between the agencies involved in ODA and committed youth, or a lack of information and awareness (as was noticed in Section 2.3). There may also be a difference in view on the role of market mechanisms as a means to achieve prosperity in poor countries. These views are often either based on past, sometimes indeed too ideological, practices of the World Bank and the IMF, or on insufficient information.

Information for communication with, and involvement of, committed youth in the daily practices of the World Bank and the IMF are essential elements to fill the void. That the void needs to be filled is beyond doubt. The present situation of ODA is like that of a house built on a marsh: highly unstable. The World Bank and the IMF are aware that they lack a foundation of support among the young in the donor countries. However, their responses have been, until now, too little and too late.

What is needed is a youth corps of the World Bank and the IMF, and a youth network which carries weight in the decision-making of the two sister organizations. This is a radical shift as both organizations exhibit a professional climate that is highly technical and does not easily admit elements of political and social support. In the above conception, the IMF and the World Bank would set aside about 10 per cent of their budgets for a youth corps and a youth network. The youth network would be actively involved in following World Bank and IMF policies and would discuss them, but would also be involved in the preparation of part of the agenda for the Development Committee and the Finance Committee, the two ministerial meetings of the 24 ministers responsible, respectively, for the World Bank and the IMF. The youth corps would allow participation of youngsters in the development work in poor countries, in order to learn and to deepen commitment.

The World Bank has a chance to gain ground for efficient and effective development assistance through an organized and engaged World Bank youth network and youth corps. What I have in mind is to transform the energy of youngsters in the developed world from dissent and demonstration into an actual involvement in the policymaking and in the practice of development cooperation in poorer countries. The delineation of where 'young' starts and ends may be flexible. Essential is organization of the debate and organization of possibilities for youngsters to spend time in developing countries in development projects.

10.3 IMPROVE THE RULES OF GLOBALIZATION

Globalization is not a choice of individuals or a policy option of countries. It is a process of rising expectations on the part of the citizens of the world of access to goods and services which are available elsewhere, in combination with decreased costs of travel or the transmission of information, and of goods and services over long distances. The tragedy of the globalization of the recent past has been that expectations increased in poor countries, while by and large divergence increased as well. In part, this is caused by the rules of globalization. These rules are derived mostly from the self-interest of the rich countries, presumably not realizing the tremendous, negative consequences for developing countries.

The present rules have proved to work against convergence. With this recognition, the Western world is in a dangerous position of hypocrisy. It now knows that its policies slow down development in developing countries. Hence, it should act quickly and radically to improve the rules of globalization to make globalization inclusive.

Abolish the trade restrictions in rich countries on agricultural imports from poor countries. It is only recently that the world has started to recognize the tremendous magnitude of the loss of income of developing countries resulting from the trade restrictions of the rich world. The rich world utilizes the full array of market interventions in agriculture: agricultural subsidies of the magnitude of $1 billion per day, export subsidies and import restrictions. Not only are these interventions denied to the developing countries which want to entertain a strong link with donors, they also cause a loss of income to developing countries of around $200 billion per year, or four times the annual amount of development assistance.

There is a tremendous discrepancy between the solidarity in the rich world and the drive to do away with the hypocrisy on agricultural interventions: the farmer's lobby (no more than 5 per cent of the population) seems to win over the interests of the population at large (time and again). There is another corollary to the realization of the magnitude of the income loss in developing countries due to trade restrictions. The 'real' minister of development cooperation is not the minister who holds the portfolio, but rather the minister of agriculture. His or her impact on development could be much larger than that of the minister of development cooperation.

Enforce the international (OECD) anti-corruption rules. The 1990s were the decade of the (re-)discovery of the determining role of governance for development. The World Bank and other institutions showed with thorough research that corruption is not the grease that oils the wheels. Rather the contrary, as it blocks the wheels of society's dynamics and the economy.

However, the next step has not yet been taken: to measure where corruption is located and where it originates. There is ample evidence that a substantial part of corruption is induced by multinational enterprises. They sometimes pride themselves on beating the competition by 'knowing the ropes', which all too often means finding the right channels for the bribery of top officials. There is also ample evidence that 'small' corruption lives by the grace of 'big' corruption in the top parts of society. In that connection (between the inducement by MNEs of corruption at the top, and the 'osmosis of corruption' to all levels of society), it is urgent to start to police the OECD anti-corruption convention as part of the improved rules of globalization. The OECD convention in itself was an excellent start: MNEs agreed to step back from the race to the bottom caused by competing for contracts through bribery. This was a wise decision as it was good for developing countries and cost-saving to MNEs. However, there was no agreement on the policing of this agreement, and hence it was an agreement without teeth (except in the case of the US, where firms can also be prosecuted for corruption outside the country). It is now imperative that the rules of globalization be improved through a proper policing agreement for corrupt behavior by MNEs.

Augment the flows from rich to poor countries. This is part of the MDGs – the compact between rich and poor countries. The public will support such an increase if it is accompanied by a youth network and a youth corps of the IMF and the World Bank, while the focus of development assistance is increased. Stopping the reverse flows (i.e. the flows from poor to rich countries) is a top priority.

10.4 USE THE POWER OF THE DIASPORA AND PREVENT BRAIN DRAIN

In June 2003, India announced that it no longer considered itself a country in need of development assistance. It would take full responsibility for its own development, including the lifting out of poverty of 400 million Indians who live in poverty. India could take this decision because the Indian government has managed to create a financial reserve of $75 billion by means of its exports, but also because it is greatly helped by the remittances of Indians abroad and (to a lesser extent) by FDI. Figure 10.4 depicts the remittances from abroad in billions of dollars for the top 20 countries who receive remittances.

Another way of looking at remittances is as a percentage of the GDP of the country to which the money is remitted (see Figure 10.5). For all twelve countries listed in the figure, remittances exceed 10 per cent of GDP. Remittances are also substantial in other countries, often superseding the official development assistance. In 2002, workers' remittances reached US $80 billion, up from $60 billion in 1998 (World Bank, Global Development

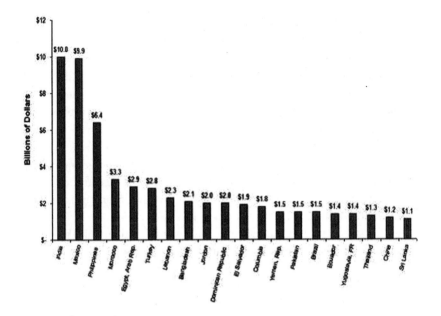

Source: The American Immigration Law Foundation
http://www.ailf.org/ipc/policy_reports_2003_pr002_remittances.asp

Figure 10.4 Top 20 developing country recipients of workers' remittances, 2001

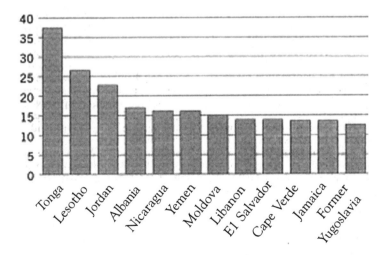

Source: NRC Handelsblad, December 18, 2003

Figure 10.5 Top 12 Recipients of remittances (% of GDP), 2001

Finance, 2003), if we only take the remittances through official channels. The transaction costs involved in using these channels are high. The World Bank estimates these costs at 13 to 20 per cent. Many 'guest workers' therefore make their transfers through unofficial channels, the so-called 'hawalas' (transfer offices which only charge small commissions). The estimate of the total of remittances through official and unofficial channels was $280 billion in 2000, showing great stability over the years and steadily rising.[2] Remittances go directly to people in developing countries, without any bureaucratic overheads: they are – in that way – highly effective ways of development assistance.

For India, remittances of approximately $10 billion a year through official channels are part of the story of rapid development. Another part is the return of a substantial number of Indians as Box 10.1 shows.

The Indian situation is the best one can hope for and aim at: the influx of remittances, of private capital and of human capital, spurred by private sector investments.

The combined effects of remittances, the return of human capital and FDI can be an iron triangle for rapid development. The organizations of ODA, like

Box 10.1: The Impact of the Diaspora in Karnataka

It is quite a coincidence to stay in the same room of the same hotel (Taj Mahal) five years later, but this is where any similarities with my previous visit ends. Back then, Bangalore, the capital of the State of Karnataka, was a sleeping giant, while now, in 2002, it is awakening.

Karnataka's population of 60 million exceeds that of any EU country, with the exception of Germany (82 million). Bangalore is building a techno-city just outside the present city. It also houses a top laboratory of Unilever (in India: Hindustanlever). All this happened with a substantial involvement of Indians with PhDs from Anglo-Saxon universities who have done well on the international labour market and have decided to come back. They now find in India the quality of equipment they are used to (and which is needed to be on the cutting edge). Their salaries in India may not be the same as they once earned on the international market, but they are sufficient to make a good living.

The chief minister of Karnataka (Chandra Babu Naidu) is a driving force behind the development of an investment climate that is not only attractive for domestic investment, but also for foreign domestic investment. At the same time a new angle on foreign domestic investment emerges: the return of well-trained professionals. One might call it the return or flow back of human capital, realizing that the same factors that make domestic financial capital return 'home' also apply to human capital.

the World Bank, have only recently come to realize that their effectiveness can be greatly enhanced by creating the climate for such a triangle, in particular a climate for the return of human capital or the prevention of an exodus.

For the private sector, the return of human capital may depend on the investment climate. For the public sector this is more complicated. We see at the moment a situation in which maybe close to half of the trained medical doctors in sub-Saharan Africa are working in rich countries. The exodus of a poor country's well-trained staff to the rich world continues to take place.

While development cooperation has rediscovered local human 'capacity' as one of the major constraints on development, on the capacity of governments, and on service delivery (in higher education, in health and elsewhere), development agencies like the World Bank have taken a strong interest in 'capacity creation.' But they have so far insufficiently focused on the dynamics of 'capacity': what makes people leave or can actually bring domestic capacity back. 'Civil service reform,' one of the topics of development cooperation between the World Bank and developing countries, for example, hardly takes into account the effects of its 'contribution' to the loss of capacity, of people deciding to leave because of salaries and working conditions which are too remote from those on the international labour market where these people can offer their services.

The role of the diaspora has not yet fully been recognized in donor countries, nor in the developing countries (perhaps with the exception of India). Donors often encourage the brain drain as an easy way to reduce shortages of trained manpower (the economic will have quite separate silos for development cooperation apart from those for their own general development. Preventing the exodus is not easily accomplished. Some countries have a culture of emigration, certainly for the elite. Morocco is a case in point. Take the front page of any French language newspaper in 2002. Day after day it will carry advertisements offering the services of an agent to procure a visa for the US, Canada or the EU. Many of Morocco's intellectuals and scientists have left the country.

The exodus is the result of push-and-pull factors.[3] The push out of the country is the result of instability, insufficient chances for children and unsatisfactory working conditions, while the pull from the developed world is the result of higher wages. The push may be reduced by better governance, but the pull can only be addressed by leaving more room in developing countries for a dual labour market, in which an international labour market (with internationally competitive wages) coexists with a national labour market. The latter is not easy to accept or delineate politically, yet it seems to be essential to achieve convergence. Employment opportunities for well-trained staff have to improve.

10.5 LOANS AND GRANTS

In the approach to reaching the MDGs (or to coming closer to reaching them for most countries) the debate on loans versus grants feels like speaking about the quality of multi-grain bread while next door a person is dying from hunger.

Loans to low-income countries, however concessional (meaning, however low the interest rate), might be better replaced by grants. In itself the notion of a loan has some appeal. It requires thinking about development assistance in terms of an investment with a return. It helps, in that way, selection between one program and the next. However, low-income countries are in need of broad sector – and budget-support. The time of investment in a factory or a dam by the development community is over. Such investments can be taken care of by private investors. Expansion and improvement of the health and education systems are highly profitable, and yet it makes very little sense to provide the donor support as a loan with all the concomitant hassle.

The real debate is on long-term loans (from the World Bank and the IMF) to middle-income countries (per capita incomes above US $865 and below the 'graduation' level of US $5185). The Meltzer Commission (and with it many thoughtful economists like the ex-chief economist and Harvard economist Kenneth Rogoff, writing in *The Economist*, July 24, 2004) argue that the existence of private (and highly liquid) markets makes this kind of lending superfluous: the IBRD (the Bank's wing for middle-income countries) does not fulfil a role and the IMF could limit its work to short-term liquidity lending to countries in crisis.

But let us look at this debate from the perspective of the MDGs. The present trends in middle-income countries are definitely not always encouraging (see World Bank web site). Many middle-income countries will fail to reach the MDGs unless major shifts take place. Could these countries finance these shifts on the private capital market? That would be out of the question: a private bank would like to see a physical asset as a mortgage. It will be the public, concessional lending of the IBRD and the IMF that can help out. In other words: I believe that the longer-term lending role of the World Bank and IMF for middle-income countries should remain. But at the same time, I propose that it should be better aimed, namely at the kind of sector reform and expansion which can bring countries closer to reaching the MDGs.

10.6 A CHANCE FOR THE WORLD BANK

The windows of opportunity for better chances for the world's poor are closing, presumably because war-talk is taking hold. War means that the world will be split up into enemies and friends, a simplifying separation of the good and the bad. Good is in our camp, bad is in their camp. War brings along the gaming to bring the non-decided into 'our' camp. This was the gaming in the Cold-War era, in which Mobutu became one of the richest people in the world with huge assets in Switzerland, derived from loans and grants that were given to Zaire under the cloak of development cooperation. Mobutu is but one extreme example. In general, development cooperation in the 1970s and 1980s was more a matter of buying friendship, whatever the policy quality of the country, than of supporting governments dedicated to the improvement of their people's fate. The new Mobutus are already visible in Central Asia where an alliance with dictators is sought for in the fight against terrorism, creating the basis for sustained dictatorship, corruption and exploitation.

This end of the interbellum between the Cold War and the War on Terror paradoxically comes at a moment when finally the world had reached an agreement on what works in development. It is the country's determination to achieve progress whether measured in economic growth or in the Millenium Development Goals, which makes the difference. If the country sits on its hands, if the élite of politicians and businessmen are working for themselves rather than for the country or its enterprises, then there will be no progress regardless of the level of inflow of knowledge or of funds from donors. If – on the contrary – the country wants to move, then it should get all the possible external support it needs and can absorb. The international community made this their paradigm and philosophy at the end of the second millennium, and formally signed up to this approach in Monterrey (Mexico), in March 2002.

But then world economic growth fizzled out in the years 2001 and 2002. In 2002 the world economy grew by 1.9 per cent, a slight increase from 1.3 per cent in 2001, but below the 2.7 per cent annual average in the 1990s. The war in Iraq became the centrepiece of the world's attention in 2003. Moreover, it drained resources in rich countries which otherwise could have been used to speed up development in poor countries. Oil prices rose and are still high as an indication of uncertainty around the globe.

Where does this leave development agencies and the World Bank? In Chapter 6 we presented conclusions on ways to improve the effectiveness of the World Bank. The sum total of our argument has been that it is not just the World Bank which has to change, but that there is an urgent need for a new Bretton Woods-like charter on development cooperation. Such a new charter includes a new context for development cooperation (the new 'rules of the globalization game') as well as new rules for the development agencies.

A new Bretton Woods-type agreement should set forth a route whereby development cooperation is anchored into a serious commitment of the rich world to give the poor countries leeway in a number of ways:

- In trade; the Geneva agreement of August 2004 has been an excellent step in reducing the trade barriers in rich countries against agriculture imports from poor countries.

- In fighting the corruption in developing countries that is brought about by foreign companies, and effectively policing the OECD convention of 1997. This essentially would imply that corruption of a firm taking place in country X will result in prosecution of that firm, even if it is based in another country than X. The international community should step up considerably its prosecution of the kind of corruption that leads to or fuels civil conflicts. An example is the diamond trade, which caused or contributed to the atrocious civil conflict in Sierra Leone. Financing rebel forces (often in return for claims to mine mineral resources) should be prosecuted internationally.

- In development cooperation, it should be agreed that harmonization is the rule. Partners in development cooperation who have chosen to work in a certain country put their money (grants and loans) into one pot. The money is allocated according to *one* national plan (which might be the PRSP or an equivalent). The spending of the money is accounted for in *one* internationally agreed procedure. This would have a tremendous effect on the efficiency of the official development assistance, maybe as much as doubling it, because the transaction costs on the part of donor and receiver would be substantially reduced. The Rome declaration (February 2003) on harmonization is a good step but desperately needs implementation.

- In development cooperation, scaling-up the efforts to reach the MDGs is imperative. Countries, which satisfy basic requirements for a policy environment conducive to human development should get all the financial support they need. The 'Fast Track Initiative' for Education for All of the World Bank and UNESCO is an example. The support of donors should be long-term (maybe as long as 10 years) and for recurrent expenditures.

- In development cooperation, there is as a rule no room for individual projects or programs beyond capacity creation. Capacity creation should be the guide for any exceptions to this rule. Clear performance indicators and evaluation criteria should be set beforehand. This should go hand in hand with attention to *maintaining* capacity and preventing brain drain. Capacity creation includes the analytical capacity of the country: public or private thinktanks.

- Transparency on the international evaluations of the quality of governance could indeed be a driving force for improvement of the quality of governance. Ensuring this transparency is more part of the UN's responsibility than that of the World Bank or the IMF. It is the joint responsibility of the Bretton Woods and the UN agencies to chart development cooperation with countries with poor governance.

- The IMF and the World Bank are too close and too overlapping to continue as separate institutions. They should merge under a new Bretton Woods agreement. Loans for poor countries should be abolished in favour of grants with a commensurate change in the financing by donors.

Such a new Bretton Woods agreement requires perseverance and boldness. Let Emily Dickinson inspire us:

To make a prairie

To make a prairie, it takes a clover and one bee.
One clover, and a bee,
And reverie.
The reverie alone will do
If bees are few.

– Emily Dickinson

There is a good chance for the World Bank, if it follows the last lesson: perseverance and boldness.

Notes

Chapter 2: Poverty Remains a Universal Concern

1 Narayan, Deepa et al, *Crying Out for Change*, Oxford University Press and the World Bank, 2000. Narayan, Deepa, *Can Anyone Hear Us?*, Oxford University Press and the World Bank, 2000. Narayan, Deepa and Patti Petesch (eds), *From Many Lands*, Oxford University Press and the World Bank, 2002.

2 The exact value is not easy to gauge. Should for example the transfer of Japanese funds, which have to be used to buy in Japan school furniture for Tanzania be valued for its full costs of the purchase or for the value of what such school furniture costs in Tanzania?

Chapter 3: Globalization does not Automatically Lead to Convergence

1 Pritchett, L. *Divergence, Big Time*, Policy Research Paper 1522, World Bank, 1995.

2 Atinc, T.M. 'How the East Asia crisis changed the social situation', Katherine Marshall and Olivier Butzbach (eds), *New Social Policy Agendas for Europe and Asia*, World Bank, 2003, pp. 66–7.

3 Working Paper 3792, World Bank, 2004.

4 Stiglitz, J. 'Two principles for the next round or, how to bring developing countries in from the cold', *The World Economy*, Vol. 23, No. 4, (2000), pp. 437–454.

5 Office of International Affairs, *Global Dimensions of Intellectual Property Rights in Science and Technology*, (1993), http://books.nap.edu/books/0309048338/html/357.html#pagetop.

6 Transparency International *Global Corruption Report*, 2003.

7 European Commission Green Paper, July 2001.

8 Financial Times, July 3, 2003.

9 Collier, P. and Hoeffler A. *Military Expenditure: Threats, Aid, and Arms Races*, Development Research Group, World Bank, 2002.

10 Addison, T., Le Billon P., and Murshed M.S., WIDER Discussion paper, No. 51, 2001. http://www.wider.unu.edu/publications/publications.htm.

11 Ritzen, J. 'Tertiary education in poor Countries: post-Monterrey perspectives' Institute of Social Studies, the Hague, October 9, 2002, Dies Natalis Address.

12 OED report: 'Tertiary Education, Lessons from a Decade of Learning', World Bank 2002.

13 Carrington W.J. and E. Detragiache "How Extensive is the Brain Drain", in *Finance and Development*, June 1999, Vol. 36, No. 2, p. 7.

Chapter 4: Shifts in Development Paradigms

1 Ritzen, J., W. Easterly and M. Woolcock *Social Cohesion, Institutions and Economic Growth: Economics and Politics* (Forthcoming in 2005).

2   Burnside, C., and Dollar D. 'Aid, policies, and growth: revisiting the evidence',
     Working Paper 3251, World Bank, 2004.
3   Hanna, Nagy and Robert Picciotto (eds) *Making Development Work, World Bank
     Series on Evaluation and Development*, Vol. 4, New Brunswick NJ: Transaction,
     2002.
4   Principles of Development Effectiveness, DAC, 1992.
5   Buckley, Robert, *Annual Review of Development Effectiveness*, World Bank, 1999.

Chapter 5: Decision-Making at the World Bank

1   *Quotations from* D.E. Moggridge, *Maynard Keynes: An Economist´s Biography*,
     London: Routledge, 1992, p. 730.
2   Simms, A., Big, T., & Robbins, N. *New Economic Foundations*, 2000. Available at
     http://www.neweconomics.org.
3   http://www.pkarchive.org/crises/SavingAsia.html.

Chapter 6: The Different Faces of the World Bank

1   Jochen, K. *Bankers with a Mission*, Oxford: Oxford University Press, 1996, p. 204
2   Williamson, J. *Did the Washington Consensus Fail?* Institute for International
     Economics, 2002
3   Stiglitz, J. *Globalization and its Discontents*, New York: Norton, 2002
4   Ndulu, B. 'Inclusiveness, accountability and effectiveness of Development
     Assistance', paper presented at ABCDE Conference, Bangalore, 2003 (World
     Bank web site).
5   Kessides, I.N. *Reforming Infrastructure: Privatization, Regulation and Competition*,
     World Bank, 2004.
6   Wade, R. 'Globalization at work: the fight over capital flows' *Foreign Policy, Winter*
     1998–9.
7   Devarajan, Shantayanan, '*Growth is not enough*', Memo, World Bank, 2002.
8   *See Ndulu.*

Chapter 7: Partners in Development Assistance

1   McCarthy, F. Desmond 'Linking macroeconomic and social policy: the Irish
     experiment', in Katherine Marshall, Olivier Butzbach (eds) *New Social Policy
     Agendas for Europe and Asia*, World Bank, 2003, p.127.
2   http://www.munfw.org/archive/45th/ecosoc3.htm
3   Ibid.

Chapter 8: Civil Society and Development

1   'Public opinion research, global education and development cooperation reform,
     in search of a virtuous circle: lessons from the OED evaluation', *Lessons and
     Practices*, no.18, August 28, 2002.
2   Reinneka, R. and Svenson, J. 'Explaining leakage of public funds', Research Paper,
     The World Bank, 2000.
3   see http://www.cceurope.org.

Chapter 9: Successes and Failures

1   See footnote 2 in Chapter 3.

2   Migdal, Joel *Strong Societies and Weak States*, Princeton University Press, 1988.

3   See footnote 1 in Chapter 3.

4   Koch, D. *Herfkens' Selectivity Policy Examined* (*Selectiviteitsbeleid onder de loep*, in Dutch), Internationale Spectator, 57–2, February 2003.

5   The excellent report of the World Bank (2000) 'Can Africa Claim the 21st Century?' makes rightly a pitch for good infrastructure policies: poor infrastructure is one of the main causes of Africa's low competitiveness. (p. 137).

6   WDR Poverty 2000–2001.

7   Walton, M and Rao, V. (eds) *Culture and Public Action*, Stanford University Press, 2004.

8   McCarthy, F. Desmond 'How the Celtic tiger did it: Ireland's Rapid Convergence with the Industrial World' Contribution to 10th EADI General Conference http://www/eadi.org/ge2002/McCarthy.pdf/ see Linking Macroeconomic and Social Policy: The Irish Experiment, in Katherine Marshall, Olivier Butzbach (editors).

Chapter 10: A Chance for the World Bank?

1   Third Annual Report on IDA's country assessment and allocation process, April 2002.

2   IMF, Balance of Payments Yearbook, World Bank, Global Development Finance, 2003.

3   Ritzen, J., Keynote Address, Institute of Social Studies, The Hague (the Netherlands), October 7, 2002.

INDEX